# Analyzing Prose

SCRIBNER ENGLISH SERIES

# Analyzing Prose

## Richard A. Lanham

UNIVERSITY OF CALIFORNIA,
LOS ANGELES

CHARLES SCRIBNER'S SONS    NEW YORK

*Copyright © 1983 Richard A. Lanham*

Library of Congress Cataloging in Publication Data
Lanham, Richard A.    Analyzing prose.
(Scribner English series)
1. English language—Style. 2. English language—
Rhetoric. I. Title. II. Series.
PE1421.L295 1983   828'.08   82-20488
ISBN 0-684-17834-6

1 3 5 7 9 11 13 15 17 19   F/C   20 18 16 14 12 10 8 6 4 2

*Printed in the United States of America.*

# Contents

# Preface

Raymond Chandler once remarked that "American is an ill-at-ease language." What makes you at ease with your language is liking it for its own sake, and this we have never done. Words were, like everything else, to be used and thrown away. At their best, they ought to evaporate entirely, constitute the ideal transparent medium for meaning. Start to look *at* words just for pleasure and you're a sissy, a poet. Not surprisingly, this tradition of see-through language has not left us especially good at analyzing prose. We are in fact, English teachers included, wonderfully inept at describing the "good writing" we all say we cherish. We don't know what to look for, nor what to call it when it trips us up. And so, mostly, we don't look at all. When we do, nine times in ten it is only to make sure we've been correct, written "good English," no spelling errors showing, no pronoun references unzipped, no modifiers dangling. If everything seems o.k., if we've come smiling from the world's great verbal snare uncaught, there's an end to it. What else can you say?

It is not only historical accident that we try so hard to avoid looking *at* prose. Prose has always been difficult to describe. From the beginning, and that means from Aristotle, we've always made a fundamental mistake. We've always confused evaluative judgments with descriptive ones. And we've always preferred evaluation to description. "Sincere," "fast-moving," "lean," "urbane," "hard-hitting," "lucid," "terse," "turgid," "sturdy"—you have seen these terms used everywhere to describe prose. How often have you heard someone talk about a hypotactic nominal style which frequently uses alliterative isocolon? It is not only that hypotaxis and isocolon are technical terms and the others popular. No, we prefer evaluative to descriptive terms because the evaluative ones talk about us, about our feelings toward the words, rather than about the words themselves. So evaluative is our nomenclature for prose that, in ordinary conversation, value judgments are the only kind usually made. And they are almost always—as with value judgments about behavior—both persistently scolding and impossibly vague. Yet we think we are talking about words and not about ourselves. We don't even know what an impartial description of written discourse looks like, much less how it differs from our usual moralizing epithets. We don't know, that is, what kind of statement we are making.

This beginner's guide to prose analysis starts therefore with description. Both description and evaluation are necessary and inevitable. To argue for one or the other exclusively would be like arguing for breathing-in over breathing-out. But evaluation falls thick as snowflakes in Siberia and description lurks only in old books, so description needs the stress. Prose to be sure will remain infinitely various, each style, like each of us, unique. But as with people, categories do exist, basic types, patterns, strategies. *Analyzing Prose* offers just these, a chart of basic types, a taxonomy.

A classification of basic types means a set of names for the classes, a nomenclature. Such a nomenclature has been available, in the classical rhetorical writings, for over two thousand years. Rhetorical analysis, using the classical terms at least, seems awfully old-fashioned nowadays. But if a better set of terms has gained common acceptance, I don't know of it. And in fact the traditional terms, unreasoned and unmethodical though they are, often work well enough, at least as an introductory way into prose analysis. Just because our discussions of prose style are so often evaluative rather than descriptive, perhaps the old descriptive terms, though cumbersome, might be profitably resurrected. That, at least when they fit, is what I've tried to do here. Where simple English terms work just as well—"noun style" or "verb style," for example—I've used those.

Books about prose style are almost all concerned with literary texts and written for literary scholars. This one draws its examples from all over and hopes to find its audience there too. After all, in our current literacy crisis it is not only the schoolmarms who are lecturing us about the writing problem. Politicians, bureaucrats, educators, businessmen, even the military, all get in on the act. If this debate is going to continue, it ought to be focused by some simple exploratory lessons in how to analyze and describe, and hence really to see, the written utterance which so vexes us. People who are

nds-on
h lend
 way.
nalysis
several
hought
t. Two
ed and
e were
n there
s.

L.
es
2

w need to know something about written
al commandments. They need, in fact, a
o do university students, those who teach
o to teach high school students. I have tried
l. The kind of descriptive analysis set forth
ghtforward; anyone who needs to think or
ble to understand it.

nts in the last two chapters is more diffi-
new ground. The argument is complex
rose are complex phenomena; there is no
whole modern confusion about prose style
escriptive statements and evaluative state-
ision can be dissolved if evaluative state-
erstand evaluative statements about prose
criptive analysis worth doing in the first
n antiquarian exercise. The Introduction
last two chapters develop the arguments

tbooks in any age) try to provide the stu-
eophyte intelligence from the speculative
nties. I have always thought this a dread-
nce of our students and—even worse—it
A textbook should provide a comprehen-
 about a subject; but it should also intro-
 matrix came from. Is that world, like
orienting, bewildering, exhilarating, and
 disabling injustice when we present to
g simplicities. That is what anesthetized
ton revolutionized it. And it is what over
e from the teaching of rhetoric. Studying
s sense only if something really depends
behave and whether we can as a species
e I've tried to argue in the Introduction

d to quote at sufficient length so that the
style tastes like as a steady diet. I've had
an go back to examples which I've cited

for one purpose and use them for another. Prose analysis is
activity; you need to do it yourself. I've tried to provide examples
themselves to different kinds of analysis. By all means use them

These chapters developed from a graduate seminar in pro
which I've given for UCLA Teaching Assistants during the
years. If those classes had not been so much fun I would never ha
to bring this kind of detailed, old-fashioned analysis out of the
students especially, Eric Sigg and Rick Eden, read drafts and an
emended. And almost all the TAs immediately took the techniqu
practicing and tried them out on their freshmen. The warm rece
cheered me up most of all. For this relief, good friends, much th

R
Los A

Οἶος ὁ βίος, τοῖος ὁ λόγος.
(As with life, so with words.)
GREEK PROVERB

# Analyzing Prose

INTRODUCTION

# The Domain of Style

For all our talking about how we write prose—and we talk about it a lot—
surprisingly little descriptive analysis goes on. Basic rhetorical analysis used
to be a high school subject in nineteenth-century America and for much of
Europe's history it was an elementary subject as well. Now even graduate
students can scarcely handle ordinary terms like "periodic sentence" or
"hypotaxis and parataxis." As a result when we talk about prose style we
often really don't know what we are talking about. We are simply not
trained to look at the words on the page.

The reasons for this failure go deep into American attitudes toward language. We have always thought—De Tocqueville noted it with disquiet—
that only ideas matter, not the words that convey them. Words linger in the
air only as a temporary contrivance for transferring ideas from mind to
mind. To look *at* them, rather than *through* them to the ideas beneath, is to
indulge ourselves in harmless antiquarian diddling or, still worse, to treat
ordinary language like poetry. Today especially, when so many larger
issues, social, economic, and political, seem to surround the national—
indeed world—literacy crisis, it seems almost atavistic to worry about the
basic rhetorical patterns, with their overlapping circular definitions and off-
putting Greek and Latin nomenclature. Since this traditional kind of analysis is both so old and so old-fashioned, it requires for a modern audience
some explanation and justification. The last two chapters of the book try to
supply both in detail. Perhaps, though, it might help to set forth these con-
cluding arguments in a brief way here, to sketch for the reader the boundary
conditions of our introduction to prose analysis.

We might begin by considering what we usually think prose style is all about. We may call this conception, building on its three central values of clarity, brevity, and sincerity, the "C-B-S" theory of prose. The C-B-S theory argues that prose ought to be maximally transparent and minimally self-conscious, never seen and never noticed. Analysis works against both these virtues. It makes us look *at* words and not *through* them. Analysis, in fact, can logically deal only with what can be seen, what is or is made self-conscious; such elements, in the C-B-S view, can logically be only mistakes. "Rhetoric" in such a view very naturally becomes a dirty word, pointing to superficial ornament on the one hand and duplicity on the other. It becomes, that is, everything which interferes with the natural and efficient communication of ideas. "Rhetoric" is what we should get rid of in prose, not what we should analyze.

However can we justify rhetorical analysis, then? Well, we might begin by pointing out the problems and confusions implicit in the C-B-S theory. The three basic terms, for example, though difficult to confute in the abstract, prove marvelously unhelpful when you come to actually write something. There are so many ways of being clear! So many different audiences to be clear to! When I tell you to "Be clear" I am simply telling you to "Succeed," "Get the message across." Again, good advice but not much real help. I have not solved your problem, I've simply restated it. "Clarity," in such a formulation, refers not to words on a page but to responses, yours or your reader's. And the writer has to write words on a page, not ideas in a mind.

And so too with "brevity." How brief? Well, as brief as possible but not so brief that the message doesn't get across. But messages vary so. If my wife comes into my study while I am writing this Introduction and I tell her "Beat it!" that is brief enough, but carries a message I tremble to convey. If I say, instead, "Yes, Dear, absolutely, I'll be right there, the camellia does need watering, just give me five minutes more, can you?" I have hardly been brief but I have still been as brief as that particular placatory message allowed. Brevity, then, depends on the message, and that home truth, as with clarity, restates the problem rather than solving it.

And how about "sincerity"? If I tell a student always to be sincere in writing a paper and that student submits a paper telling me how stupid he thinks the assignment is, I'm likely to rejoin, "Well, not *that* sincere! I meant sincere within limits." Of course. But what are the limits? The problem is finding the right kind of sincerity. Once again, we return to the writer's problem, not its solution.

The C-B-S theory of prose style seems not only unhelpful but a violation of our common sense. Suppose we really behaved according to these tenets, said exactly what we thought to everyone, with no sugar on top, always showed exactly what our feelings were? We would not last long in society; in fact we'd probably be locked up. "To be social," Robert Frost reminded us, "is to be forgiving," and in the rigorous application of the C-B-S theory there is precious little forgiveness. There are times in life when one must be absolutely clear, brief, and sincere, but not many; the whole of civility lies in learning how few they be.

The C-B-S theory violates not only our common sense about human behavior but much that we have learned about behavior in a more formal way in the last century. Sincerity as a central evaluative term implies that there is a central self to be sincere to, a "real me" halfway between the ears. Yet social psychologists since George Herbert Mead have argued that we do not inherit a central self at birth, but build one up by degrees, through incessant practice of social roles. Even the most integrated of us holds not one self but many; every day we must "get our act together." And so when we are told to "Be sincere," which self must we be sincere to?

"Clarity," too, as an all-purpose touchstone, seems to be contradicted by what we now know about human perception. We perceive the world actively and recreatively; we don't just register naturally a world already "out there." To perceive the world is to compose it, to make sense of it. The mind, to use the philosopher Karl Popper's revealing terms, acts like a "searchlight," not a "bucket." The reality we are being "clear" about dwells within us as well as "out there." The "successful communication" that "clarity" points to is finally our success in getting someone else to share our view of the world, a view we have composed by perceiving it. And if this is true of perception it must be true of prose too. To write is to compose a world as well as view one. Prose can never be purely transparent because there is no self-subsisting model out there to be transparent to.

"Brevity," also, contradicts fundamentally a basic theme in modern thought, the socially cohesive function of language. We don't communicate through simple gestures and monosyllabic grunts, because when we talk we are communicating attitudes as well as facts, redefining and reaffirming our social relationships as we go about our daily business. We make, through language, such reaffirmation part of our daily business. Brevity, in most human communication, remains a variable governed by social relationships as much as by factual baggage. One is "brief" in all kinds of ways, and

Polonius' objection, "This is too long," always means "Too long for this person, place, and time." Language always carries an enormous amount of contextual information, information about human relationships, about, as Gregory Bateson has put it, "What kind of a message a message is." "Brevity," applied in a simple-minded way, ignores this information and thus dehumanizes human communication.

The C-B-S theory always seems to contradict all that we say is good in literature and thus runs an enormous rift between "literature" on the one hand and "ordinary prose" on the other. This gap is sometimes described as between "prose" on the one side and "poetry" on the other. Prose must be entirely transparent, poetry entirely opaque. Prose must be minimally self-conscious, poetry the reverse. Prose talks of facts, of the world; poetry of feelings, of ourselves. Poetry must be savored, prose speed-read out of existence. This dichotomy proves very confusing. How can the same verbal patterns and attributes be good in poetry and bad in prose? Do these two kinds of languages point to two completely different kinds of human behavior? Students especially are bewildered by this distinction. "How can Shakespeare get away with what I get pummeled for in English 1? What gives?" One of the main strands in modern thinking about ordinary language is its essential "poeticality," the complex, layered series of messages that it carries in a single set of words. Our C-B-S pattern of thinking must ignore all this.

Perhaps the most drastic limitation of C-B-S thinking as a general theory of prose stems from its limited range. The history of prose style shows clarity, brevity, and sincerity to be not only rare attainments but even rarer goals. People want to do all kinds of other things through their prose—show off, fool you, fool themselves, run through all the feints and jabs of human sociality. If we push C-B-S thinking to its logical conclusion—and we seldom do—all this complex purpose must be classified as a gigantic mistake.

No wonder students are confused fundamentally by how they are taught to write. They are taught the C-B-S theory for their own writing. Yet when they come to study literature, which a rigorous C-B-S theory would have to revise out of existence, they are taught an opposite theory. And neither theory is brought into consonance with the commonsense rules of ordinary social life. How much easier chemistry and physics seem. There you really have a textbook, an argument from first principles, a periodic table of the elements, basic rules for matter. In the higher reaches, these principles may bend a little but at least they exist to start with. A student knows where to begin. How different with the teaching of writing. A student is given a body of theory, assumed to be a set of first principles but not taught as such; a body of theory riddled with contradictions which the student is forbidden to point out; a body of thinking manifestly inadequate to all that the student will learn about human behavior in every other course in the curriculum; a body of theory which, if actually carried out either in the classroom or in ordinary life, would destroy human sociality (imagine, just one day in which you said exactly what you thought to everyone). No wonder students, and corporations and governments too, hunger for simplistic rules, numerical readability formulas.

The C-B-S theory often does work, of course. We do live in an age of "Official Style" jargons and very often you need to translate them into transparent plain English. You can even, as I tried to show in my earlier volumes in this series, *Revising Prose* and *Revising Business Prose,* do the translating in a formulaic, rule-based way. Living in an age cursed by copiers and high-speed printers we must develop speed-reading techniques. A lot of verbal jungle-clearing must be done. The practical purposes of the world demand it.

Yet it is just in these practical purposes that the limitations of the C-B-S theory really lie. An ideal of silent and transparent prose assumes that we are basically creatures of practical purpose, that we build houses to get out of the rain, wear clothes to keep warm, buy a new car to get to Cucamonga and back. But are we really such purposive creatures? What do we do to our houses? Live in them in quiet content or spend years of weekends fixing them up? How do we pick our clothes? Buy the first thing that fits, or spend hours pursuing something that seems really "us"? And what about cars? The automobile industry represents surely the most practical, purposive, bottom-line part of America. The modern American economy was built on it. And yet do we cherish a C-B-S attitude toward the automobile, ask it only for transport to Cucamonga? Henry Ford thought so and produced both the Model T and the Model A with the same no-frills, basic transportation, any-color-so-long-as-it's-black philosophy. He sold a lot of cars when it was a "T" or nothing at all, but what did people do once they got the car home? They started playing around with it, souping it up, "personalizing" it. They started making it something *beyond* basic transportation, and thus began the great after-market car accessories industry. Meanwhile, Alfred Sloan at General Motors went the other way. He arranged all the cars GM produced into an orderly and multicolored social hierarchy, with Cadillac at the top and Chevy at the bottom. He sold status first and transportation second. And GM nearly put Ford out of business. People took black only when that was the only color they could get. The automotive industry, the great monument to the primacy of practical purpose, turns out to be driven by other motives as well, by social competition on the one hand and pure decorative play on the other. When it comes down to a test, practicality usually proves the weakest of the three.

We all share this simplistic view of human motive, don't we? Like to think of ourselves as basically commonsensical and purposive creatures? Other people, of course, spend their whole lives keeping up with the Joneses or strutting around like peacocks just for the hell of it. That's why they need satirists like Thorstein Veblen, with their incessant mocking of status games and ornamental play. But not us. And it is easy to see why we like to delude ourselves in this way. To think of ourselves as essentially purposive creatures is to flatter ourselves with a self which is independent, if not of external circumstance, then at least of our fellow men. We are intensely status-conscious creatures, condemned to a lifetime of striving for position. This means that we live inevitably in other men's minds. Every statement that we make is, at some remove, a statement about human relationship, about relative standing.

We are also creatures who enter the world with an awful lot of leftover evolutionary baggage. A lot of things come up that we just "feel like doing," and are going to do whether we have a "reason" to do them, whether it "makes sense" to do them, or not. When we're young we play at these things and when we're older we play them out for real. The pioneering students of animal behavior like Konrad Lorenz christened this kind of behavior "vacuum behavior" because it would happen even in a behavioral vacuum. A response wanted to happen so badly it hardly needed a stimulus; a young man is out "looking for trouble"; a young woman "in love with love" needs only someone to fasten it on. In verbal behavior, these play impulses manifest themselves very early on. The infant likes to babble in rhythm, the young child likes to repeat words endlessly, turning them around and around, playing with them like a new toy. And as we get older the pleasures of rhyme, pun, balance, climax come into their own, as well as the love of verbal shapes for their own sake.

When we want to deprecate these two kinds of behavior, competition and vacuum behavior, game and play, as motives for writing, or as ingredients in verbal style, we use the same word for both—"rhetoric." "Rhetoric" is everything in a message which aims not to deliver neutral information but to stimulate action. And rhetoric is the whole domain of ornament, of verbal play, that impulse which always seems to move in on purposive communication like an ornamental border gradually taking over the page in a medieval manuscript. "Rhetoric" was not always a dirty word. Its bad press really comes from what we might call the "Newtonian Interlude" in Western history, the period from the seventeenth through the nineteenth centuries when the world was clearly "out there" and all of us clearly "in here" and the relationship between the two more a neutral exchange of information than an explosive family reunion. The Newtonian Interlude has now become a thing of the past everywhere except in our thinking about prose composition. Evolutionary biology, from its microfocus in the discovery of DNA to its macrofocus in the controversial hypothesis of sociobiology, seeks to acknowledge and explain our evolutionary inheritance, to welcome game and play into the legitimate domain of human motivations. Psychology depicts an interactive perceiver, literary criticism a participatory reader who both plays with and competes with the text he reads. Historians are coming to view themselves as imaginers of history who by their very historical vision decide what counts as a "fact" and what not. They become if not historical novelists then inevitably novelistic historians. Some sociologists and anthropologists have begun to think society a dramatic text with a recognizable repertoire of social roles.

Teachers of writing still cling, however, to a Newtonian idea of verbal behavior, to the C-B-S theory of style. And this in spite of its manifest self-contradictions and its discontinuity with the other disciplines of behavioral inquiry. Partly this is so because it is partly true, as we've seen. But much more we persist because the practical-purpose view of behavior flatters us so, allays our ontological insecurities, our worries about the stability of the self, makes us into simpler and more straightforward creatures than we are. And too because it encourages action. Self-consciousness can be paralytic, as Hamlet found out; we just don't want to risk this. Thinking is hard enough as it is. To orchestrate it with other and conflicting motives can—and in the much-discussed "writer's block" often does—lead to fearful paralysis.

But if we allow the full tripartite range of human motive, play and competition as well as purpose, to enter the domain of verbal style, some extraordinary revelations occur. We no longer, for a start, must repudiate nine-tenths of what we seek to explain. The history of English prose style no longer seems a dark story illuminated by the lighthouse of Dryden's prose at one horizon and George Orwell's at the other. As we shall see, the playfulness of John Cage's typographical experiments or of Kenneth Burke's "Flowerishes" can take their place within the legitimate range of stylistic motivation along with manifest attempts to persuade, like Churchill's speeches or like *Variety's* invidious listings of movie grosses in Chicago. The whole range of prose behavior for the first time makes sense.

And so do the literature/non-literature and prose/poetry splits, both being now part of one spectrum of verbal experience which allows all three motives in an infinite variety of mixtures. Poetry and prose do differ, as we'll see, but not in a fundamental, dichotomous way. And with the poetry/prose distinction clear in our minds, we can see that other fearsome dichotomy—style/content—a little more clearly as well. "Style" usually means the game-and-play part of the message, but sometimes the competitive or the playful part of the message really *is* the message and so style becomes content. Nothing especially "decadent" or even puzzling about this. It happens all the time.

We can begin to see the pedagogy of writing in a new light too. First, the great problem of motivating students: the C-B-S way of thinking puts us all—students and teachers—in a dreadful bind. School is by its nature both a competition and a playground. It is games and play that socialize students, teach them to create and tolerate a society. If these kinds of motive are outlawed for the teaching of writing, not much is left for the composition course, since it has by its nature no "content" or "message" of its own. If we think of journal-writing as a "sincere" expression of self, we blind ourselves to its true function as a way to release the kinds of "selves" the student is currently learning to play and hence to be. When we ask for a "sincere" style from students—and then give them *a good grade* for it—we put them in a double bind: we ask them to "be sincere" in the way that they think the teacher wants them to be.

Most high school and young university students are adolescents and it is during adolescence that the motives of game and play predominate. If we outlaw them we lend to the whole proceeding an abiding air of flattery and falseness that is always felt even if seldom understood. The pedagogy suggested by a full mixture of motive is both easier to understand and more at peace with itself. Purpose enters through studying the forms of expository discourse; persuasion enters as a systematic analysis of our evolutionary baggage, of the actions that "want to happen" and how written and spoken language release these and use their force.

Now we can begin to see why we feel prose composition so important an activity. We need to communicate information efficiently, for certain. But if this is all we try to do, we won't do even this. If we simplify human motive into naive purpose, if we ignore game and play, they will come back to haunt us. If, like Henry Ford, we offer any color so long as it is black, we'll find our customers fleeing to General Motors in the foreseeable fuchsia. To think of prose only within the C-B-S framework encourages a simplistic practicality which can have disastrous results in the practical world. What proves to be really practical in the practical real world is a full and shrewd conception of why people behave as they do. Whether you are trying to sell them an automobile or get them to save electricity, you'll find that appeals to plain purpose seldom do the trick. The really persuasive people have an instinctive grasp of the radical diversity of human motives, of the ever-changing mixture of purpose, game, and play. And it is precisely this mixture that prose style in its fullness always expresses, and that prose analysis can teach. That is why we think the teaching of writing to be so centrally important, important—though we're hard put to say why—far beyond the needs of practical purpose.

And so we can see why prose analysis is worth bothering about. Prose style models human motive. Every statement about style is, if we know how to interpret it, a statement about behavior. Thus the study of style is not a peripheral or cosmetic accompaniment to the exposition of self-standing ideas but a choreography of the whole dance of human consciousness, a dance in which practical purpose and information form but one part. The real practicality in prose analysis is the intuitive grasp of motive which analysis can impart to us. We will know what kind of message a message is. This knowledge proves to be the most practical knowledge of all. It is what every employer looks for in his general managers and long-range planners and senior executives. It is the stuff of which great politicians are made. On a less exalted level it provides the "sense" in common sense.

If we ignore the play and game ranges of human motive, they will come back to plague us. It is at least arguable that this has happened in the literacy crisis itself. Our resolutely purposive C-B-S attitude toward language banished game and play. But that also banishes all the fun and so we start playing games with the "scientific" language, making it more specialized than it needs to be, more restricted to a special audience. We start, that is, inventing the jargons which so vex us today, invent them to demarcate human relations and impulses rather than simply the impersonal and unfeeling conveyance of information.

"Clarity," we found, really meant only "success" in communication; this success almost always means a successful mixture of motives rather than a purity of purpose. When we analyze prose we are really trying to factor out the causes of this success we call "clarity," see how motives have been harmoniously mixed for a particular purpose. And, when you think of it, is this not just what we say a "liberal education" as a whole ought to bestow on us? A sense of how to hold and use what we have learned, a skill for "clarity" in the higher sense of the word? "Wisdom," the philosopher Alfred North Whitehead said, "is the way knowledge is held." The difference between the C-B-S theory of style and the larger mixed-motive one I've been describing is really the difference between being well-informed and being wise, knowing *how* to use information, knowing *what kind of message* a message is. The study of prose style then, properly conceived, shows us what is most centrally "humanistic" about the humanities, what is truly "liberal" in a liberal education.

If this is true, we can perhaps begin to glimpse how instruction in writing fits into the larger curriculum. It is not simply that to read and write about complex subjects you must know how to read and write. Without the judgment of motive stylistic analysis can bestow, a student won't know how to put together the various subjects of the curriculum, the various worlds passed through. Devising an ideal curriculum has been the great humanist pastime for two and a half millennia, but all these ideal designs have been patterns designed from the outside in, a series of disciplines, activities, courses, that must be passed through in a specific order to produce—well, to produce what? Finally, just the intuitive sense of human motive we have been discussing. But it has always been difficult—and today it seems impossible—to fit students into the constraints of a rigid external pattern. The study of prose style provides the same kind of training but *from the inside*. It provides the students with a gyroscope, a compass, a map of human motive, rather than a totally-planned guided tour.

This gyroscope acts as an internal as well as an external guide. Learning to write is like growing up. You model a dozen styles before you find, or make up, one that suits you. Acts of analysis, of self-introspection, alternate with acts of creation. We alternately cherish our self-consciousness and abandon it. This kind of oscillation hardly seems to come natural to us, either in behavior or in its verbal analysis. We have to contrive, through religion or psychiatry or a fraternity party, both our times of introspection and of self-abandonment. And likewise with how we write. The most difficult trick of all is to learn when to involve the analytical powers and when to forget them and write out whatever inside you demands to be written out. Writers get blocked for all kinds of reasons, but the root problem remains the same as on the larger stage of life. The selective pattern of remembering rules and forgetting them, of self-consciousness and spontaneity, does not come naturally. We have to work at it, to remind ourselves that life is neither all creation nor all revision, that it inevitably happens event by event, draft by draft.

But if this life-giving diastole and systole is to occur, both stages of the process must be in robust health. We must know how to assemble and how to take apart. These are not the same activities, though as necessary to one another as breathing out and breathing in. Historically, Western thinking about language and language instruction has stressed analysis far more than creation, bowed briefly to invention and then spent hundreds of pages analyzing the figures of speech. And more often than not, the rhetoricians simply assumed that what you could analyze you could create, that taking apart was the same kind of activity as putting together. We now know this is not true, and Western thinking has since the Romantic period steadily stressed creation instead of analysis. This stress has gone so far that in contemporary America we have almost forgotten how to analyze. We don't know what to say about a passage of prose. We lack a fundamental terminology. We can't even tell a descriptive statement from an evaluative one. *Analyzing Prose* tries to redress the balance a little, to bring breathing-in and breathing-out into a more equitable balance.

But if we do this only in a neutrally descriptive way, if we offer only a descriptive terminology, we will be simply recreating the persistent error of classic rhetorical theory: the assumption that description of stylistic features constitutes its own reason for being, that the connection of style with behavior can safely be left to someone else. The legitimate question that must follow any act of stylistic description is, "So what?" "What difference does it make?" To ask this essential question, though, immediately moves us from description to evaluation. It asks us to supply an analogue in behavior for every stylistic judgment, to move, for example, from the noun-style/verb-style opposition to a meditation on human action *vs.* human thought. We must always do this sooner or later. The hard question is "When?" I've chosen to explicate description in the first eight chapters and let the behavioral analysis enter by implication. The last two chapters reverse this order and talk directly and explicitly about the behavior to which prose style stands analogous. But in both sections I've tried to stay close to the basic questions: "So what?" "What difference does it make?"

I've tried, thus, to answer questions which are very old but that are also on the lips of every modern student. When Socrates objected to the teachings of the Greek rhetoricians, he returned again and again to a single fundamental objection. Rhetoric had no τέχνη, no central body of knowledge, no legitimate area of concern, no room of its own. It was at best only an external cosmetic. We've been living with this Platonic objection ever since—it forms the core, as we have just seen, of the C-B-S theory of style—but we are now in a very good position to answer it. The τέχνη of rhetoric is just the mixture of human motive we have been examining. It comprehends purpose but it is not restricted to purpose; it includes game and play as well. And about game and play especially, we are learning a great deal in all the disciplines which deal with human behavior. The whole of evolutionary biology, in fact, can be taken as a single great answer to Socrates' question: What is the τέχνη of rhetoric? What is the domain of style? What can it be but the whole complex motivational structure of Homo sapiens? And it is that whole structure of motive which we are examining, explicitly or implicitly, when we analyze prose. No wonder it sometimes seems confusing.

Beneath the confusion, though, we can for the first time glimpse the real place of traditional rhetoric in a modern prose world. We can make this point best, perhaps, by restating the basic arguments underlying rhetorical analysis. If words do not matter, only ideas; if all prose should be wholly transparent, not seen and not heard; then rhetorical analysis can be at best an exposé of errors, at worst a dispute about trifles. If, however, the opposite is true, if words matter too, if the whole range of human motive is seen as animating prose discourse, then rhetorical analysis leads us to the essential issues and answers the essential questions about prose style. Classical rhetorical theory assumed a full range of human motive, game, play, and purpose in ever-shifting combinations. We are now discovering just how right and how relevant that mixture is, and hence how useful, here and now, classical rhetoric can be.

·PART ONE·

# Descriptive Analysis

# I

# Noun and Verb Styles

Our exercise in a descriptive terminology for prose starts by recognizing that no generally accepted descriptive terminology for prose exists, no basic set of hierarchical categories, genus, species, phylum, etc. We cannot take all prose styles and divide them into basic groups which themselves divide into subgroups and so on. Stylistic study badly needs such a basic framework, if one could be discovered, but trying to find it would take us far from our present purpose. We'll have to content ourselves with the commonly used categories. They work well enough as it turns out, but they often overlap. Since it is easier to see contrasted pairings than overlapping ones, our informal taxonomy uses basic contrasts. These are not the only contrasts we could use. They've been chosen because, easy to see, they offer the easiest way into prose analysis. This is how you begin to analyze prose anyway. No standard procedure, no check list of questions for every style; you take an outstanding feature and see where it leads.

Easiest to see is the difference between action and stasis.

> *Either:*    I came. I saw. I conquered.
> *or:*         Arrival; Reconnaissance; Victory.

A style based on verbs, on *action;* a style based on nouns, on *stasis.*

Here is a typical modern noun style. The writer is discussing theatricality in Western culture:

> The connection between behaviour in the socially real world and dramatic performance is a double link. Much of everyday social behaviour and socially

15

consequential action is itself composed, and often in a fashion which is recognised at the time as "theatrical" or is revealed as such afterwards. When we construct special buildings or settings for ritual occasions of many kinds, from judicial proceedings to love-making, when we set scenes and dress up or dress down for a social occasion there is a resemblance, which may not be admitted even to ourselves, to the enactment of composed theatrical performances by professional actors. Tacitly or explicitly we constantly draw on symbolic references and typifications shared by playwright, actors and audience. This is the basis of the adoption of dramaturgic terminology by social scientists and of its elaboration in the "mere analogy" of the analysis of social behaviour as more or less skilled performance, by Erving Goffman, and as "symbolic interaction" by Blumer, Becker and others.

The second connection runs, so to speak, the other way. Drama is a presentation of *interpretations* of everyday social behaviour and of consequential action which are, or are offered for, good currency. Moreover, because, as the audience, people can be shown more of the course, causes and consequences of action than they can ever know in the socially real world, the theatre provides usable paradigms for conduct. The excellence of the playwright as composer of theatrical action lies in this. The emergence of modern drama from religious ritual by way of Miracle plays and Moralities is not simply a fact of inconsequential chronology. First, in the Miracles there was the presentation in "ideal types" of conduct, good, evil, wayward, mundane or spiritual, in confrontation, and eventually representation of stereotype figures working out recognisable or plausible strategies of action in order to engage themselves in or disengage themselves from recognisable or plausible social relationships of situations; all these constitute an evolutionary or epigenetic pattern familiar enough in the interpretation of contemporaneous historical changes.

All social structures maintain themselves by means of an apparatus of institutional forms which provide individual members of the society with codes of behaviour and grammatical rules for reading the behaviour of others. (Elizabeth Burns, *Theatricality* [New York: Harper & Row, 1972])

A basic pattern appears here: noun + "is" + prepositional phrase. Sometimes the prepositional phrases precede the "is":

> The connection *between* behaviour
>            *in* the socially real world
>                        and dramatic performance
>    *is* a double link.

Sometimes they follow it:

Drama *is* a presentation
> *of* interpretations
> *of* everyday social behaviour and
> *of* consequential action which are, or are offered
> *for* good currency.

Or they come both fore and aft:

> The emergence  *of* modern drama
> > *from* religious ritual
> > *by* way
> > *of* Miracle plays and Moralities
>
> *is* not simply a fact
> > *of* inconsequential chronology.

If you circle the "is"s and the prepositions throughout the passage, you'll see how this pattern dominates. The prepositional phrase strings create a pronounced (da da *dum,* da da *dum,* da *dum*) monotony which makes the action disappear into the nouns. In the sentence just diagrammed, for example, both natural actor and natural action have been hidden. The actor, *modern drama,* cowers in a prepositional phrase; the action, *emerge,* hides in "emergence." The whole pattern follows from adopting the noun strategy. Rewrite in a verbal style and the prepositional phrases vanish:

Modern drama did not emerge from religious ritual . . . accidentally.

Or, as in the sentence before,

Drama presents and interprets ordinary social behavior and its consequences.

The noun strategy, then, suppresses action in two ways: verb sinks into noun and the sentence's forward motion sinks into the da da *dum* prepositional-phrase-string monotony. Most working prose nowadays uses precisely this monotonous noun-style pattern. Since it so strongly opposes action and movement, bureaucrats love it. Often, as here when used to describe *social action,* it works against its subject.

So, oddly enough, does the following verbal style, a passage (from Virginia Woolf's novel *To the Lighthouse*) which defines a noun, "night."

*[handwritten margin note: opposes action]*

But what after all is one night? A short space, especially when the darkness dims so soon, and so soon a bird sings, a cock crows, or a faint green quickens, like a turning leaf, in the hollow of the wave. Night, however, succeeds to night. The winter holds a pack of them ·in store and deals them equally, evenly, with indefatigable fingers. They lengthen; they darken. Some of them hold aloft clear planets, plates of brightness. The autumn trees, ravaged as they are, take on the flash of tattered flags kindling in the gloom of cool cathedral caves where gold letters on marble pages describe death in battle and how bones bleach and burn far away in Indian sands. The autumn trees gleam in the yellow moonlight, in the light of harvest moons, the light which mellows the energy of labour, and smooths the stubble, and brings the wave lapping blue to the shore.

It seemed now as if, touched by human penitence and all its toil, divine goodness had parted the curtain and displayed behind it, single, distinct, the hare erect; the wave falling; the boat rocking, which, did we deserve them, should be ours always. But alas, divine goodness, twitching the cord, draws the curtain; it does not please him; he covers his treasures in a drench of hail, and so breaks them, so confuses them that it seems impossible that their calm should ever return or that we should ever compose from their fragments a perfect whole or read in the littered pieces the clear words of truth. For our penitence deserves a glimpse only; our toil respite only.

The nights now are full of wind and destruction; the trees plunge and bend and their leaves fly helter skelter until the lawn is plastered with them and they lie in gutters and choke rain pipes and scatter damp paths. Also the sea tosses itself and breaks itself, and should any sleeper fancying that he might find on the beach an answer to his doubts, a sharer of his solitude, throw off his bedclothes and go down by himself to walk on the sand, no image with semblance of serving and divine promptitude comes readily to hand bringing the night to order a making the world reflect the compass of the soul. The hand dwindles in his hand; the voice bellows in his ear. Almost it would appear that it is useless in such confusion to ask the night those questions as to what, and why, and wherefore, which tempt the sleeper from his bed to seek an answer. (*To the Lighthouse* [New York: Harcourt Brace Jovanovich, 1949])

The passage starts out to define a noun ("But what after all is one night? A short space . . .") but then immediately comes a series of verbs which form the central backbone. Maybe a diagram will help here, too:

> . . . the darkness *dims* so soon
> so soon a bird *sings*
> a cock *crows*

or a faint green *quickens*
   like a leaf turning
   in the hollow
   of the wave.
Night, however, *succeeds* to night.
  The winter *holds* a pack of them
   in store and
    *deals* them equally,
   evenly,
   with indefatigable fingers.
They *lengthen;*
they *darken.*

Notice how Woolf's sentences usually get off to a quick subject-verb start? "The winter holds . . ."/"They lengthen"/"They darken"/"The autumn trees gleam"/"Also the sea tosses itself"/"The hand dwindles"/"The voice bellows." Try translating them into a noun style and see what happens. First go shape and rhythm, built as they are on the basic quick-start subject-verb pattern the noun style begins by dissolving. For the subject-verb pattern sets up several other repetitive patterns that, taken together, form the passage's basic structure. A phrase may simply recur (as in "*The autumn trees,* ravaged . . ."/"*The autumn trees* gleam") but usually the phrases resemble each other only in structure and length:

mellows the energy of labour
smooths the stubble
brings the wave
*or* the hare erect
the wave falling
the boat rocking
*or* for our penitence deserves a   glimpse only
our toil          respite only
*or* they lie packed in gutters and
choke rainpipes and
scatter damp paths
*or* the hand dwindles in his hand
the wave bellows in his ear

Arranging phrases and clauses in units of equal length and structure is called *isocolon;** Virginia Woolf uses it as her basic organizational pattern

*See the Glossary at the end of the book for definitions of rhetorical terms.

here. Sometimes obviously, as in the examples above; sometimes, as follows, much less so. A diagram backlights the pattern:

> The autumn trees, ravaged as they are,
> take on the *flash of tattered flags*
> kindling in the      *gloom of cool cathedral caves*
> where                *gold letters on marble pages*
> *describe death in battle* and how
> *bones bleach and burn* far away in Indian sands.

Notice how the isocolon is reinforced by alliterations:

> *fl*ash . . . *fl*ags
> *g*loom . . . *g*old
> *c*ool *c*athedral *c*aves
> *b*ones *b*leach and *b*urn

She uses alliteration in this way throughout the passage. She also, once or twice, uses a pattern that inverts the basic parallelism. It is called *chiasmus,* turning the parallelism into a mirror (*ABBA* instead of *ABAB*):

> A   B          B            A
> yellow moonlight, in the light of harvest moons
>
> A         B        B     A
> darkness dims so soon, and so soon a bird sings

We saw that choosing a noun style leads to a pattern, a characteristic syntax. The verb style too suggests a consequent pattern, a series of parallel phrases appealing to eye and ear. But suggests, not compels. A verb style may not proceed in this way or a noun style may. A decision about one element, though, usually does decide about others. And because a logic prevails in the interconnection between elements, styles do come in basic types. This logic emerges especially clearly when translating one style into another, making a noun style verbal, for example. When the central strategic choice shifts, other changes follow. Consider the Burns passage on theatricality analyzed earlier. Here is a line-by-line translation into a verb style.

## NOUN STYLE

The connection between behaviour in the socially real world and dramatic performance is a double link.

## VERB STYLE

Socially "real" behaviour and dramatic performance overlap.

## NOUN STYLE

Much of everyday social behaviour and socially consequential action is itself composed, and often in a fashion which is recognised at the time as "theatrical" or is revealed as such afterwards.

## VERB STYLE

When we act in real life we often recognize it, either at the time or later.

## NOUN STYLE

When we construct special buildings or settings for ritual occasions of many kinds, from judicial proceedings to love-making, when we set scenes and dress up or dress down for a social occasion there is a resemblance, which may not be admitted even to ourselves, to the enactment of composed theatrical performances by professional actors.

## VERB STYLE

When we build ritual settings, from law-courts to boudoirs, when we dress up or down, we resemble—admit it or not—professional actors.

## NOUN STYLE

Tacitly or explicitly we constantly draw on symbolic references and typifications shared by playwright, actors and audience. This is the basis of the adoption of dramaturgic terminology by social scientists and of its elaboration in the "mere analogy" of the analysis of social behaviour as more or less skilled performance, by Erving Goffman, and as "symbolic interaction" by Blumer, Becker and others.

VERB STYLE

And since, knowingly or not, we use dramatic symbols, social scientists can assess our behavior as drama (Goffman) or as symbolic interaction (Blumer, Becker and others).

Concentrate on verbs and the strings of prepositional phrases vanish. Their departure in turn allows the sentence to assume a more varied shape. With the prepositional phrases still on board, the sentences can have only one shape, the "is + prepositional phrase" string we've seen:

> This is the basis    *of* the adoption
> *of* dramaturgic terminology
> *by* social scientists and
> *of* its elaboration
> *in* the "mere analogy"
> *of* the analysis
> *of* social behaviour
> *as* more or less skilled performance
> *by* Erving Goffman and
> *as* "symbolic interaction"
> *by* Blumer, Becker and others.

This formula holds a noun stylist by the throat. Changing from noun to verb style breaks the stranglehold. (Notice how I've moved from description to an evaluative metaphor?) And not by accident is the verb style translation half as long. The "is + prepositional phrase" formula by its very form encourages repetition. Why not add another qualifying prepositional phrase or three to the string?

How strongly this formal encouragement may operate you can see in the following translation, one which moves in the opposite direction, from verb style to noun style. One of my students, Susan Dingilian, has taken a passage of my prose where I'm striving to avoid the noun-style pattern, and deliberately courted it instead. (I'm talking, in this example, about an earlier version of the stylistic spectrum discussed in chapters 9 and 10.)

VERB STYLE

Posit the two extremes of our spectrum. Both are unliterary. At the extreme left, childish babble, nursery rhymes, pure pleasure in words. Words here are things. You play with them. They have shape, sound, corporeality. At the other end, a mathematical equation, pure significance, all sign. Pleasure flows from concepts. Nonsense rhyme presents a perfectly opaque surface, equations a perfectly transparent one. (*Style: An Anti-Textbook* [New Haven: Yale University Press, 1974])

NOUN STYLE

A perception of the two extreme poles of this spectrum of language is derived from a conception of the range of language under consideration. The unliterary quality of the kinds of discourse found on each pole of the spectrum must first be understood, however. The left pole of this spectrum is characterized by the presence of the babble associated with children and the presence of children's nursery rhymes; in terms of the attitudes associated with this pole of the spectrum, there is a general preference for the derivation of pleasure from language. Language on the left pole of the spectrum is characterized by the reification of words; in other words, words are given a tangible quality. In accordance with this theory, words are found by the reader to be the objects of play. A categorization of the properties of this kind of language reveals in it the existence of a principle of contour, an audible quality, and a sense of physical corporeality. On the pole to the extreme right of the spectrum, there is an abundance of symbols, notably the equations associated with the practice of mathematical inquiry, which appear to exist for the sake of their denotative quality; transparent signifiers and their readily comprehensible signifieds are to be found on this pole of the spectrum. On this pole, concepts constitute the body of ideas from which pleasure is derived. From this discussion it is apparent that the verbal surface of types of prose like nonsense rhymes is characterized by opacity; transparency is more characteristic of the surface texture of mathematical equations, however.

Another force has supervened in the translations beyond the noun-verb change—translation itself. Translation, like revision, makes us pay attention to the verbal surface and this attention changes things almost by itself. The Burns style, for example, pays no attention to sound patterns. If we attend to them nevertheless, the prose becomes almost unreadable. Look at the tongue-twisting ending pattern *(homoioteleuton)* in "tacit*ly* or explicit*ly* we constant*ly* . . ." or at the "p" and "s" alliteration in a paragraph just after the one we've been discussing:

To regard the same evolutionary *p*attern as *p*art of the *p*rocess of *s*ecularisation is to *s*hift to a *p*ers*p*ective which *is* *s*ignificantly but not qualitatively different. *Secularisation* as a *process* by which *publicly sacred* institu*tion*s, formal religious *p*ractice*s* and ob*s*ervance*s,* and Church organi*sation* gradually empty of authority, regular and *sanctioned performances* dimini*sh,* and acknowledged member*ship* decline*s,* has its counterpart in the *sanctification* of *s*e*c*ular life. The double *process* of the *s*e*c*ulari*s*a*tion* of the *s*a*c*red, and the *s*an*c*tifi*cation* of *s*e*c*ular life in the h*i*storical period (the *s*ixteenth *c*entury) with which we are centrally concerned at this point occurs . . .

To read such prose, we must turn off our ears. Virginia Woolf used alliteration too, but to reinforce a pattern. We are meant to notice it. She used similar endings too (equa*lly,* even*ly;* length*en,* dark*en*) but again means them to be noticed as part of a larger design, as extended parallelism. This difference in stylistic self-consciousness makes Woolf seem to control her verb/parallelism strategy, while Burns seems controlled by her "is + prepositional phrase" formula. The two passages differ as much, then, in their stylistic self-consciousness as they do in their noun/verb use. An inner logic may be operating here, too. Verb styles tend to be self-conscious. Styles conceived, like the British Empire, in a fit of absence of mind, tend to be noun styles. The "is + prepositional phrase" formula, at least in our time, seems to come naturally.

Let's look at a less extreme style than either of these, one about halfway between noun and verb. Here is John Dean beginning his Watergate chronicle:

"Would you be interested in working at the White House?" Bud Krogh asked me casually.

It was a warm afternoon in May 1970, and we were walking toward a park bench that was well shaded by the aged trees surrounding the Ellipse. Bud had invited me to his White House office and, when I arrived, had suggested that we take a stroll so that we could talk, but I had had no idea what he wanted to talk about. I was pleasantly surprised by the question.

"Why do you ask?" I countered, trying to check my impulse to give way to flattery.

As I listened to Bud telling me he had recommended me for President Nixon's White House staff, I was also paying attention to the little voice in the back of my head that was telling me to act reserved, to remember the negative impressions I had collected about the White House: friends haggard and drained from long hours of pressure, able men reduced to "gophers" and errand boys, breaking their necks whenever one of the President's top aides had a whim. That was not for me even if it was the White House. My job at the Justice Department was relaxed and enjoyable, with importance and promise for advancement. "Bud, thank you," I said, "but I really like it at Justice."

I did not want to act coy, just properly cautious, so that he would carry back the message that I would not be lured by just any job. He was scouting, and I wanted to find out exactly how interested the White House was. As always, I was masking my inner calculations and feelings, this time behind an appearance of friendly sincerity. So was Krogh. We had both come a long way in the government at thirty.

Speaking as if he were musing on whether I could move my desk down the hall, Bud inquired whether I thought the Attorney General, John N. Mitchell, would let me move to the White House.

"I really don't know," I replied. (*Blind Ambition* [New York: Simon and Schuster, 1976])

The verbs in this passage don't stand out but they work hard. He varies them nicely (another evaluative term), active and passive, simple and progressive, active and passive participles, a sprinkling of infinitives. Taken together with a skillful variation in sentence-length they get Dean's narrative off to a fast start. Could you write this kind of narrative in the Burns noun style? Two things, at least, would prevent it. A passage like this depends for its effect on a colloquial rhythm prepositional-phrase strings would destroy. Nor could the word choice—all those Latinate noun phrases like "socially consequential action" and "adoptions of dramaturgic terminology"—create a convincing image of conversation. For these reasons, too, the noun style tends to be a written, not a spoken, style.

Could you, using translation again as a device to look *at* the words rather than *through* them, write on a Burns topic in a Dean style? Make social science sound like conversation? Here is someone trying:

My problem is that I have been persecuted by an integer. For seven years this number has followed me around, has intruded in my most private data, and has assaulted me from the pages of our most public journals. This number assumes a variety of disguises, being sometimes a little larger and sometimes a little smaller than usual, but never changing so much as to be unrecognizable. The persistence with which this number plagues me is far more than a random accident. There is a design behind it, some pattern governing its appearances. Either there really is something unusual about the number or I am suffering from delusions of persecution.

I shall begin my case history by telling you about some experiments that tested how accurately people can assign numbers to the magnitudes of various aspects of a stimulus. In the traditional language of psychology these would be called experiments in absolute judgment. Historical accident, however, has decreed that they should have another name. We now call them experiments on the capacity of people to transmit information. Since these experiments would not have been carried out if information theory had not appeared on the psychological scene, and since the results are analyzed in terms of the concepts of information theory, I shall have to preface my discussion with a few remarks about this theory. (George A. Miller, "The Magical Number Seven, Plus or Minus Two," in *The Psychology of Communication* [New York: Basic Books, 1975])

More action by half than the Burns passage. Look at the verbs: "persecuted," "followed me around," "intruded," "assaulted," "assumes disguises," "plagues me." The scientist uncharacteristically enters in his own person—"I have been persecuted"—and this invites active, transitive verbs to follow. He casts his discussion as a personal narrative, a case history, and deliberately invites the reader—"I shall begin my case history by telling you"—to form part of the conversational group. Very like Dean, then, beginning his case history. And the style wants to go the same way—lots of verbal action, varied sentence-length and conversational rhythm, colloquial diction. But it doesn't quite get there. He starts fast but then the prepositional-phrase strings begin: "*to* the magnitude *of* various aspects *of* a stimulus," "*in* terms *of* the concepts *of* information theory." And the diction inevitably becomes more specialized. As a result, the style does not get where it wants to go, hangs irresolute between Burns and Dean. Let me, by revising the first paragraph, push it closer to Dean.

"My problem is that I have been persecuted by an integer." No revision needed here. The "my X is that" or "the fact of the matter is that" opening, usually a filler that keeps the sentence from starting fast, here really works. "My problem" is just where the passage ought to begin, and delaying the entrance of the faintly melodramatic "I have been persecuted by an integer" strengthens the self-conscious comedy.

For seven years this number has followed me around, has intruded in my most private data, and has assaulted me from the pages of our most public journals.

The changes here underline the incipient parallelism which, as in the Woolf passage, often develops logically from a verb-style choice:

| | | |
|---|---|---|
| followed | me | around |
| intruded in | my | most private data |
| assaulted | me | from our most public journals |

Because the sentence begins with a comic reference to the magical number seven, the comedy wants to be sustained, and so we emphasize the parallelism between "most private data" and "most public journals." In a change like this, the verb-style logic cuts filler words and needless qualifications rather than, as in the noun-style prepositional-phrase strings, encouraging them. The verb style wants to move fast.

This number assumes *a variety of* disguises, *being* sometimes a little larger
or
*and sometimes a little* smaller *than usual*, but never *changing so much*
*as to be* unrecognizable.

REVISION

This number assumes disguises, sometimes a little larger or smaller, but never unrecognizable.

Again, simply following the verb style's internal logic, pushing it where it wants to go:

It                                                with
*The persistence   with which this number* plagues me *is far* more than *a*
persistence
random *accident.*

REVISION

It plagues me with more than random persistence.

A          lurks
*There is a* design  behind it, some pattern governing *its appearances.*

REVISION

A design lurks behind it, some governing pattern.

Either *there* really is *something* unusual *about* the number or I am suffering *from* delusions of persecution.

REVISION

Either the number really is unusual or I am suffering delusions of persecution.

These changes confirm the passage's verb-style logic, reinforce the try for a colloquial personality. The whole paragraph now, original and revision:

ORIGINAL

My problem is that I have been persecuted by an integer. For seven years this number has followed me around, has intruded in my most private data, and has assaulted me from the pages of our most public journals. This number assumes a variety of disguises, being sometimes a little larger and sometimes a little smaller than usual, but never changing so much as to be unrecognizable. The persistence with which this number plagues me is far more than a random accident. There is a design behind it, some pattern governing its appearances. Either there really is something unusual about the number or I am suffering from delusions of persecution.

REVISION

My problem is that I have been persecuted by an integer. For seven years this number has followed me around, intruded in my most private data and assaulted me from our most public journals. This number assumes disguises, sometimes a little larger or smaller, but never unrecognizable. It plagues me with more than random persistence; a design lurks behind it, some governing pattern. Either the number really is unusual or I am suffering delusions of persecution.

Revision, like translation, often serves to expose a style's interior logic—make it, as here, more like itself.

Could you write—to take an extreme example of translation-as-analysis—a Burns-like or Miller-like scientific report in Woolf's self-consciously mannered style? Not likely. It has, though, been done at least once. Gilbert White was an eighteenth-century English country clergyman and amateur naturalist. Here, in his *Natural History of Selborne* (New York: Penguin, 1977) he describes the flight of birds.

A good ornithologist should be able to distinguish birds by their air as well as by their colours and shape; on the ground as well as on the wing; and in the bush as well as in the hand. For though it must not be said that every species of birds has a manner peculiar to itself, yet there is somewhat in most genera at least, that at first sight discriminates them, and enables a judicious observer to pronounce upon them, with some certainty. Put a bird in motion . . . *et vera incessu patuit* . . .

Thus kites and buzzards sail round in circles with wings expanded and motionless; and it is from their gliding manner that the former are still called in the north of England gleads, from the Saxon verb *glidan,* to glide. The kestrel, or windhover, has a peculiar mode of hanging in the air in one place, his wings all the while being briskly agitated. Hen-harriers fly low over heaths or fields of corn, and beat the ground regularly like a pointer or setting-dog. Owls move in a buoyant manner, as if lighter than the air; they seem to want ballast. There is a peculiarity belonging to ravens that must draw the attention even of the most incurious—they spend all their leisure time in striking and cuffing each other on the wing in a kind of playful skirmish; and, when they move from one place to another, frequently turn on their backs with a loud croak and seem to be falling to the ground. When this odd gesture betides them they are scratching themselves with one foot, and thus lose the centre of gravity. Rooks sometimes dive and tumble in a frolicsome manner; crows and daws swagger in their walk; wood-peckers fly *volatu undoso,* opening and closing their wings at every stroke, and so are always rising or falling in curves. All of this genus use their tails, which decline downward, as a support while they run up trees. Parrots, like all other hookclawed birds, walk awkwardly and make use of their bill as a third foot, climbing and descending with ridiculous caution. All the *Gallinae* parade and walk gracefully and run nimbly; but fly with difficulty with an impetuous whirring, and in a straight line. Magpies and jays flutter with powerless wings, and make no dispatch; herons seem encumbered with too much sail for their light bodies, but these vast hollow wings are necessary in carrying burdens, such as large fishes and the like; pigeons, and particularly the sort called smiters, have a way of clashing their wings, the one against the other, over their backs with a loud snap; another variety, called tumblers, turn themselves over in the air. Some birds have movements peculiar to the season of love; thus ringdoves, though strong and rapid at other times, yet in the spring hang about on the wing in a toying and playful manner; thus the cock-snipe, while breeding, forgetting his former flight, fans the air like the windhover; and the greenfinch in particular, exhibits such languishing and faltering gestures as to appear like a wounded and dying bird; the kingfisher darts along like an arrow; fern-owls or goat-suckers, glance in the dusk over the tops of trees like a meteor; starlings as it were swim along, while missel-thrushes use a wild and desultory flight; swallows sweep over the surface of the ground and water, and distinguish themselves by rapid turns and quick evolutions; swifts dash round in circles; and the bank-martin moves with frequent vacillations like a butterfly. Most of the small birds fly by jerks, rising and falling as they advance. Most small birds hop; but wagtails and larks walk, moving their legs alternately. Skylarks rise and fall perpendicularly as they sing; woodlarks hang poised in the air; and titlarks rise and fall in large curves, singing in their descent. The whitethroat uses odd jerks and gesticulations over the tops of hedges and bushes. All the duck kind waddle; divers and auks walk as if fettered; and stand erect on their tails; these are the *Compedes* of Linnaeus. Geese and cranes, and most wild fowls move in figured flights, often changing their position. The secondary *remiges* of *Iringae,* wild ducks, and others, are very long, and give their wings, when in motion, a hooked appearance. Dabchicks, moor-hens, and coots, fly erect, with their legs hanging down, and hardly making any dispatch; the reason is plain, their wings are placed too forward out of the true centre of gravity; as the legs of auks and divers are situated too backward.

White faces a task common enough in the Age of Science. He has to compile a descriptive list, communicate a body of repetitive data alike in source and extent. A modern ornithologist would doubtless transmit such information in a chart or subheaded list. But White, ornithologizing before see-through prose had dominated science, felt free to write a self-conscious literary prose. Because he is discussing the flight of birds, he builds his passage on a skeleton of active verbs which describe this flight:

> kites and buzzards sail around
> Hen-harriers fly low
> Owls move in a buoyant manner
> Rooks sometimes dive and tumble
> daws swagger
> woodpeckers fly *volatu undoso*

This basic pattern of verbal assertion he varies with alternative verb forms. The windhover "has a peculiar mode of hanging," instead of "hangs peculiarly"; the whitethroat "uses odd jerks and gesticulations" instead of "jerks and gesticulates"; pigeons "have a way of clashing their wings" instead of "clash them"; ravens don't simply "strike and cuff" each other, they "spend all their leisure in striking and cuffing each other on the wing." But the basic subject-verb-qualification (bird-flies-thus) pattern underlies the whole passage. In the Woolf passage, a pronounced parallelism followed from the basic verb-style choice. Here, too, self-conscious parallelism of phrases (iso-colon) occurs continually. In the opening sentence:

> A good ornithologist should be able to distinguish birds
> by their air as well as     by their colours and shape
> on the ground as well as     on the wing and
> in the bush as well as     in the hand

The need for a third element in the pattern (the "thus" qualification in the "bird-flies-thus" formula) leads White into the prepositional-phrase string danger we've confronted in noun styles. He handles it by grouping them in this self-conscious parallelism. And he chooses, as did Woolf, to underline it with alliteration. He uses it, for example, to bind together the bird and his manner of flight:

> *t*umblers *t*urn
> *g*oat-suckers *g*lance
> *s*tarlings *s*wim
> *sw*allows *sw*eep

And he will often divide and balance his syntax, too, exactly to fit the infor-mation offered.

MAIN ASSERTION #1

> All the *Gallinae* parade
> (qualification)     and walk gracefully
> (qualification)     and run nimbly

MAIN ASSERTION #2

> (Contrast to #1)     but fly
> (qualification)     with difficulty
> (qualification)     and in a straight line

The prose does not openly diagram the information but it leads the reader's eye and ear in that direction.

White writes both a noun style and a verb style, then, and balances the two. And the balance shows in the parallelism and contrast that devolve from it. "Bird-flies-thus" becomes thus a central backbone for the passage, a principal pattern then varied to give the list an interest it would otherwise lack. Push this basic form—noun-verb-qualification—in the opposite direction and you end up outside the range of prose altogether, in the world of chart and graph. In such a world noun and verb are converted into the horizontal and vertical coordinates and the qualification comes from the reader's relating the two. This interpretive eye, as we shall see later, is evoked by more than one kind of prose.

# II

# Parataxis and Hypotaxis

A style's characteristic manner of connecting provides an easy way to recognize it. Whatever units a writer chooses to work with—phrases, clauses, or complete sentences—he must relate them equally or unequally. He can tell us how they are related—A *caused* B, B *came after* A—and thus subordinate one to the other, by cause, time, or whatever, or he can simply juxtapose them and leave the relationship up to us. When Caesar wrote "I came; I saw; I conquered" *(Veni, vidi, vici.)* he was leaving a great deal up to us. We were to infer that, for Caesar, diagnosing the situation ("I saw") and defeating the enemy ("I conquered") were no more difficult than simply appearing on the scene ("I came"). He boasts without seeming to by putting three different kinds of action on the same syntactic level. This syntactic democracy is called *parataxis*. If Caesar had written instead, "Since it was I who arrived, and I who saw how the land lay, the victory followed as a matter of course," he would have said outright what the tight-lipped "came-saw-conquered" formula only invites us to say about him. The second formulation is *hypotaxis*. Hypotaxis lets us know how things rank, what derives from what. If Caesar had been Eisenhower, and written a hypotactic, a less intensely egotistical prose, he might have said something like "Since I got there early and soon saw what ought to be done, why, it was easy to conquer France." Both paratactic and hypotactic styles can work in complex ways but the principle remains the same. Is the ranking done for us (hypotaxis) or left up to us (parataxis)?

Perhaps the most consistent, philosophically reasoned paratactic style in our time has been written by Ernest Hemingway. Here is the famous tight-lipped syntactic reserve:

Now in the fall the trees were all bare and the roads were muddy. I rode to Gorizia from Udine on a camion. We passed other camions on the road and I looked at the country. The mulberry trees were bare and the fields were brown. There were wet dead leaves on the road from the rows of bare trees and men were working on the road, tamping stone in the ruts from piles of crushed stone along the side of the road between the trees. We saw the town with a mist over it that cut off the mountains. We crossed the river and I saw that it was running high. It had been raining in the mountains. We came into the town past the factories and then the houses and villas and I saw that many more houses had been hit. On a narrow street we passed a British Red Cross ambulance. The driver wore a cap and his face was thin and very tanned. I did not know him. I got down from the camion in the big square in front of the Town Mayor's house, the driver handed down my rucksack and I put it on and swung on the two musettes and walked to our villa. It did not feel like a homecoming. (*A Farewell to Arms* [New York: Charles Scribner's Sons, 1929])

Although the passage includes a complex sentence or two, the basic pattern emerges from the alternation of simple and compound ones. "I did X *and* I did Y." No causal relationships are spelled out even when they scream to be:

We crossed the river and I saw that it was running high. It had been raining in the mountains.

The obvious "*Because* it had been raining in the mountains, the river was running high," Hemingway declines to elaborate. When a syntactic pattern becomes so pronounced as this, we suspect that the syntax has become allegorical, has come to be *about* connection, *about* a refusal to subordinate. The narrator here registers things passively, as they impinge upon his consciousness. He refuses, the syntax suggests, to make complex, unequal connections, to relate, to explain X in terms of Y. Instead, only the simplest, and at best temporal, relationship: X and Y, or, first X and then Y. When you feel a style making this allegorical appeal, it helps to diagram the pattern speaking to us, highlight it while downplaying the other element.

The chart (p. 35) dramatizes a basic seesaw rhythm. The "and" connection runs through it like a backbone. This Hemingway hero does not reflect on the world he passes through; he notes and endures it. The chart also illuminates some other stylistic elements. We noticed in the last chapter that

Now in the fall the trees were all bare *and* the roads were muddy.
I rode to Gorzia from Udine on a camion.
We passed other camions on the road *and* I looked at the country.
  The mulberry trees were bare *and* the fields were brown.
There were wet dead leaves
  on the road from the rows of bare trees *and* men were working on the road,
tamping stone in the ruts from piles of crushed stone along the side of the road between the trees.
We saw the town with a mist over it that cut off the mountains.
  We crossed the river *and* I saw that it was running high.
It had been raining in the mountains.
We came into the town
past the factories and then the houses and villas *and* I saw that many more houses had been hit.
On a narrow street we passed a British Red Cross ambulance.
  The driver wore a cap *and* his face was thin and very tanned.
I did not know him.
  I got down from the camion in the big square in front of the Town Mayor's house
  the driver handed down my rucksack *and* I put it on
  *and* swung on the two musettes
  *and* walked to our villa.

It did not feel like a homecoming.

every style possesses an inner logic. A basic decision—for a noun style, a verb style, or here for parataxis—encourages subsidiary elements to follow. Parataxis most obviously encourages *anaphora,* a pattern of similar sentence-openings. Here there are three basic ones, the "I + verb" formula, the "We + verb" formula, and the "indefinite pronoun/noun + was" formula:

> I rode from Gorizia
> I looked at the country
> I saw that it was running high
> I saw that many more houses
> I did not know him
> I got down from the camion
> I put it on
> and
> We passed other camions
> We saw the town
> We crossed the river
> We came into the town
> We passed a British Red Cross ambulance
> and
> The trees were all bare
> The roads were muddy
> The mulberry trees were bare
> The fields were brown
> There were wet dead leaves
> Men were working
> It had been raining
> his face was thin
> It did not feel like a homecoming.

A series of short phrases or clauses equalized by parataxis seems almost to invite these repetitive openings. We are reminded, on the one hand, of Scripture's iterative ritual repetition—a list of "Thou shalt not's" or of "begats." On the other hand, the humble laundry list comes to mind. When you think of it, ordinary workday prose is often taken up with lists. They represent parataxis par excellence. Hemingway here draws on both resemblances, sacred and mundane. We feel the parataxis to be emotionally charged, deliberately held in check and understated, as in Scripture. But we also feel the dry breath of empty lists, of an exhausted and passive narrator who can *list* the countryside he passes through but feels too exhausted to understand it, and to suggest this understanding through subordination.

The list mentality shows in the verbs, too, forms of "to be" more often than not. Things simply are or he simply looks at them. And when they "are," we have the prepositional-phrase strings we saw in the last chapter as devolving from "to be":

> There *were* wet dead leaves
>   on the road
>   from the rows
>   of bare trees
> and men *were* working
>   on the road, tamping stone
>   in the ruts
>   from piles
>   of crushed stone
>   along the side
>   of the road
>   between the trees.

These prepositional-phrase strings, as we've noticed earlier, can be extremely monotonous. (Monotonous can be a neutral descriptive term— one-toned—but notice how easily, as here, it falls over into evaluation?) Here the basic paratactic rhythm, the syntactic democracy, seems to flow into them and subsume them into the basic pattern. As a result, we don't notice them so much.

The insistent parataxis of this passage illustrates yet another tendency inherent in paratactic styles, the movement toward verse. Often, printing such a style as verse will almost make it into verse. Verse-making is not quite that easy, to be sure, but the disconnected, syntactically equal units gravitate in this direction, Scripture again a familiar example. It is often said that a paratactic style is easier to write than a hypotactic one, that it comes more naturally. Hemingway's prose suggests that this may be too simple. There is, of course, the Shakespearean Mrs. Quickly example, a garrulous old biddy you hear on the bus: "And then I says to Fred, I says . . . and he says and so I says. . . ." But parataxis can be a contrived, patterned, self-conscious style, one whose syntax can carry, as we have seen, an allegorical meaning of its own. It is easy to write a laundry list, but not so easy to write like Hemingway without falling into parody. Try it.

The "and" pattern Hemingway used introduces another pair of basic terms—*asyndeton* and *polysyndeton*. An asyndetic style does without connectors. (That is just what the Greek means—"without connections.") A polysyndetic style makes a great many connections. You need both terms to pin down Hemingway's parataxis because he seems basically asyndetic and only symbolically polysyndetic. The "and" connector is emphasized but it is almost the only one. Its very poverty intensifies the *asyndetic* world, a world where connections are not possible.

Chronicle history provides the most obvious example of a polysyndetic style: first A happened *and* then B *and* then C, et cetera. Here is a famous piece of chronicle polysyndeton, Malory's description of the truce broken by the accidental drawing of a sword and of King Arthur's subsequent fight with Mordred. I've emphasized the connectors:

*And* so they met as their appointment was, *and* were agreed *and* accorded thoroughly. *And* wine was set, *and* they drank together. *Right so* came out an adder of a little heath bush, *and* it stung a knight in the foot. *And so when* the knight felt him so stung, he looked down *and* saw the adder; *and* anon he drew his sword to slay the adder, *and* thought no other harm. *And when* the host on both parts saw that sword drawn, *then* they blew trumpets and horns, *and* shouted grimly, *and* so both hosts dressed them together. *And* King Arthur took his horse *and* said, "Alas, this unhappy day!" *and* so rode to his party, *and* Sir Mordred in like wise.

*And* never since was there a more dolefull battle in no Christian land, *for* there was but rushing and riding, thrusting and striking, *and* many a grim word was there spoken of one to another, *and* many a deadly stroke. *But* ever King Arthur rode throughout the battle many times *and* did full nobly, as a noble King should do, *and* at all times he fainted never. *And* Sir Mordred did his duty that day *and* put himself in great peril.

*And* thus they fought all the long day, *and* never stinted until the noble knights were laid to the cold earth. *And* ever they fought still until it was near night, *and by then* was there an hundred thousand laid dead upon the earth. *Then* was King Arthur wrathful out of measure, *when* he saw his people so slain from him. . . . *Then* King Arthur looked about *and* was aware where stood Sir Mordred leaning upon his sword among a great heap of dead men.

"*Now,* give me my spear," said King Arthur unto Sir Lucan, "for yonder I have espyed the traitor that this woe hath wrought.". . . *Then* the King got his spear in both his hands, *and* ran toward Sir Mordred, crying and saying,

"Traitor, now is thy death-day come!"

*And when* Sir Mordred saw King Arthur he ran unto him with his sword drawn in his hand, *and* there King Arthur smote Sir Mordred under the shield, with a foin of his spear, throughout the body more than a fathom. *And when* Sir Mordred felt that he had his death's wound he thrust himself with the might that he had up to the burr of King Arthur's spear, and *right so* he smote his father, King Arthur, with his sword, holding it in both his hands, upon the side of the head, that the sword pierced the helmet and the outer membrane of the brain. *And* therewith Mordred dashed down stark dead to the earth. (Sir Thomas Malory, *Le Morte d'Arthur* [New York: Bramhall House, 1962])

The "and—then" pattern comes across in silent reading as more monotonous than it does when the passage is read aloud. A good storyteller can convert such ritual "and"s and "then"s into pauses or rests, some long and some short, which punctuate his narrative and build suspense. The polysyndetic pattern, simple as it is, in skilled hands turns into a performative advantage, a discretionary opportunity to slow down the narrative or speed it up, to color it with intonation or pregnant pause. Try reading the passage aloud. You can, by coming down hard on the "and"s, reduce the passage to a maddening monotony, or you can syncopate them out almost completely. Malory is not alone in claiming this flexibility. The connectors—*and, then, but, however*—often work in a polysyndetic style as much rhythmically as syntactically, telling the voice where to rise or fall, hurry up, or go slow. When, as with Malory, the connector is a simple repeated one—"and"— we often feel echoing the ritual harp beat of oral epic, a basic mensuration against which the improvising poet juxtaposes his ever-changing inventions.

Dickens provides us with an equally famous example of the opposite pattern, *asyndeton*, when he begins *Bleak House:*

LONDON. Michaelmas Term lately over, and the Lord Chancellor sitting in Lincoln's Inn Hall. Implacable November weather. As much mud in the streets as if the waters had but newly retired from the face of the earth, and it would not be wonderful to meet a Megalosaurus, forty feet long or so, waddling like an elephantine lizard up Holborn Hill. Smoke lowering down from chimney-pots, making a soft black drizzle, with flakes of soot in it as big as full-grown snowflakes—gone into mourning, one might imagine, for the death of the sun. Dogs, undistinguishable in mire. Horses, scarcely better—splashed to their very blinkers. Foot passengers, jostling one another's umbrellas, in a general infection of ill-temper, and losing their foothold at street corners, where tens of thousands of other foot passengers have been slipping and sliding since the day broke (if this day ever broke), adding new deposits to the crust upon crust of mud, sticking at those points tenaciously to the pavement, and accumulating at compound interest.

Fog everywhere. Fog up the river, where it flows among green aits and meadows; fog down the river, where it rolls defiled among the tiers of shipping and the waterside pollutions of a great (and dirty) city. Fog on the Essex marshes, fog on the Kentish heights. Fog creeping into the cabooses of collier-brigs; fog lying out on the yards and hovering in the rigging of great ships; fog drooping on the gunwales of barges and small boats. Fog in the eyes and throats of ancient Greenwich pensioners, wheezing by the firesides of their wards; fog in the stem and bowl of the afternoon pipe, of the wrathful skipper, down in his close cabin; fog cruelly pinching the toes and fingers of his shivering little prentice boy on deck. Chance people on the bridges peeping over the parapets into a nether sky of fog, with fog all around them, as if they were up in a balloon, and hanging in the misty clouds.

Gas looming through the fog in divers places in the streets, much as the sun may, from the spongy fields, be seen to loom by husbandman and plough-boy. Most of the shops lighted two hours before the time—as the gas seems to know, for it has a haggard and unwilling look.

The raw afternoon is rawest, and the dense fog is densest, and the muddy streets are muddiest, near that leaden-headed old obstruction, appropriate ornament for the threshold of a leaden-headed old corporation—Temple Bar. And hard by Temple Bar, in Lincoln's Inn Hall, at the very heart of the fog, sits the Lord High Chancellor in his High Court of Chancery. (*Bleak House* [New York: Penguin, 1977])

Here the syntax imitates the saccades—the discontinuous leaps—which the eye makes in surveying a scene. The eye can move, and the fog, but very little else. An asyndetic style is often, as here, paratactic as well, and the anaphora which parataxis often brings with it occurs here, too. Not only all those sentences beginning with "fog" but the less obvious pattern of noun + qualifier: "smoke lowering," "dogs indistinguishable," "foot-passengers jostling," "gas looming." Sometimes Dickens uses an ending pattern, too, as in:

|  |  |
|---|---|
| The raw afternoon | is rawest and |
| the dense fog | is densest and |
| the muddy streets | are muddiest . . . |

A similar-ending pattern like this is called *epanaphora*. (Classical rhetoric also used a term which described an ending pattern like raw*est*, dens*est*, muddi*est*—*homoioteleuton*.) Dickens breaks the asyndetic pattern in a carefully strategic, climactic way. We get a verb rather than a participle in the Megalosaurus analogy, but it comes in what is still a dependent clause; we get another in "if this day ever broke" but again separated parenthetically from the main movement—all those paratactic, asyndetic participles. We hunger for an independent verb but get none until the last two paragraphs. In them, Dickens constructs a very elaborate rhetorical climax. The persistent asyndeton has created a ritualistic repetition, and when we finally come to a finite verb, it occurs in the parallel clauses we have just seen. Look at them again:

The raw afternoon    is rawest, and
the dense fog        is densest, and
the muddy streets    are muddiest . . .

The isocolon both summarizes the three images Dickens builds upon—rawness, mud, fog—and begins a climactic structure that ends with High Court of Chancery. The second stage again uses *isocolon*.

                                near that    leaden-headed old obstruction,
appropriate ornament for the threshold of a    leaden-headed old corporation—
                                             Temple Bar.

The third, now with a connective "And," begins with yet another repetition; one where the weight of connection shifts from conjunction to preposition:

            Temple Bar
And hard by  Temple Bar,
    in    Lincoln's Inn Hall,
    at    the very heart of the fog,
    sits  the Lord  High Chancellor
    in his          High Court of Chancery.

Plenty of connectives here. Dickens has reserved the *polysyndeton* for a climactic paragraph. This opening section of *Bleak House* resembles, in its almost formulaic, climactic repetitions, the high-style openings of classical epic. And basic to this elevated opening stands the calculated juxtaposition of asyndeton and polysyndeton.

A polysyndetic prose is often a hypotactic one. Parataxis, as with Hemingway, can be either asyndetic or the opposite. Hypotaxis, however, most often goes with polysyndeton. Using a classic combination of these two patterns, Lord Brougham spoke to the House of Lords during the second reading of the Reform Bill of 1832:

My Lords,—I feel that I owe some apology to your lordships for standing in the way of any noble lords who wish to address you: but after much deliberation, and after consulting with several of my noble friends on both sides of the House, it did appear to us, as I am sure it will to your lordships, desirable, on many grounds, that the debate should be brought to a close this night; and I thought I could not better contribute to that end than by taking the present opportunity of addressing you. Indeed, I had scarcely any choice. I am urged on by the anxiety I feel on this mighty subject, which is so great, that I should hardly have been able to delay the expression of my opinion much longer; if I had, I feel assured that I must have lost the power to address you. This solicitude is not, I can assure your lordships, diminished by my recollection of the great talents and brilliant exertions of those by whom I have been preceded in the discussion, and the consciousness of the difficulties with which I have to contend in following such men. It is a deep sense of these difficulties that induces me to call for your patient indulgence. For although not unused to meet public bodies, nay, constantly in the habit, during many years, of presenting myself before great assemblies of various kinds, yet I do solemnly assure you, that I never, until this moment, felt what deep responsibility may rest on a member of the legislature in addressing either of its houses. And if I, now standing with your lordships on the brink of the most momentous decision that ever human assembly came to, at any period of the world, and seeking to arrest you, whilst it is yet time, in that position, could, by any divination of the future, have foreseen in my earliest years, that I should live to appear here, and to act as your adviser, on a question of such awful importance, not only to yourselves, but to your remotest posterity, I should have devoted every day and every hour of that life to preparing myself for the task which I now almost sink under,—gathering from the monuments of ancient experience the lessons of wisdom which might guide our course at the present hour,—looking abroad on our own times, and these not uneventful, to check, by practice, the application of those lessons,—chastening myself, and sinking within me every infirmity of temper, every waywardness of disposition, which might by possibility impede the discharge of this most solemn duty:—but, above all, eradicating from my mind everything that, by any accident, could interrupt the most perfect candour and impartiality of judgment. (Cheers)

Such a style seems, above all, *ranked:* first-rank statements, second-rank elaborations, third-rank qualifications. Again, a diagram which exaggerates these relationships a little makes them easier to see (p. 43). The "taxis" of hypotaxis comes from the Greek word for drawing up ranks in battle and the diagram does just this, shows the elements of the sentence drawn up one under another. A sentence like this may obviously be broken down in other ways. Here I've cut across both syntactical and rhythmic units to emphasize

RANK #1

I feel

it did appear to us

I thought

RANK #2

that I owe some apology

but after much deliberation and
after consulting

as I am sure it will
desirable

that the debate should be brought to a close
I could not better contribute
than by taking the present opportunity

RANK #3

to your Lordships
for standing
in the way
of any noble lords who wish to address you

with several
of my noble friends
on both sides
of the House
to your Lordships

on many grounds
this night and
to that end
of addressing you.

the essential hypotaxis, the "ranking under." Other strong patterns, though, work in it too. Look, for example, at the paratactic anaphora in this sentence:

```
Indeed,  I had scarcely any choice.
             I am urged on by the anxiety
             I feel on this mighty subject
                   which is so great that
             I should hardly have been able to delay the expression of my
                   opinion much longer
         if     I had
             I feel assured that
             I must have lost the power to address you
```

Again, a choruslike ritualistic repetition combined with list-making.

We so much take for granted reading as horizontal movement that we have trouble seeing what charting so often emphasizes: the *vertical* coordinate upon which so much depends in prose style. A hypotactic style encourages you to read from top to bottom as well as from left to right. Here is another of Brougham's sentences, diagrammed to bring out this vertical coordinate. I've chosen a four-column categorization, though you could argue that five or six are needed. Each top-to-bottom reading represents a rank, each left-to-right reading a movement down from one rank to another. I've tried, within columns, to rank similar elements under one another (see pp. 46–47). The left column, read by itself top-to-bottom, establishes the top-ranking basic assertion. The columns to the right add specific details. Students of style have long referred to the similarities of phrasing and structure—the participles in column 2, for example: "standing," "seeking," "gathering," "looking," "chastening," "sinking," "eradicating"—as examples of "parallel construction." Since in normal print they become horizontally parallel rarely and by accident, it must have been our intuitive awareness of the vertical axis which has kept this puzzling and seemingly inapplicable term in circulation.

We've found that basic stylistic decisions like parataxis or hypotaxis bring with them their own inner logic, a set of subsidiary patterns following naturally from the main one. Maybe we can talk about something like an *outer* logic too, a natural relationship between a fundamental stylistic decision and the reality it seeks to describe. In the Hemingway passage the coincidence was perfect. But it always is for fiction, since fiction, inasmuch as it is fiction, creates the reality it describes. Because nonfictional prose describes a reality external to itself, other issues arise, issues of *decorum* (suitability of style to subject) and sincerity. What terms like decorum and sincerity mean we'll be considering later on, but we can begin to focus them a little by looking at an unusual kind of parataxis, the "school style" of textbooks.

Here is a page from a third-grade textbook:

### Pittsburgh Needs New Workers

As steel mills grew bigger, they needed more workers. But they needed a different kind of worker. The small mills had needed skilled workers. The big new mills needed unskilled workers, too.

The steel companies sent men to Eastern Europe to hire unskilled workers. Thousands of them came to Pittsburgh to work in the mills.

Most of the people who worked in the mills were crowded together. They lived in broken-down houses. They walked on dirty streets. And they breathed smoke and soot from the factories and mills. They called Pittsburgh the "smoky city." But they put up with it. Those dirty industries gave them an income.

### Pittsburgh Has Hard Times

Trouble came to our country in the 1930s. Factories were producing more goods than people could afford to buy. Some factories had to slow down. Some just closed. Thousands of people lost their jobs. The demand for steel dropped. Pittsburgh suffered more than many other cities did. Seven out of every ten workers there had jobs in the steel industry.

### America Goes to War

America entered World War II in 1941. The Army, Navy, and Air Force needed supplies. They needed guns, tanks, planes, and ships. These supplies were all made from steel.

Once again, the steel mills worked day and night. The people of Pittsburgh were back at work, earning high wages.

At the end of the war, the demand for steel was still high. But other cities had steel mills. During the war, they had found cheaper sources of power than coal. And after the war, they bought scrap metal which could be melted down to make steel products. Pittsburgh now needed new industries.

A special case, obviously. A style adapted to third graders. The adaptation, though, seems less in vocabulary or concept than in *syntax,* the premise

| 1 | 2 | 3 | 4 |
| --- | --- | --- | --- |
| And if I | now standing | with your lordships<br>on the brink<br>of the most momentous<br>decision | that ever human assembly came to<br>at any period<br>of the world |
|  | and seeking to<br>arrest you | whilst it is yet time<br>in that position<br>by any divination<br>of the future<br>in my earliest years |  |
| could |  |  |  |
| have foreseen<br>that I should live<br>to appear here | and to act as your<br>adviser | on a question<br>of such awful<br>importance | not only to yourselves<br>but<br>to your remotest posterity |

I should have
    devoted every day
    to preparing myself
        for the task

            which I now almost
            sink under
            gathering

                    and every hour

                        of that life

            from the monuments
            of ancient experience
            the lessons of wisdom

                            which might guide our course
                            at the present hour

            looking abroad

                    on our own times

                        and these not uneventful
                        by practice

                    to check
                    the application
                    of those lessons

            chastening myself
            and
            sinking within me

                    every infirmity of temper
                    every waywardness of
                    disposition

                            which might by possibility
                            impede the discharge
                            of this most solemn duty

            but above all
            eradicating

                    from my mind
                    everything that
                    could interrupt

                        by any accident
                        the most perfect candour and
                        impartiality of judgment.

being that third-graders are too young to understand subordination. True or not, what of our adult response? How, for example, would an adult version (unless the word "adult" has been destroyed by the pornographers) of the first paragraph read?

ORIGINAL

As steel mills grew bigger, they needed more workers. But they needed a different kind of worker. The small mills had needed skilled workers. The big new mills needed unskilled workers, too.

REVISION

As steel mills grew bigger, they needed more workers, but a different kind of worker, unskilled rather than skilled.

Or the second:

ORIGINAL

The steel companies sent men to Eastern Europe to hire unskilled workers. Thousands of them came to Pittsburgh to work in the mills.

REVISION

The steel companies sent men to Eastern Europe to hire unskilled workers for the Pittsburgh mills.

Or a third passage later on?

ORIGINAL

Factories were producing more goods than people could afford to buy. Some factories had to slow down. Some just closed.

REVISION

Because factories were producing more goods than people could afford to buy, some factories had to slow down and others to close.

In each case, the third-grade parataxis hides a causal relation which finds its natural adult expression in hypotactic subordination. The style seems for the adult reader to work against its own inner logic. And outer logic too, since a social history like this one builds on causality and to leave it out, as parataxis by its nature does, sets style and subject at loggerheads. Parataxis, as we've seen, leaves connections—causal, temporal, whatever—up to the reader. Child psychologists may think parataxis the natural language of childhood—I don't know—but it seems odd to leave connection-making up to the minds least equipped to make connections. For adults, certainly, such prose seems fake, duplicitous. The argument says one thing, the syntax another.

Here is another passage, this time from a sixth-grade text. Presumably, if parataxis is the natural syntax of childhood, we would expect more hypotaxis here.

Groups that wanted the jetport had to think about all this when they looked for a place to build. They decided on an area just north of Everglades National Park. Then they had to get their plan approved by county, state, and federal governments.

Other groups, however, did not want the jetport built near Everglades National Park. They said the jetport would harm the plants and animals. The park is a wildlife refuge, which means that no one can hunt the animals or damage the plants in it. People can go there to enjoy the beauty of the park and to see many kinds of rare birds and trees.

What might happen to the park if the jetport were built near it? The animals and plants of the park must have fresh, unpolluted water. The water source for the park is outside the park boundaries, in the swamps and marshes north and west of the planned jetport. The pollution from the jets and from chemicals used at the jetport would pollute the water flowing into the park. And the roar of the jets would badly frighten birds and other animals.

### Pressure and Conflict

Conservations groups were very worried. These groups are interested in preserving the natural beauty of the environment. They did not want the park ruined. Some conservation groups opposing the jetport site were local or state groups. But national conservation groups were concerned, too.

Everglades is a national park—all the people of the United States own it. As an American citizen, you share in owning all the national parks. As one of the owners of the Everglades National Park, you could let the government know how you feel about the plan to build a jetport near your park. You could write your Representative and Senator to tell them how you feel. If a great many people contact them, will they pay more attention? Why do you think so?

There is a little more subordination ("when they looked for," "which means that") but not much. And the parataxis that remains often, as in the third-grade example, seems to fragment sentences that naturally belong together:

SIXTH-GRADE VERSION

Some conservation groups opposing the jetport site were local or state groups. But national conservation groups were concerned, too.

ADULT VERSION

National conservation groups, as well as local and state ones, opposed the jetport site.

Or the second and third sentences:

SIXTH-GRADE VERSION

They decided on an area just north of Everglades National Park. Then they had to get their plan approved by county, state, and federal governments.

ADULT VERSION

After they had decided on an area just north of Everglades National Park, they had to get their plan approved by county, state, and federal governments.

Is it only this artificial parataxis that makes the passage seem so fake? Or the simplistic diction and word repetition? Or the spelling out of much that for an adult audience would have been left unsaid? Could you rewrite the passage in a mature style which sixth-graders still could understand? If you have a sixth-grader handy, try it.

Here's a final textbook example, this time from grades nine to twelve:

### The Romans Built on Greek Culture

The roots of Western civilization can be traced to the blend of Greek and Roman culture, known as *classical culture,* that flourished during the *Pax Romana.* The Romans admired Hellenic culture and borrowed widely from the Greeks. In the process, certain elements of the culture were changed. For example, Roman sculpture became more lifelike than the Greek; Roman architecture, more elaborate. In addition, the Romans themselves made many contributions of their own that, when added to the Greek heritage, helped form a truly Greco-Roman culture. Perhaps the greatest single achievement of the Romans was the creation of a body of laws suitable for governing a world state.

**Roman law held the peoples of the empire together.** In modern-day Italy, France, Spain, and Latin America, law codes based on Roman legal principles are still in use. Law in the modern English-speaking countries was also greatly influenced by Roman law.

Roman law developed from the Laws of the Twelve Tables—those written laws won by the plebeians so that they would know how they would be ruled. As Rome expanded, laws governing noncitizens were added. The decisions of different magistrates in the provinces were kept, and these *legal interpretations* helped other judges decide cases. Sometimes, the existing laws of a conquered place influenced the magistrate's decision. In this way, local rules and customs became a part of the larger body of Roman law. Roman laws became international, particularly the laws dealing with commerce. When Augustus was emperor, professional law schools were established to teach the law. Later, in the 6th century A.D., Justinian, emperor of the eastern empire, had this huge body of laws *codified,* that is, organized into a system that could more easily be used.

**The Latin language was a lasting gift to civilization.** The Romans spoke a language called Latin. It is one of the Indo-European languages, as are German, Slavic, Greek, and Sanskrit. The Romans did not develop writing until the 7th century B.C., when they adopted an alphabet used by the Etruscans. Writing with an alphabet is much easier than writing with picture forms, as in Chinese, the oldest system of writing still in use. Today, the so-called Roman alphabet is the most widely used alphabet in the world.

During the years of Roman civilization, two forms of Latin developed. One was literary Latin, the form used in writing. The second was the *vernacular* [vər nak´ yə lər], or simplified, spoken language used in people's everyday dealings with each other. Literary Latin continued to be more formal and is highly prized for its logic and exactness.

Yes, a few changes, but still unmistakably the paratactic school style, the textbook style a modern student can spot at a hundred yards. Again, spelling out the obvious. "The Romans spoke a language called Latin" rather than "The Romans spoke Latin," or rather than nothing at all. Again, the child-like habit of repeating words, here especially "law." And defining "codified" and the pronunciation key for "vernacular" further identify textbook prose. Again style contradicts subject. But the most childlike element must be the impossibly high level of generalization. This creates the passage's central childish tone, and the parataxis reinforces it. Complex issues like these demand subordination.

This last passage aims at an audience of young adults. If we suppose that third-graders cannot detect this fake parataxis, can we make the same supposition for high school kids? Surely just the opposite. Their powers to detect stylistic falsity, in all kinds of behavior, will never be greater than in adolescence. Stylistic conformity sometimes seems their primary interest. And yet their connection with books, with the very act of reading, comes through a kind of prose false since the third grade. Their books still talk baby talk. In this sense we can speak of a prose style as fake, insincere. Parataxis itself can be called "bad" here because it has been used to keep children from growing up, to keep twelfth-graders reading like ninth-graders so that, in the self-expanding way of bureaucrats, there will have to be a thirteenth grade, and a fourteenth.

Whether a paratactic style is more "natural," in the sense of coming earlier in our evolutionary history, we'll have to learn from the anthropologists. What has happened with textbook parataxis, however, poses a different problem. Parataxis has been assumed to be more "natural," "childlike," than hypotaxis, and a particular pedagogy built on that assumption. The assumption may be false and the pedagogy debilitating but the larger moral taught should be that stylistic patterns are always being taken as allegorical, as "naturally" pointing to one thing or another. Sometimes we can find "nature" in such a conclusion, as when we said that parataxis is not a suitable vehicle for describing social causality; sometimes, however, we find only an arbitrary assumption. And it is hard to tell which is which.

# III

# The Periodic Style and the Running Style

Out of the parataxis-hypotaxis exposition emerges the fundamental pairing for prose style, periodic style and running style. "Periodic" is one of those traditional but confusing words we ought to throw away but can't. Etymologically, περίοδος (periodos) means "a way around," "a circuit," a racetrack turning. A "periodic sentence" must then have something to do with such a meaning. It doesn't. By περίοδος Aristotle seems to have meant what we mean by "sentence," a unit, with a beginning, middle, and end, small enough to be read as a single unit (*Rhetoric,* III.9). Not much help, this, an etymology for "periodic sentence" that comes down to "sentence sentence." It could apply to anything from "Ouch" to the Gettysburg Address. Whatever we decide a periodic style means for English prose, it has nothing to do with περίοδος.

The "running" in "running style" manages to be even more loose and baggy a term than "periodic." It has an Aristotelian source, too—he talks about the λέξις εἰρομένη (lexis eiromenē), or strung-together style—but happily the Greek term has stayed out of English. If the periodic style is basically hypotactic, the running style is basically paratactic, incremental, shapeless. It just goes on. Not much help either, this definition. It could point to almost anything not, well, not periodic. And has.

But terms like these don't stay in circulation unless they point to *something*. And these two terms point to something fundamental, a basic difference in how one human intelligence presents itself to another. I can show you my mind in two ways, in present time and in the past. In present time, you see the machine in all its giddy unsplendor as it lurches from crisis to crisis, first tripping over one argument then bumping into another, unbalanced and unsymmetrical and unhandy, now mulling over and thinking out, alternating argument with pronouncement, often—to use the unflattering but apposite cliché, finding out what the mind thinks by seeing what the hand writes.

To imitate thus the mind in real-time interaction with the world is to write in some form of running style. The serial syntax registers first the first thing and then the second thing second, simple chronological sequence always calling the tune and beating the tempo. Such a syntax models the mind in the act of coping with the world. The coping is all small-scale, minute-to-minute tactics, not seasonal grand strategy. There is no time to reflect on grand strategy; the reader is on patrol with the writer, sharing immediate dangers and present perplexities. Things happen as they want to, not as we would have them. Circumstances call the tune.

The periodic style reverses all this. The mind shows itself after it has reasoned on the event; after it has sorted by concept and categorized by size; after it has imposed on the temporal flow the shapes through which that flow takes on a beginning, a middle, and an end. The periodic stylist works with balance, antithesis, parallelism, and careful patterns of repetition; all these dramatize a mind which has dominated experience and reworked it to its liking. It is tempting to say that the periodic style humanizes time and we can say this, so long as we remember that to "go with the flow" is as human as to oppose it, that humankind's bewilderment before raw event is as characteristic as the will to impose order on it.

Styles in prose then are rather like styles in gardens. The periodic style is like the vast formal garden of a Baroque palace, all balanced squares and parallel paths. The land is rearranged in ways that the visual cortex can easily sort out. The running style, on the other hand, is like the informal garden which shapes nature without seeming to. Nature is not dominated and reformed but simply helped on the way it wanted to go anyway. We can wander—since there is no beginning, middle, and end—but again without fear of getting lost.

Periodic style and running style, then, point to two basic ways the mind relates itself to time and hence to human experience. But just because these patterns are so basic they can be realized in many different verbal forms. The terms periodic style and running style are thus bound to remain imprecise. But each does bring with it basic verbal patterns we can see and describe and they do have a dynamic relationship we can trace. Let's look at some examples, first of the two styles and then of their relationship.

The best definition of "periodic sentence" I know is also the simplest. The great classicist H. J. Rose in his *A Handbook of Latin Literature* (London: Methuen, 1936) called it "the long and frequently involved type of sentence, needing skill to handle it properly, in which the construction begun with the first word is not completed until the last." "Construction" here we'll take to mean sense as well as syntax. In a periodic sentence, things don't fall into place until the last minute, and when they do, they do with a snap, an emphatic climax. The juggler catches all the pieces, and takes his applause. In a periodic style, sometimes the periodism is contained in a single grammatical sentence and sometimes it runs over into a larger unit, but the architecture is the same whether the scale is small or large. When it is large, and more than one sentence is involved, the construction is usually called a *period.* H. J. Rose himself could build a beautiful period, as when he described the younger Seneca. After a brief introductory flourish ("Of his works the writer finds it hard to judge fairly, owing to the loathing which his personality excites") comes this salvo:

> That a man in exile should flatter basely those who have power to recall him is understandable; Ovid did as much. That a prime minister in difficult times should show himself neither heroic nor self-consistent is no more than is to be expected of the vast majority of statesmen. That the influential adviser of an impressionable and unbalanced young prince should allow his master's favors to take the form of making him prodigiously wealthy is not remarkable; we may discount the tales of Seneca using extortion to add to his riches. That, having flattered, he should bespatter with abuse the object of his sometime adoration is certainly not commendable, but shows no deep depravity, merely a desire to swim with the current. That, being the most popular author of the day and master of an eloquence calculated to make the worst case appear passable, he should frame an elaborate justification of a matricide, may be passed over as one of the hard necessities of his position; but when the man who has done and is doing all this takes the tone of a rigid moralist and a seeker after uncompromising virtue, preaching, from his palace, simplicity and the plainest living with almost the unction of a St. Francis praising Holy Poverty, refusing all knowledge that does not tend to edification, and proclaiming, in verse worthy of a better man than Nero's hack, that the true king is he who fears nothing and desires nothing, the gorge of the reader rises and he turns for relief to some one who either made his life fit

his doctrine or, if he behaved unworthily of the best that was in him, at least laid no claim to be a spiritual guide.

Longer than one sentence, technically, but we could fix that up with semi-colons. And it doesn't matter whether the period stretches over one sentence or several. The main thing is the *suspension,* both of syntax and sense, until the end. The basic design looks like this:

A. a) *That* a man in exile . . . is understandable;

$a_1$) Ovid did as much.

b) *That* a prime minister in difficult times . . . is no more than

$b_1$) the vast majority of statesmen.

c) *That* the influential adviser . . . is not remarkable;

$c_1$) we may discount the tales of Seneca using extortion.

d) *That,* having flattered, . . . is certainly not commendable

$d_1$) but shows no deep depravity.

e) *That,* being the most popular . . . may be passed over

$e_1$) hard necessities of his position

B. *but when*

the man who has done and is doing all of this takes the tone of a rigid moralist and a seeker after uncompromising virtue,

*preaching* from his palace . . .

*refusing* all knowledge that . . .

*proclaiming* in verse worthy . . .

THE GORGE OF THE READER RISES

and he turns for relief to someone who

*either* made his life fit his doctrine

*or* if he behaved unworthily of the best that was in him, at least laid no claim to be a spiritual guide.

What fun to watch this balancing act. The secret of a periodic structure is *pacing,* slowly building up steam for a thundering climax like THE GORGE OF THE READER RISES. If the secret is pacing, the center is drama, the suspense as the syntactical spring is wound tighter and tighter and finally—ah, got him!—released. Rose has, as his first movement, set up an antiphonal chorus, first a *that* statement (a), then the balancing qualification ($a_1$). Then, after five of these antiphons (the pattern shifts slightly at $e_1$), the second movement begins with *but when,* and continues through three long parallel phrases depending on present participles which refer back to "the man." Then the climax. Then a coda which lets us back down gradually to ordinary utterance.

Some tangible ingredients for a "periodic" style at last: 1) *suspension,* and suspension over a number of complex statements; 2) *parallelism* of phrases and clauses—all those "That"s and later the three participles; 3) *balance,* the antiphonal chorus; 4) *climax,* the final thrust that nails Seneca to the wall. And to these we must add a last quality that exudes from periodic structure, *virtuoso display.* Rose does not just hack his man down. He fences him into pieces *con brio.*

With the basic pattern before us, look at a passage where suspension works differently. It comes from a seventeenth-century collection of religious meditations by William Drummond:

### A Reverie on Death

Having often and diverse times, when I had given myself to rest in the quiet solitariness of the night, found my imagination troubled with a confused fear, or sorrow or horror, which, interrupting sleep, did astonish my senses, and rouse me all appalled, and transported in a sudden agony and amazedness: of such an unaccustomed perturbation not knowing, not being able to dive into any apparent cause, carried away with the stream of my then doubting thoughts, I began to ascribe it to that secret foreknowledge and presaging power of the prophetic mind, and to interpret such an agony to be to the spirit, as a sudden faintness and universal weariness useth to be to the body, a sign of following sickness; or as winter lightnings, earthquakes, and monsters are to commonwealths and great cities, harbingers of wretched events, and emblems of their sudden destinies.

Hereupon, not thinking it strange, if whatsoever is human should befal me, knowing how Providence overcomes grief, and discountenances crosses; and that, as we should not despair in evils which may happen to us, we should not be too confident, nor lean much to those goods we enjoy; I began to turn over in my remembrance all that could afflict miserable mortality, and to forecast everything which could beget gloomy and sad apprehensions, and with a mask of horror show itself to human eyes; till in the end, as by unities and points mathematicians are brought to great numbers and huge greatness, after many fantastical glances of the woes of mankind, and those incumbrances which follow upon life, I was brought to think, and with amazement, on the last of human terrors, or (as one termed it) the last of all dreadful and terrible evils, Death. (from Henry Craik, *English Prose Selections,* vol. 1 [London, 1893], p. 227)

*Having often*          (and diverse times,)

  when I had given myself to rest          (*in* the quiet solitariness *of* the night,)

*found my imagination troubled*          (*with* a confused fear,

                                                        or sorrow

                                                        or horror,)

  which,          (interrupting sleep,)          did astonish my senses,

                                                        and rouse me all appalled,

                                                        (and transported)          (*in* a sudden agony and amazedness)

*of* such an unaccustomed perturbation not knowing,

                                        not being able to dive *into* any apparent cause,

                                        carried away (*with* the stream *of* my then doubting thoughts)

I *began*

  to ascribe it to that secret foreknowledge

                                        and presaging power *of* the prophetic mind, and

*to interpret such an agony to be*

  to the spirit, (*as* a sudden faintness and universal weariness useth to be *to* the body,)

*a sign of following sickness;* or

  (*as* winter lightnings, earthquakes, and monsters are to commonwealths and great cities)

*harbingers of wretched events,*          (and emblems *of* their sudden destinies.)

Hereupon,

          (1)

  not *thinking* it strange, if whatsoever is human should befal me,

          (2)

  *knowing* how Providence overcomes grief, and

                                        discountenances crosses; and

(3)

(*knowing*) that, as we should not despair in evils which may happen to us,

    (3a)

    (3b)

    we should not be too confident,

        (3c)

        nor lean much to those goods we enjoy;

I began

    (1)

    to turn over in my remembrance all that could afflict miserable mortality, and

    (2)

    to forecast everything which could beget gloomy and sad apprehensions, and

        with a mask of horror show itself to human eyes;

till

    (1)

    in the end, as by unities and points mathematicians are *brought to* great numbers and huge greatness,

    (2)

    after many fantastical glances of the *woes* of mankind,

        and those *incumbrances* which follow upon life,

I was brought to think,

        and with amazement, on

    (1)

    the last of human terrors, or (as one termed it)

    (2)

    the last of all dreadful and terrible evils,

Death.

Both sentences are built around a core which has been opened at many points and parentheses inserted. The first sentence core: "Having found my imagination troubled, I began to ascribe it to secret foreknowledge and to interpret it as a sign of following sickness." The second, a little harder to extract: "Hereupon I began to turn over in my remembrance all that could afflict miserable mortality, till I was brought to think on Death." This skeleton sentence, stretched and tensioned by three parentheses, creates suspension, but one different in shape and rhythm from H. J. Rose's period. Rose signals his skeleton with those "that"s and parallel participles. Here the skeleton lies buried in the parentheses. The style extends itself outward from its core (in our diagram, the left edge) by parenthetical extensions. Its internal logic wants to qualify and extend, and it does so on several levels. Do you notice, first, how every noun attracts a qualifying adjective: "quiet solitariness," "confused fear," "sudden agony," "apparent cause," "doubting thoughts," "secret foreknowledge," "sudden faintness," "universal weariness," and so on? Above this works a polysyndetic "and" pattern of additional specification:

often—and diverse times
astonish my senses—and rouse me all appalled
and transported
secret foreknowledge—and presaging power

and so on. The prepositional phrases work in the same way, adding parenthetical specification. So "given myself to rest" is qualified by "in the quiet solitariness" and this in turn further specified by "of the night." In the H. J. Rose period, the lower ranks of the sentence all present themselves as thought out beforehand. Not here. Just the opposite. The parenthetical qualifications seem *ex tempore,* seem to follow a mind in the act of meditating, of exploring possibilities. Parallelism ("to be to the spirit"; "to be to the body," for example) is played down, not up. Imbalance, not balance, establishes the dominant pattern. Try reading the passage aloud. We don't know when to raise the pitch of the voice, or how high, to indicate all those parentheses within parentheses. The syntax gives you no visual clues—no parallelism, no antiphonal chorus.

The second sentence-paragraph, its suspension arranged exactly as in the first, starts with a word that leaves the sense hovering—"Hereupon"—then moves to an "I began" in mid-sentence which has its sense completed, in turn, in a climactic "Death." And the two sentences work as a single unit, too, stretching from the first word, "Having," to the last word, "Death." "Death" works strongly as a climax, the end of the meditation as it is the end of life. Or is it an *anti*climax? Notice that last parenthesis—"(as one termed it)"—just before "Death." It seems to deflate the whole climax, to suggest that Death is not the most terrible of evils. We only *think so* to scare ourselves by dwelling upon it. The twistings and turnings of the syntax represent twistings and turnings of the mind, tergiversations that are ironical or unnecessary vexations man offers to himself. How does this irony affect how we analyze the style? The style has become self-consciously allegorical, modeled a mind tending to run away with itself, trap itself in its own convolutions. This "running" we may tentatively put down as one of the meanings of the "running" style, a following of the mind as it worries a problem through. To the extent that Drummond is ironical here the passage, to answer the question just asked, comes to be *about* the running style, about the traps, in sense and syntax, the mind sets for itself.

In Drummond, then, we see the basic suspension and climax of the period, but with internal elements that begin to liquefy, to run. The liquefaction goes further, the nascent internal logic of suspended running style grows more pronounced, in the later style of Henry James. James, as William Allen White wrote in his *Autobiography,* seemed to speak the same way: "He talked, as he wrote, in long involved sentences with a little murmur—mum-mum-mum—standing for parentheses, and with those rhetorical hooks he seemed to be poking about his mind, fumbling through the whole basket of his conversational vocabulary, to find the exact word, which he used in talking about most ordinary matters. He seemed to create with those parentheses." Here is a passage from *The Wings of the Dove* creaking with parentheses. See what White was talking about?

> It was really a matter of nerves; it was exactly because he was nervous that
> he *could* go straight; yet if that condition should increase he must surely go
> wild. He was walking, in short, on a high ridge, steep down on either side,
> where the proprieties—once he could face at all remaining there—reduced
> themselves to his keeping his head. It was Kate who had so perched him, and
> there came up for him at moments, as he found himself planting one foot

exactly before another, a sensible sharpness of irony as to her management of him. It wasn't that she had put him in danger—to be in real danger with her would have had another quality. There glowed for him in fact a kind of rage for what he was not having; an exasperation, a resentment, begotten truly by the very impatience of desire, in respect to his postponed and relegated, his so extremely manipulated state. It was beautifully done of her, but what was the real meaning of it unless that he was perpetually bent to her will? His idea from the first, from the very first of his knowing her, had been to be, as the French called it, *bon prince* with her, mindful of the good humour and generosity, the contempt, in the matter of confidence, for small outlays and small savings, that belonged to the man who wasn't generally afraid. There were things enough, goodness knew—for it was the moral of his plight—that he couldn't afford; but what had had a charm for him if not the notion of living handsomely, to make up for it, in another way? of not at all events reading the romance of his existence in a cheap edition. All he had originally felt in her came back to him, was indeed actually as present as ever—how he had admired and envied what he called to himself her direct talent for life, as distinguished from his own, a poor weak thing of the occasion, amateurishly patched up; only it irritated him the more that this was exactly what was now, ever so characteristically, standing out in her.

It was thanks to her direct talent for life, verily, that he was just where he was, and that was above all just *how* he was. The proof of a decent reaction in him against so much passivity was, with no great richness, that he at least knew—knew, that is, how he was, and how little he liked it as a thing accepted in mere helplessness. He was, for the moment, wistful—that above all described it; that was so large a part of the force that, as the autumn afternoon closed in, kept him, on his traghetto, positively throbbing with his question. His question connected itself, even while he stood, with his special smothered soreness, his sense almost of shame; and the soreness and the shame were less as he let himself, with the help of the conditions about him, regard it as serious. It was born, for that matter partly of those conditions, those conditions that Kate had so almost insolently braved, had been willing without a pang, to see him ridiculously—ridiculously so far as just complacently—exposed to. How little it could be complacently he was to feel with the last thoroughness before he had moved from his point of vantage. (Henry James, *The Wings of the Dove* [New York: Penguin, 1974])

Everything exfoliates from the central strategy of parenthetical qualification. So much qualification has come into play, however, that the large central suspension has snapped. In its place, James uses a pattern of almost ritualistic repetition, of compulsive *anaphora*. The dominant sentence-beginning and phrase-beginning pattern looks like this:

It was really a matter of nerves . . .
it was exactly because . . .
He was walking . . .
It was Kate who had . . .
It wasn't that she . . .
what he was not having . . .
It was beautifully done . . .
what was the real meaning . . .
he was perpetually . . .
his idea had been to be as the French call it . . .
There were things enough . . .
it was the moral of . . .
It was thanks to her . . .
where he was . . .
that he was . . .
*how* he was . . .
how he was and how little . . .
He was for the moment . . .
that was so large a part . . .
It was born . . .

And I've left several derivative forms out! Still, compulsive ritualistic repetition, as mannered and self-conscious a style as English affords. But instead of never repeating the phrase that keeps us suspended, James repeats it constantly.

We may have surprised here a general rule for style. Stuff a style so full of parentheses that the hypotactic suspension breaks, and you return to extreme parataxis. Instead of repeating nothing, keeping everything up in the air, you repeat everything. And repeat it as a kind of internal summary, a reminder of where you are. The parenthesis strategy gets redoubled, expanded, into restatement and repetition. I'll chart first the obvious parentheses and then the repetitions and restatements.

Parentheses: It will be simplest here if I just add them where appropriate. Notice that James, to soften the parenthetical appearance of the style, never uses ( ) in this passage? Again, I'm bearing down on the parenthetical strategy, exaggerating it to make it show.

It was (really) a matter of nerves; it was (exactly) because he was nervous
that he *could* go straight; yet (if that condition should increase) he must surely
go wild. He was walking, (in short), on a high ridge, (steep down on either

side), where the proprieties—(once he could face at all remaining there)—reduced themselves to his keeping his head. It was Kate who had so perched him, and there came up for him at moments, (as he found himself planting one foot exactly before another), a sensible sharpness of irony as to her management of him. It wasn't that she had put him in danger—(to be in real danger with her would have had another quality). There glowed for him (in fact) a kind of rage for what he was not having; an exasperation, a resentment, begotten truly by the very impatience of desire, in respect to his postponed and relegated, (his so extremely manipulated) state. It was beautifully done of her, but what was the real meaning of it unless that he was perpetually bent to her will? His idea from the first, (from the very first) of his knowing her, had been to be, (as the French call it), *bon prince* with her, mindful of the good humour and generosity, (the contempt) in the matter of confidence, for small outlays and small savings, that belonged to the man who wasn't generally afraid. There were things enough (goodness knew)—(for it was the moral of his plight)—that he couldn't afford; but what had had a charm for him if not the notion of living handsomely, (to make up for it), in another way? of not (at all events) reading the romance of his existence in a cheap edition. All he had originally felt in her came back to him, (was indeed actually as present as ever)—how he had admired and envied (what he called to himself) her direct talent for life, as distinguished from his own, a poor weak thing of the occasion, amateurishly patched up; only it irritated him the more that this was exactly what was now, (ever so characteristically), standing out in her.

It was thanks to her direct talent for life, (verily), that he was just where he was, and that he was (above all) just *how* he was. The proof of a decent reaction in him against so much passivity was, (with no great richness), that he at least knew—(knew, (that is),) how he was, and how little he liked it as a thing accepted in mere helplessness. He was, (for the moment), wistful—(that (above all) described it); that was so large a part of the force that, (as the autumn afternoon closed in), kept him, (on his traghetto), positively throbbing with his question. His question connected itself, (even while he stood), with his special smothered soreness, his sense almost of shame; and the soreness and the shame were less as he let himself, (with the help of the conditions about him), regard it as serious. It was born, (for that matter) partly of the conditions, (those conditions that Kate had (so almost insolently) braved), had been willing, (without a pang), to see him ridiculously—(ridiculously (so far as just complacently))—exposed to. How little it *could* be complacently, he was to feel with the last thoroughness before he had moved from his point of vantage.

The dominant seesaw rhythm models the hesitation about what, in fact, it *is* (or *was*) which constitutes the passage's central theme. Again, the style has become allegorical, a style about the hesitation and qualification it creates.

Word repetition intensifies this basic parenthetical pattern: we have already seen the starring "it was" anaphora. Now the supporting cast:

> matter of nerves
> he was nervous
>
> go straight
> go wild
>
> in danger
> in real danger
>
> from the first
> from the very first
>
> small outlays
> small savings
>
> her direct talent for life
> her direct talent for life
>
> his special smothered soreness, his sense almost of shame
> the soreness and shame
>
> the conditions
> those conditions
>
> see his ridiculously
> ridiculously so far as
>
> just complacently
> *could* be complacently

Some of these repetitions are isocolons, equal in length and structure, and so could be called parallel, but the parallelism doesn't strike us. The small-scale repetition comes across instead. James uses a periodic style, then, only on a smaller scale: "his postponed and relegated, his so extremely manipulated state." No large-scale suspensions; no big climax. The liquefaction we saw beginning in Drummond here takes a turn toward parataxis, back, oddly enough, toward Hemingway. It can continue this way, toward discrete self-contained units, or it can liquefy more, become entirely an affair of hesitant stops, starts, and requalifications. Two passages to illustrate the two tendencies: first, one from Raymond Chandler and then an excerpt from a crazy seventeenth-century novel called *Ornatus and Artesia,* by Emmanuel Ford.

Here's the Chandler passage, a section—all self-contained paratactic units—from *Farewell My Lovely:*

I walked back through the arch and started up the steps. It was a nice walk if you like grunting. There were two hundred and eighty steps up to Cabrillo Street. They were drifted over with windblown sand and the handrail was as cold and wet as a toad's belly.

When I reached the top the sparkle had gone from the water and a seagull with a broken trailing leg was twisting against the offsea breeze. I sat down on the damp cold top step and shook the sand out of my shoes and waited for my pulse to come down into the low hundreds. When I was breathing more or less normally again I shook my shirt loose from my back and went along to the lighted house which was the only one within yelling distance of the steps.

It was a nice little house with a salt-tarnished spiral of staircase going up to the front door and an imitation coachlamp for a porchlight. The garage was underneath and to one side. Its door was lifted up and rolled back and the light of the porchlamp shone obliquely on a huge black battleship of a car with chromium trimmings, a coyote tail tied to the Winged Victory on the radiator cap and engraved initials where the emblem should be. The car had a right-hand drive and looked as if it had cost more than the house.

I went up the spiral steps, looked for a bell, and used a knocker in the shape of a tiger's head. Its clatter was swallowed in the early evening fog. I heard no steps in the house. My damp shirt felt like an icepack on my back. The door opened silently, and I was looking at a tall blond man in a white flannel suit with a violet satin scarf around his neck.

There was a cornflower in the lapel of his white coat and his pale blue eyes looked faded out by comparison. The violet scarf was loose enough to show that he wore no tie and that he had a thick, soft brown neck, like the neck of a strong woman. His features were a little on the heavy side, but handsome; he had an inch more of height than I had, which made him six feet one. His blond hair was arranged, by art or nature, in three precise blond ledges which reminded me of steps, so that I didn't like them. I wouldn't have liked them anyway. Apart from all this he had the general appearance of a lad who would wear a white flannel suit with a violet scarf around his neck and a cornflower in his lapel.

He cleared his throat lightly and looked past my shoulder at the darkening sea. His cool supercilious voice said: "Yes?"

"Seven o'clock," I said. "On the dot."

"Oh yes. Let me see, Your name is—" he paused and frowned in the effort of memory. The effect was as phony as the pedigree of a used car. I let him work at it for a minute, then I said:

"Philip Marlowe. The same as it was this afternoon."

He gave me a quick darting frown, as if perhaps something ought to be done about that. Then he stepped back and said coldly:

"Ah yes. Quite so. Come in, Marlowe. My house boy is away this evening."

He opened the door wide with a fingertip, as though opening the door himself dirtied him a little.

I went in past him and smelled perfume. He closed the door. The entrance put us on a low balcony with a metal railing that ran around three sides of a big studio living room. The fourth side contained a big fireplace and two doors. A fire was crackling in the fireplace. The balcony was lined with bookshelves and there were pieces of glazed metallic-looking bits of sculpture on pedestals.

We went down three steps to the main part of the living room. The carpet almost tickled my ankles. There was a concert piano, closed down. On one corner of it stood a tall silver vase on a strip of peach-colored velvet, and a single yellow rose in the vase. There was plenty of nice soft furniture, a great many floor cushions, some with golden tassels and some just naked. It was a nice room, if you didn't get rough. There was a wide damask-covered divan in a shadowy corner, like a casting couch. It was the kind of room where people sit with their feet in their laps and sip absinthe through lumps of sugar and talk with high affected voices and sometimes just squeak. It was a room where anything could happen except work. (*Farewell My Lovely* [New York: Random House, 1976])

We've been here before—the compound Hemingway rhythm all over again. No need to re-do the same analysis (an "and" backbone here, too). But you see the style in a different way when you come to it from James. Here the parentheses have taken over entirely from the main suspension, the qualifications have become the main utterance. This parataxis represents one extreme which stands opposite to the periodic style.

Here's the Ford:

There dwelleth not far hence one Allinus, *that* mortally hateth my father, and all that belong to him, *whose son* Ornatus was, whom if I should commend, you might think me too cruel to refuse his love so unkindly, *only thus much* I will say of him, he was every way worthy to be beloved, *though* my fancy could never be drawn to like of him: *who* upon what occasion I know not, *but* as Adellena told me, made his love known to her, *which* she likewise told me of: *but* I refusing to hear her, answered her plainly, that I was greatly offended with her, for making any such motion, and forbade her for ever to speak of him again. *But* now this day you have heard what she hath told me, which I can hardly believe to be true, *or* that Ornatus would be so rash without wisdom to enter into such extremes. *But* if it be so (*as* I would it were not) it grieveth me for him, and I wish that I had not refused to hear his suit, *though* I am not willing to yield thereto *for* I would not have it said of me, *nor* my name so much blazed, that my cruelty procured him to that extremity, *though* his wisdome might have foreseen such mischief, and the more moderately have tempered his love.

Ornatus taking occasion, said: I *neither* know this gentleman, *nor* how constant his love was, *but* thus much my mind persuadeth me, *that* had not his love been great, he would not have grieved so much at your unkindness: *but* love is of this force, *that* it turneth the mind into extremes, or utterly breaketh the heart: *which* fire belike it had in him, else would he not have done himself so much harm. *But* it may be (as you say) Ornatus hath not done himself outrage, *but only* abandoning company, liveth in despair and so meaning to die: *which* if it be, then in my fancy, you might do well to let him by some means understand that you did pity him. Stay there, quoth Artesia, you must first know, whether I can do it, or no: *for* if I should say, I pity with my lips, and not find it so, it would drive him to more despair: *and therefore* I will leave off to do that, *until* I can find whether I can do so, or no.

These her speeches drove Ornatus into a perplexed doubt, what to think, *being* no way assured of her love, *nor yet* utterly despairing thereof, *for that* her speeches give likelihood of both. *Therefore* he durst not speak too boldly, *least* she should suspect him, *but only* rested in good hope to find comfort, and by other means to try her.

*Then* taking his lute, he began to play sweetly, *as would have* ravished a comfortable mind, with great content: *to hear which* harmony, pleased Artesia so well, *that when* he left, she would request him, calling him Sylvia, to play again. *Whilest* he sat playing, Artesia sitting close by his side, fell fast asleep: *which* he perceiving, left off his play, to surfeit himself with beholding her sweet beauty *in which* he took such delight, as almost ravished his senses; *sometimes thinking, whilest* she slept, to imprint a kiss upon her sweet ruddy lip; *but* fearing thereby to wake her, and lose that delightful contemplation, he desisted: beholding each part of her visible form, which was most divine, his mind was affected with inward suppose, *what* perfection her hidden beauties did comprehend, *which* his fancy persuaded him, he did in conceit absolutely contemplate. *Then* seeing her stir, he suddenly catched up his lute again, striking his sweet note, to continue her in that slumber, *and then* again laying by the same, to enter into his former contemplation: comparing his delight to exceed all heavenly joy; and wishing, though Artesia could not love him, *that* she would always grant him so to behold her. (*Ornatus and Artesia* [London, 1607])

Here one clause flows into another, itself connected to a third, *ad infinitum*. Instead of the discrete compound paratactic units from which Chandler builds his prose, every unit is braided into every other. The style continually pivots on the connecting words I've italicized, pushing off against the last element in a new direction. This style, too, can be seen as developing dynamically from the periodic parenthesis. With James the parenthesis is always closed; after it, we return to the main assertion. Here, parentheses are always opened but never closed. One opens after another, each leaning on the previous element like a string of dominoes. Chandler's parataxis develops the Jamesian parenthetical strategy into a series of discrete independent units; Ford fabricates a string of half-parentheses each dependent on the preceding one and none complete. This incompleteness makes it run on, like a perpetually bubbling fountain. To call it a running style seems almost inevitable—and, for a change, descriptive.

These two theoretical extremes form the basic categories which stand opposite to the periodic style: short elements either self-contained or evolving from one another in dependent relationship. When self-contained, they project discipline and control; when dependent, the garrulous, rambling, associative syntax of conversation. The second we usually call "running." For the first, though it has a common theoretical ancestry with "running," we have no better name than parataxis or the "clipped" style, perhaps as good a name as any.

Prose styles rarely come in pure forms, "purity" being usually a tacit assumption to ignore complications for the sake of analysis. Maybe examples of *mixed* styles will make the patterns easier to see.

Here's a balanced combination of clipped and running styles, a sixteenth-century lament on the woes of inflation from Hugh Latimer's masterly "Decay of the Yeomanry":

My father was a yeoman and had no lands of his own, only he had a farm of three or four pound by year at the uttermost, and hereupon he tilled so much as kept half a dozen men. He had walk for a hundred sheep; and my mother milked thirty kine. He was able, and did find the king a harness, with himself and his horse, while he came to the place that he should receive the king's wages. I can remember that I buckled his harness when he went unto Blackheath field. He kept me to school or else I had not been able to have preached before the king's majesty now. He married my sisters with five pound, or twenty nobles apiece, so that he brought them up in godliness and fear of God. He kept hospitality for his poor neighbours, and some alms he gave to the poor. And all this he did of the said farm, where he that now hath it payeth sixteen pound by year or more, and is not able to do anything for his prince, for himself, nor for his children, or give a cup of drink to the poor.

The "clipped" style's control here perfectly combines with the easy associative movement from subject to subject. Or we might look at a modern example of the same balance. Again, a mind recollecting the past, letting the memories come back, but selectively, not in a flood. Sidney Bechet, in *Treat It Gentle* (New York: Da Capo, 1975), is recalling the origins of jazz:

But Jazz didn't come from a peephole. You know, you take a woman. Say she's got a light dress on; maybe it's summer—if you look through her dress and see she's a woman, it's not her fault; it's not her fault you're looking to see how she is. And if she moves, and you watch her, all the time thinking about having her, that isn't her fault either. That's your mind putting something else on something very natural; that's a fact and shouldn't be made out of shape. And that's Jazz too. If people want to take a melody and think what it's saying is trash, that ain't the fault of the melody. Sure, there's pieces like *Easy Rider* or *Jockey Blues* that have got lyrics you'd call "dirty." Lots of them, they're exhibition-like, they're for show—a novelty to attract attention. But it's not those lyrics or those blues that really enter into your heart. The ones that really do that, they're about sad things—about loving someone and it turns out bad, or wanting and not knowing what you're wanting. Something sincere, like loving a woman, there's nothing dirty in that.

See how the Jamesian parenthesis begets both running and clipped styles? I'm not making a case for historical influence here, obviously, but for a closed circle of elements, of basic patterns constantly shifting into one another, sometimes in an orderly evolutionary way, sometimes not. And you can just as well reverse this development, start with disconnected patterns and see them slowly becoming more and more formally subordinated until the full period is born. The basic cycle must be from hypotaxis to parataxis and back, and the central catalyst in the oscillation seems to be parenthesis.

It's a case, though, that would take more proving than we've time for here. Again, we're talking about categories that will help us *see* a prose surface rather than look *through it.* Any categories like parenthesis that do this are, for present purposes, good enough.

Let's put together our accumulated analytical powers on a style which balances nicely the three basic patterns, periodic, clipped, and running. It is an informal obituary for Edward Villiers by the great nineteenth-century diarist Charles Fulke Greville:

> November 7th.—Last night came intelligence from Nice that Edward Villiers was dead. He went there in a hopeless state, was worse after his arrival; then an abscess in his lungs broke, which gave a momentary gleam of hope, but he expired very soon after. I had great regard for him, and he deserved it. He was a man little known of the world in general, shy, reserved to strangers, cold and rather austere in his manners, and being very short-sighted, made people think he meant to slight them when he had no such intention. He was not fitted to bustle into public notice, and such ambition as he had was not of the noisy and ostentatious kind. But no man was more beloved by his family and friends, and none could be more agreeable in any society when he was completely at his ease. He was most warm-hearted and affectionate, sincere, obliging, disinterested, unselfish, and of scrupulous integrity, by which I mean integrity in the largest sense, not merely that which shrinks from doing a dishonourable or questionable action, but which habitually refers to conscientious principles in every transaction of life. He viewed things with the eye of a philosopher, and aimed at establishing a perfect consistency between his theory and his practice. He had a remarkable acute and searching intellect, with habits of patient investigation and mature deliberation; his soul was animated by ardent aspirations after the improvement and the happiness of mankind, and he abhorred injustice and oppression in all their shapes and disguises with an honest intensity which produced something of a morbid sentiment in his mind, and sometimes betrayed him into mistaken impressions and erroneous conclusions. The expansive benevolence of his moral sentiments powerfully influenced his political opinions, and his deep sympathy with the poor not only rendered him inexorably severe to the vices of the rich, but made him regard with aversion and distrust the aristocratic elements of our institutions, and rendered him an ardent promoter of the most extensive schemes of progressive reform. But while he clung with inflexible constancy to his own opinions, no man was more tolerant of the opinion of others. In conversation he was animated, brilliant, amusing, and profound, bringing sincerity, single-mindedness, and knowledge to bear upon every discussion. His life, though short, uneventful, and retired, was passed in the contemplation of subjects of the highest interest and worthiest to occupy

the thoughts of a good and wise man, and the few intimacies he cultivated were with congenial minds, estimable for their moral excellence or distinguished by their intellectual qualities and attainments. The world at large will never know what virtues and talents have been prematurely snatched away from it, for those only who have seen Edward Villiers in the unrestraint and unreserve of domestic familiarity can appreciate the charm of his disposition and the vigor of his understanding. No stranger would have divined that under that cold and grave exterior there lay concealed an exquisite sensibility, the most ardent affections, and a mind fertile in every good and noble quality. To the relations and friends, who were devotedly attached to him, the loss is irreparable and will long be deplored, and the only consolation which offers itself is to be found in the circumstances of his end. He was surrounded by kind and affectionate friends, and expired in the arms of a wife whose conduct he himself described to have been that of a heroine as well as an angel. He was in possession of all his faculties, and was free from bodily pain. He died with the cheerfulness of a philosopher, and the resignation of a Christian, happy, devout, and hopeful, and joyfully contemplating death in an assured faith of a resurrection from the dead.(*The Greville Memoirs* [New York: D. Appleton, 1875])

Greville alternates, with almost dependable regularity, the Hemingway-Chandler compound parataxis and the running style. So:

PARATAXIS

Last night came intelligence from Nice that Edward Villiers was dead.

RUNNING

He went there in a hopeless state, was worse after his arrival; then an abscess in his lungs broke, which gave a momentary gleam of hope, but he expired very soon after.

PARATAXIS

I had a great regard for him, and he deserved it.

RUNNING

He was a man little known of the world in general, shy, reserved to strangers, cold and rather austere in his manners, and being very short-sighted, made people think he meant to slight them when he had no such intention.

PARATAXIS

He was not fitted to bustle into public notice, and such ambition as he had was not of the noisy and ostentatious kind.


RUNNING AND PARATAXIS

But no man was more beloved by his family and friends, and none could be more agreeable in any society when he was completely at his ease.


RUNNING

He was most warm-hearted and affectionate, sincere, obliging, disinterested, unselfish, and of scrupulous integrity, by which I mean integrity in the largest sense, not merely that which shrinks from doing a dishonourable or question-able action, but which habitually refers to conscientious principles in every transaction of life.


PARATAXIS

He viewed things with the eye of a philosopher, and aimed at establishing a perfect consistency between his theory and his practice.


RUNNING

He had a remarkably acute and searching intellect, with habits of patient investigation and mature deliberation; his soul was animated by ardent aspi-rations after the improvement and the happiness of mankind, and he abhorred injustice and oppression in all their shapes and disguises with an honest intensity which produced something of a morbid sentiment in his mind, and sometimes betrayed him into mistaken impressions and erroneous conclusions.

Then running and paratactic styles coalesce:

> The expansive benevolence of his moral sentiments
>     powerfully influenced his political opinions and
> his deep sympathy with the poor
>     not only rendered him inexorably severe to the vices of the rich
>     but made him regard with aversion
>         and distrust
>            the aristocratic elements of our institutions

and rendered him an ardent proponent
　　　　of the most extreme schemes
　　　　of progressive reform.

Then a slight, suggested chiasmus:

　　　　　　　　　　　　　　　　　　　　A　　　B
　　But while he clung with inflexible constancy to his own opinions
　　　　　　　　　　　　　　　　　　　B　　　　　A
　　　　no man was more tolerant of the opinions of others.

Then two climactic series, built on a central parallelism:

In conversation he was animated, brilliant, amusing, and profound,
bringing sincerity, single-mindedness, and knowledge to bear upon every
discussion.

Then a period which is built on an expanded compound parataxis:

His life　　　　though short, uneventful, and retired
　　　　was passed in the contemplation of subjects of the highest interest
　　　　　　　　and worthiest ⟩

　　⤷ to occupy the thoughts of a good and wise man
*and* the few intimacies he cultivated were with congenial minds estimable ⟩

　　　　　⤷ for their moral excellence
　　　　　　or distinguished ⟩
　　⤷ by their intellectual qualities and attainments.

Notice how the symmetrical balance is varied by those dependent clauses
from the running style, which I've indicated by ⤳ ? He sets up a parallelism ("highest" and "worthiest" for example) and then runs it on into the
next element. He moves from clipped parataxis to a running-style informality to a definite, though not fully realized, period. It adds up to a nice
and almost regular alternation of the three basic structures, a style with the
ease of a running pattern, the control of a clipped one, and the climactic
emphasis that the period so naturally generates.

The periodic style usually brings with it a cluster of associated traits:

anaphora; the various patterns of antithesis and balance (isocolon, for example, and chiasmus), often sound patterns (alliterations, homoioteleuton) which underscore the balanced antitheses. Because it is so much more coherent than the other two, it is both easier to recognize and easier to analyze. As the diagramming has shown, it depends heavily on suggested visual patterns, horizontals and verticals that depend on the powerful orienting capability of the visual cortex.

In prose analysis, pairs of opposed terms seem spontaneously to generate a third term halfway between the two opposites. We'll see this happening later, for example, with the high-middle-low style distinction. And something of the sort has happened here with the "clipped" style. It has presented itself as intermediate between the two basic categories, a style that dramatizes control but not through the expansive retrospective balancing act the periodic style employs. This perpetual generation of mixed middle cases is often confusing but can't be avoided. In prose behavior no more than in any other kind do we often find the pure case, the crystalline form. Rather, we're perpetually committed to a chain of circular interpretation. We take an admittedly vague term and use it to analyze a style. The analysis feeds back on, enriches and expands, our sense of what the term means. So much so, sometimes, that we need a new term. That term in its turn is tested against prose experience and refined as an analytical tool. The more experience we have in doing this, the more likely the circle of interpretation will become an upward spiral in which analytical terms allow us to see more in a particular style and the uniqueness of that particular style tells us more about the verbal richness that the term would point to.

All this is to say that descriptive analysis, although a more straightforward affair than rendering value judgments, hardly lends itself to the impersonal objectivity of the chemistry laboratory. Even when considering fundamental terms as we've done in this chapter, analyzing prose remains always a fully human activity which enlists all our powers of thinking, feeling, and intuiting. That is why analysis will always remain inexact—but also why it remains so much fun. We might, in conclusion, point up an analogy with the noun/verb style distinction considered earlier. We can reason that the periodic style, like the noun style, shows thought to be *static,* organized into its component parts and then flash-frozen, while the running style, like the verb style, shows behavior still *in progress,* happening in the present not the past. The contrast often proves a fruitful one but it ought

not lead us to ignore the powerful internal dynamics the period can generate. It builds its design around a center of controlled violence. That is why
the great political voices, the voices of public thunder, have usually been
periodic. The running style seems more naturally to represent the moody
reflections of the private life. When it does work as a public voice, as in
Hitler's oratory for example, it often allegorizes not control but mad abandon.

# IV

# Styles Seen

The hypotactic period, with its internal parentheses, balanced phrasing, and climactic resolution, stops time to let a reader take in the complete pattern. Periodic symmetry, as the diagramming shows, appeals to the eye. The paratactic running style does not exploit the orienting power of the eye to the same degree. The basic difference suggests that verbal style does have a visual component, that some styles, or parts of styles, are meant to be seen. Prose, that is, can be iconic as well as symbolic. This iconic element sometimes creates context and sometimes becomes content. In either case it can be extremely powerful. And yet, unless we're trained to notice, it often works like a pair of eyeglasses, seen through and not noticed, yet enabling us to see. Prose is supposed to be the kind of writing where such tricks are just not done. But if you look, you can often find them.

The most obvious, and hence usually least noticed, visual elements in prose are typographical conventions. And of these, the most obvious—obviously—the difference between verse and prose. Look at this passage:

> One stands almost grateful, in the freezing air, to feel mildly alive, shovelling some earth into the broken ground while new fields lie all around, fallow, awaiting spring or summer plowings, or the jackhammers of deep winter again, to blossom in white tombstones. It is too cold and too late in the year to pluck a handful of grass and mutter of grass and dust. Up toward the eastern horizon the highway—down toward the low, grayish hills westward—runs out in a broad, constantly extending band whose traffic, even in this clear air sighs rather than roaring. The cold spade drops its dirt into earth's dry, ungrateful trough.

A typical piece of what the Germans call *kunstprosa* (art prose) and we would call "poetic" prose. A "poetic" topic too, this Hamlet-like gravedigger's mood. A running style, without any particular shape except for an oddly discordant "*down toward* the low, grayish hills," which seems to clash with the "Up toward the eastern horizon" beginning the sentence. The "blossom in white tombstone" metaphor seems a bit Faulknerian but the diction otherwise is commonplace enough. And the syntax, if a bit loose, hardly operates at the limits of prose adhesion. Fiction then, or an impressionistic essay. But look what happens when the passage is printed as the author intended:

> NEW GRAVEYARD IN NEW JERSEY
> One stands almost grateful in the freezing air
> To feel mildly alive, shovelling some earth
> Into the broken ground while new fields lie all
> Around, fallow, awaiting spring or summer
> Plowings, or the jackhammers of deep winter
> Again, to blossom sometime in white tombstones.
> It is too cold and too late in the year to pluck
> A handful of grass and mutter of grass and
> Dust. Up toward the eastern horizon, the high-
> Way—down toward the low, grayish hills westward—
> Runs out in a broad, constantly extending
> Band whose traffic, even in this clear air sighs
> Rather than roaring. The cold spade drops its dirt
> Into earth's dry, ungrateful trough.
> (John Hollander, *The New Yorker,* October 23, 1978)

What has changed? In making my prose version, I altered the words not at all and the punctuation just slightly. Yet typographical convention has transformed the passage. The *visual* change, for after all it is only that, has altered both context and content. The passage has become something that, printed as prose, it simply was not—a sonnet. Both the fourteen lines and the eleven-syllable lines (except for the last) are created by, and for, the eye. They did not exist before. And the context changes, too, snaps into a familiar focus—a sonnet on the *topos,* the commonplace subject, "death fructifies the earth." The commonplace subject made new, to be sure. This kind of plowing yields only a crop of tombstones; the solemn biblical references to the grass-and-dust generations of men become a low-style throwaway remark. The "up toward"/"down toward" now makes sense as a smoothed-out buried allusion to a "Way" (now split off by typography from its "high(way)" that runs up to Heaven and down to the grave.

But most important, our expectations have altered completely. As prose, the passage is a bit mannered, as poetry almost affectedly informal. Typographical convention has acted as the fundamental context here, changing how we read the poem so much that it changes the poem itself.

This contrived example points an important truth. To print written utterance as prose amounts, in our time, to a fundamental stylistic decision. In prose we expect not only a particular range of topics but a transparent style to express them clearly. We expect, in fact, the whole Clarity-Brevity-Sincerity syndrome so commonly thought to define good writing. But with poetry, just the opposite—all the poetic virtues. The poet need not be grammatically correct, he'll talk about feeling not fact, and he'll do so in a self-conscious metaphorical way. We expect to look *through* prose, to the subject beneath, but *at* poetry, where the language forms part of the subject. A poet can play with words, juggle sounds, in ways the prose writer must not. Prose entitles us to expect all the virtues of correctness—plain narrative sense, grammaticality, intelligible and complete syntax. A writer may strain at these or abolish them but he has then proclaimed himself unconventional and must somehow make artistic capital out of this decision. He can flout convention but it remains there—in the typography. For written discourse we now have these two basic choices, basic contexts for style, fundamental stylistic decisions: present-it-as-prose or present-it-as-poetry. Although we seldom reflect on it, this dichotomy represents an extraordinary restriction, a domineering either/or choice. Present it as poetry (right-hand margin not justified; each line begins with a capital letter) and the reader immediately applies to it the whole pattern of poetic expectation. A poet who does not want to use that whole pattern will have to let the reader know which parts don't fit. It is a "Have you stopped beating your wife yet?" predicament. If you want to occupy a middle ground somewhere between these two basic patterns of expectation, you can't just begin there. You've got to deny part of your initial typographical choice, work against the visual allegory you have chosen.

For discourse, it was not always so. The need for a writing convention forced us to these two antithetical choices. An oral storyteller, orator, or bard started out wherever he wanted to, established his own context as he went along. He could pick up a lyre and start delivering rhymed hexameters if he chose. But he need not have labeled himself either poet or prose writer, could comfortably dwell in a niche of his own making somewhere in between. The oral artist faced a choice of degree, not one between two antithetical extremes. When we come to copy out or print such effects from an age of oral presentation, we cannot help distorting them *by our very typographical convention*. They did not face the Hobson's choice we foist upon them.

Translators face this conventional distortion every day. A translator must first decide whether he will do a prose translation or a verse translation. Whichever he chooses, he will then tend to downplay the elements of the other extreme. He will translate differently and his typographical decision will encourage us to respond differently to what he translates. An ornate, poetic prose—and most prose styles are to some degree poetic—will almost always be translated as prose, and its poetic elements downplayed. If he decides to print his translation as verse, distortion comes in, *a fortiori*, from the other side. We apply all our poetic expectations. An extreme example may help make the point. The Greek sophist Gorgias (ca. 483–376 B.C.) wrote an extraordinarily poetic, ornamented prose. His prose was meant to be spoken, and so the prose/verse typographical choice did not bear heavily upon him. Furthermore, when he did write on paper, the Greek manuscript convention did not discriminate between prose and verse. No spaces of any kind were left, the reader having to sort it out himself. Supposeforexa mplethatIwritewithoutanyspacinginthiswayandletyoumakesenseofthespacin gyourself? When we print his ornamental rhetoric as prose, it looks silly. LaRue Van Hook's literal translation of Gorgias' speech in defense of Helen can serve as example:

> But if by violence she was defeated and unlawfully she was treated and to her justice was meted, clearly her violator as a terrifier was importunate, while she, translated and violated, was unfortunate. Therefore, the barbarian who verbally, legally, actually attempted the barbarous attempt, should meet with verbal accusation, legal reprobation, and actual condemnation. For Helen, who was violated, and from her fatherland separated, and from her friends segregated, should justly meet with commiseration rather than with defamation. For he was the victor and she was the victim. It is just, therefore, to sympathize with the latter and anathematize the former. ("The Encomium on Helen," from an English version by LaRue Van Hook, *Classical Weekly*, February 15, 1913)

The prose expectation makes everything look grotesque. Every manner becomes a mannerism. To get it really right we would have to hear it rather than read it, dodge the typographical dilemma entirely. Since we can't do this, let's follow a modern precedent, chart a new typographical middle ground, by observing neither left nor right margin. It doesn't, let me warn you, work very well. Not my fault. It hasn't worked very well for modern poetry either. It seems contrived, a little precious. We're trapped now, conditioned by our dichotomous typographical convention. We want the fellow to make up his mind whether he's writing prose or poetry. But here's a try:

> BUT IF   by violence
> > > she was defeated
> > and unlawfully
> > > she was treated
> > and to her
> > > justice was meted
> > > > CLEARLY
> > > > her violator
> > > > as a terrifier
> > > > > was importunate
> > > > WHILE SHE
> > > > translated
> > > > and violated
> > > > > was unfortunate.
> THEREFORE the barbarian who verbally
> > > legally
> > > actually
> > attempted the barbarous attempt    should meet with
> > > verbal accusation
> > > legal reprobation
> > > and actual condemnation.
> FOR HELEN                  who was violated
> > > and from her fatherland separated
> > > and from her friends segregated
> > > > should justly meet with commiseration
> > > > rather than with defamation.
> FOR    he was the victor
> > and she was the victim.
> > > It is just, therefore, to sympathize with the latter
> > > > and anathematize the former.

Gorgias was famous for these patterns of parallel phrases *(isocolon)* with similar endings *(homoioteleuton)*. But presenting them as modern experimental verse, I've singled them out for special attention, told you that it was all right to play games with them. By allowing you to read from top to bottom as well as left to right, I've liberated something in the prose that wanted out, the strong desire for a vertical visual coordinate. The poetic typography carries out the inner logic of Gorgias' style, lets it go where it wants to go. It wants to make lists, to put things in antithetical or complementary columns. The poetic typography allows the eye to help in this effort, to reinforce it. The "poetry" thus created ought to look familiar. I've been doing it all along by charting styles. The chart brings the eye's orienting power to bear in analyzing prose. Many prose styles continually aim—through balance, antithesis, parallelism—for a vertical visual coordinate. Often the power thus generated is stronger because not expressed visually. It must be recreated in the reader's mind. The writer has deliberately created a tension between what the eye wants to do with the style and what typography allows it to do. The struggle creates the style's power. But for a style like Gorgias', which predates this convention, charting constitutes pure expressive liberation.

The poetic format tells the reader that he is free to concentrate on the words as words, to play games with them. It frames them for contemplation. By doing so, it reminds us that whatever reality we manage to see through words is still a reality created, and continually conditioned, by them. The prose format encourages us to look *through* words. It does this by being the same for all styles, a never-changing context that aims to be never-noticed. It aims to vanish, to make us forget the mediation of words between us and the reality words create. Just the opposite for the Gorgias chart. It aims to make us self-conscious about the words, to look *at* them, to remind us that the reality is not just "out there" but that words create it. Recently a few writers whose normal medium would be orthodox prose have wanted so strongly to stress this inevitable intervention of words that they've pressed into service an intermediate typography very like our charts.

R. D. Laing, for example, found conventional prose inadequate to express the schizophrenic's imprisonment in a world of words, of verbal symbols forever confusing because the analyst took figuratively what the patient meant literally. When the schizophrenic said he felt immersed within walls of glass, that was how he felt. But the analyst, in order to understand what this meant, rather than how it felt, took it as a metaphor, as a symptom. Thus inside and outside seemed forever blocked off from each other. To express this blockage he had to make us look *at* the words rather than *through* them, to stress their obstinate opacity. So here, in a fragment from a larger unit or "poem."

One is inside
then outside what one has been inside
One feels empty
because there is nothing inside oneself
One tries to get inside oneself
    that inside of the outside
    that one was once inside
    once one tries to get oneself inside what
    one is outside:
    to eat and to be eaten
to have the outside inside and to be
    inside the outside

But this is not enough. One is trying to get
the inside of what one is outside inside, and to
get inside the outside. But one does not get
inside the outside by getting the outside inside
for;
although one is full inside of the inside of the outside
one is on the outside of one's own inside
and by getting inside the outside
one remains empty because
while one is on the inside
even the inside of the outside is outside
and inside oneself there is still nothing
There has never been anything else
and there never will be
(*Knots* [New York: Pantheon, 1970])

Laing's poem looks to the reader the way the world looks to the schizo-phrenic: it seems as if it ought to make sense and yet the more we try the more baffled we become; the more we attempt to look through the words to a conceptual argument, the more the words seem to dissolve into meaning-less repetition of a religious chant. It is a poetry which expresses the crucial importance of our knowing when to look *at* words and when *through* them. Our sanity depends on it.

Again and again in Laing's extraordinary volume of prose poems, *Knots,* he reaches for the vertical coordinate which charting exposes. So in this frag-ment from a "Jack and Jill" parable.

    Jill thinks
        Jack thinks
            Jill does not see something

> Jack does think
> Jill sees it
> but Jack does not see
> Jill thinks
> Jack thinks
> Jill does not see.

The need for the eye as balancer, for both horizontal and vertical coordinates, surfaces repeatedly:

> Jack does not see something.
> Jill thinks Jack does see it.
> Jack thinks Jack does see it and Jill does not.
> Jill does not see herself what
> she thinks Jack does see.
>
> Jack tells Jill
> what Jack thinks Jill does not see.
> Jill realizes
> that,
> if Jack thinks
> Jill does not see *that,*
> which Jill thinks she does,
> Jack does not see
> what Jill thought
> Jack saw.

Or in this relentless anaphora, crafted to express a mind imprisoned in a maddening iteration:

> *She* feels
> he is asking too much (greedy)
> to expect *her,*
> not to feel he is asking too much (greedy)
> to expect her
> not to feel he is mean and greedy
> to feel she is mean
> to feel he is greedy
> to feel *she* is mean
> to feel he is mean
> to feel she is mean
> to feel he is greedy
> to feel she is greedy

when all *she* wants is that
    *he* be more generous in his judgement about her

namely, not·to feel she is mean
      to feel he is mean
      to feel she is greedy
      to feel he is mean
   to feel she is mean
      to feel he is mean
      to feel she is greedy
      to feel he is mean
to want her to be more generous in her judgement about him
namely.

At times, the need for a vertical as well as a horizontal reading plane becomes so strong that he writes in a notation which is half musical score and half scientific chart. Its "meaning" is a plea. Laing feels just the constraints the either/or typographical convention imposes and pleads for more flexible categories, for a convention which will let the powerful and comforting orientation which vision provides express an argument about confused *mental* orientation. Schizophrenics have lost their reality coordinates. They go around in a circle. And so:

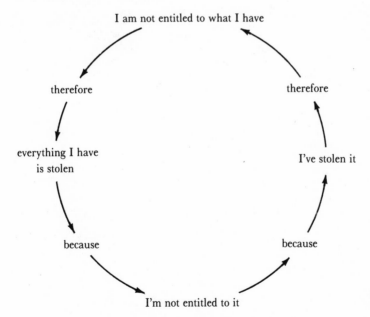

I am not entitled to what I have

therefore          therefore

everything I have         I've stolen it
is stolen

because         because

I'm not entitled to it

The strongest orientative sense we have is vision. Laing uses that power to depict the schizophrenics' inability to orient themselves, to rank things, to arrange a reality. And so these seemingly bizarre typographical vagaries which invite us to perform the poem as if it were music:

```
⎡If it is mine                                        Moderato
⎣          it is not me       .... 1
⎡It it is not mine
⎣          it is not me       .... 2
 If it is not me                    ⎤
           it is not mine⎦    .... 3
 If it is me                        ⎤
           it is mine        ⎦ .... 4
 But
        if it is mine
                it is not me   .... 1
      and if it is not me
                it is not mine   .... 3
 Therefore,
           if,
           if it is not me
                   it is not mine ....  3
      and if,
           if it is not mine
                it is not me     .... 2
      and if,
           if mine
                it is not me     .... 1
 then,
           if it's not me
                it's mine        ....  5
           If it's not me it's mine  ....  5      poco a
           If it's mine it's not me  ....  1      poco
           If it's mine it's not me  ....  1      accelerando
           If it's not me                         al fine
                It's not mine    ....  3
           if it's not mine
                it's not me      ....  2
           if it's not me
                it's mine        ....  5
 If, if it's mine
                it is not me     ....  1
```

                    if it is not me
                            it's not mine      .... 3
        *then,*
            If it's mine, it's not mine        .... 6
        *If,* if it's mine, it's not mine      .... 6
                    if (1 2 3 4/1 3/3 2 1 5/5 1 1 3 2 5 1 3)

As the reading goes ever faster the words become musical notes, devoid of content, a meaningless swirl that, like the "poem," goes on too long. Laing suggests what it feels like to be schizophrenic, rather than what it means—an effort to make sense of the world with a disordered cataloging apparatus. And so we have a mad symphonic score, a crazy list where the principal protagonists become the two typographical conventions, prose and poetry. Typography here has become fully allegorical, come to stand for a way of apprehending the world. And yet Laing's "poetry" can claim a didactic purpose too. He argues that the schizophrenic looks *at* words which we look *through.* If we are ever to understand a patient, we must learn to do both. And that requires typographical categories like these, standing between the two extremes, which can teach us how to move from the one to the other.

A similarly didactic purpose has for a long time galvanized both the music and the prose of John Cage. Like so much modern music, Cage's music is often really music criticism, makes us listen to how we listen, how listening conventions construct, as well as transmit, musical reality. The same resolute didacticism carries over into his prose. See the page (p. 88) from his compendium *Silence* (Middletown, Conn.: Wesleyan University Press, 1961).

Is this a cheap typographical trick or what? Does Cage's message demand this typographical fragmentation? What would be lost if it were printed as conventional prose? Let's try it. I'll adjust the punctuation a little, but that's all:

It is perfectly clear that walking along the river is one thing and writing music is another and being interrupted while writing music is still another and a backache too. They all go together and it's a continuity that is not a continuity that is being clung to or insisted upon. The moment it becomes a special continuity of I am composing and nothing else should happen, then the rest of life is nothing but a series of interruptions, pleasant or catastrophic as the case may be. The truth, however, is that it is more like Feldman's music—anything may happen and it all does go together. There is no rest of life. Life is one. Without beginning, without middle, without ending. The

from one another.       It is perfectly clear       that walking       a–long the river       is
one thing       and writing music       is another       and being interrupted
while writing       music is still       an–other and a backache       too.       They
all go together       and it's a continuity       that is not a continuity       that is being
clung to       or in–sisted upon.       The moment       it be–comes a
special continuity of       I am composing       and nothing else       should happen,       then the
rest of life       is nothing but a series       of interruptions,       pleasant       or
catastrophic       as the case may be.       The truth, however,       is that it is
more like       Feldman's music —       anything may happen       and it all does
go together.       There is no rest of       life.       Life is one.       Without be–
ginning, without middle, without ending       .       The concept: beginning
middle and meaning       comes from a sense of       self       which separates itself
from what it considers to be the rest of life.       But this attitude is untenable unless
one insists on stopping life and bringing it to an end       That
thought is in itself       an attempt to stop       life, for life goes on, indifferent to       the
deaths       that are part of its       no beginning, no middle,       no meaning
.       How much better to       simply get behind and push!
To do the opposite is clownish, that is:       clinging       or trying to force
life into one's own       i–dea of it, of what it should be,       is on–ly absurd.       The ab–
surdity comes from the artificiality of it, of not living,       but of
having to have       first an idea about how one       should do it and then       stumblingly
trying.       Falling down on some one of the various banana peels       is what we
have been calling tragedy. Ideas of separateness artificially elevated. The mythological
and Oriental view       of the hero       is the one       who accepts life
.       And so if one should       object to calling       Feldman a composer,
one could call him       a hero.       But we are all heroes,       if we accept what
comes,       our inner cheerfulness       undis–turbed       If we ac–cept what comes,
that (again) is what       Feldman means       by *Intersection*.       Anyone may cross it.
Here Comes Everybody .       The light has turned.       Walk on.       The
water is fine.       Jump in.       Some will refuse,       for they see that the
water is thick with       monsters       ready to devour them.       What they have       in
mind       is self–preservation.       And what is that       self–preservation but
only a preservation       from life?       Whereas life without death is no longer life       but
only self–preservation. (This by the way is another reason why recordings are not music
.)       Which do we prefer is, practically speaking, an irrelevant       question,
since life       by exercising death       settles the matter       conclusively       for

concept: beginning, middle, and meaning comes from a sense of self which separates itself from what it considers to be the rest of life. But this attitude is untenable unless one insists on stopping life and bringing it to an end. That thought is in itself an attempt to stop life, for life goes on, indifferent to the deaths that are part of its no beginning, no middle, no meaning. How much better to simply get behind and push! To do the opposite is clownish, that is: clinging or trying to force life into one's own idea of it, of what it should be, is only absurd. The absurdity comes from the artificiality of it, of not living, but of having to have first an idea about how one should do it and then stumblingly trying. Falling down on some one of the various banana peels is what we have been calling tragedy. Ideas of separateness artificially elevated. The mythological and Oriental view of the hero is the one who accepts life. And so if one should object to calling Feldman a composer, one could call him a hero. But we are all heroes, if we accept what comes, our inner cheerfulness undisturbed. If we accept what comes, that (again) is what Feldman means by *Intersection*. Anyone may cross it. Here Comes Everybody. The light has turned. Walk on. The water is fine. Jump in. Some will refuse, for they see that the water is thick with monsters ready to devour them. What they have in mind is self-preservation. And what is that self-preservation but only a preservation from life? Whereas life without death is no longer life but only self preservation. (This by the way is another reason why recordings are not music.) Which do we prefer is, practically speaking, an irrelevant question, since life by exercising death settles the matter conclusively for . . .

It makes perfectly good sense in conventional typography. We forget the columnar presentation and follow a rambling, not specially remarkable disquisition on Zen quietude and the oneness of life. Metaphorical and a bit quirky, as such discussions often are, but hardly obscure. So what have we lost? Well, we've lost Cage's main point—what *we've* lost when we unthinkingly accept the convention of prose typography. Cage points to opportunities lost, extraordinary typographical limitations taken for granted. The first thing that occurs to him, as a composer, is vertical chord-harmony, and so he suggests this. But since his subject is, at least partly, the artificiality of beginnings and endings, he breaks the left and right margins of these columns as soon as he sets them up. By doing so, he breaks the continuity of sense which prose typographical convention makes us think inevitable. All those convenient beginnings, middles, and endings prose style has cherished since Aristotle inhere in us the observers, not in reality itself. He exposes the force of our own conventional expectations by altering the stimulus which usually evokes them. The classic example of this basic technique in postmodernist art remains Cage's own piano piece *4'33"*. During this performance he sits on stage silently for four minutes, thirty-three seconds. The audience, deprived of their object of contemplation, must "listen" to their own expectations and reflect upon them. So in this prose. The world, Cage would remind us, does not resemble, necessarily or sometimes at all, the model of it prose typographical convention presents. For the convenience and explanatory power of that presentation, we pay a high price. By definition, we leave out a lot.

I'm not pleading here for wild-eyed typographical license—though Laing and Cage can teach us a good deal—so much as pointing a lesson for conventional prose styles. A number of impulses in conventional prose push toward an expanded convention and draw their power from this pressure. They want to use our eyes just as they want to use our ears. They may call attention to syntax as a conventional, arbitrary reality in ways less obvious than Cage's simply leaving space between words, typographically manhandling convention, but they want to do the same thing. Much of Western prose history can be explained in just this way, as attempts to regain the expressive power given away by prose typographical convention without actually breaking that convention. Just for this reason the diagrams we've been using, by restoring visual coordinates, seem to show immediately how a style works. Our eyes tell us what the style has been saying all along.

When the prose typographical convention is seen as a convention, it seems remarkable that it has lasted so long. Writing does remain while speech vanishes but its major advantage over speech lies in its use of our visual powers of understanding. Vision provides us with our primary orientation. "To see" in a number of languages means "to know." From Gorgias' parallelism onward, prose has wanted to use this powerful persuasion. Historians of rhetoric continually puzzle over why the isocolon habit so thrilled the Greeks when they first encountered it. Maybe it allowed them, for the first time, to "see" their argument.

A few writers have pointed to what prose typography chooses to ignore. Laurence Sterne's eighteenth-century *The Life and Opinions of Tristram Shandy* provides perhaps the best-known instance in English. Sterne wanted to remind his readers that they—he and they together—were constructing a reality, not looking through a transparent typographical window at a reality already out there. The pleasures of the eye he addresses continually, always surrounding words with accompanying gesture, framing a speaking tableau. Asterisks and italics, as well as his famous Shandean dash, create a visual equivalent of gesture, a suggestion of sound and pace. After a sentimental set-piece like the "Alas, poor Yorick" chapter (vol. 1, ch. 12), he puts his ironic counterstatement in the form of two black pages, reminding us that it is black ink which has made us weep. He puns on the connection between narrative and vision by giving us pictures, visual representations, of his "story line."

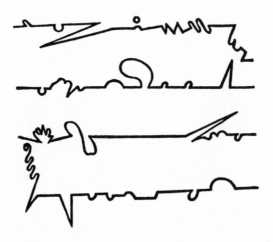

When Uncle Toby flourishes his stick rhetorically, we get a graph of it:

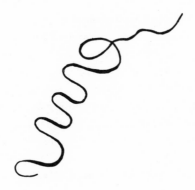

When, like Cage in *4'33"*, Sterne wants to call our attention to what *we* contribute to the novel, how reading is a two-way street, he leaves two blank pages for us to fill in ourselves (vol. 9, chs. 18 and 19). And immediately after, when asked a question so private as to raise a blush, the print blushes too.

## CHAPTER XX.

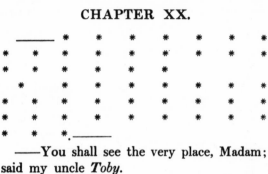

——You shall see the very place, Madam; said my uncle *Toby*.

Sterne made a game from the strong contextual force typographical convention had come to play, as he did out of everything else. Just so he'll misplace the marbled end papers so common in the bindings of his day, put them in the middle of volume 3, to remind us, like Cage, that beginnings and endings inhere in us and not in the world. Sterne wants to make us self-conscious about print, as well as about words. Necessary intermediaries to representing reality, they distort it too. We are, after all, he reminds us, *reading a book.*

In our time, Kenneth Burke has taken this lesson one step further. In a set of sublime doodles called "Flowerishes," he makes us aware of how physically we hold the book, and this by the Cage-like expedient of printing lines going in all four directions, slanting and spiraling across the page. You sit there turning the book around and around like an illiterate pretending to read. You can't get your bearings. When something makes sense, is readable, something else always does not. Burke thus models his own central thesis, that individual perspective, individual orientation, determines what world we live in. Every way of seeing, he insists, is a way of not seeing. And, lest we miss the point, he creates a visual picture of it. The "content," proverbial wisdom in various stages of quirky idiosyncracy, depends on how you look at it. On the next pages are three "Flowerishes" that appear in *Collected Poems, 1915–1967* (Berkeley: University of California Press, 1968).

★ Not knowing either how to live with money, or how to live without it ★ better when busi-

ness becomes a ritual than when ritual becomes a business ★ Person in suspense afraid of losing his faith in skepticism

On the good ship Squalling Brat, in a time of Crying Need

Beware the Ideas of March

★ the few teeth he had left, he ground them in his sleep

the enemy was accused of "stirring up fraternization"

AS OUTMODED AS LAST YEAR'S MODEL OF THE UNIVERSE — A DREARY PLACE, FULL OF OLD NEWTHINGS

Having ceased to follow the news, though he could not do much to it, it could do an awful lot to him

THE NEXT TIME THEY WANT SOME-THING, THEY'LL REMEMBER. THANK YOU FOR THE FORMER TIME

he said: "When I recall the Russian rape of Belgium in the first world war, and the Russian sneak attack on Pearl Harbor in the second, and how the Russians dropped the atom bomb on Hiroshima, I can certainly understand why our leaders should want us to arm Germany and Japan."

say "he is wrong," and they'll call you clear; say precisely how he is wrong, and they'll call you obscure

when reading so religious-and-witty a poet as Herbert, he felt so virtuous-and-distinguished, he began consigning all sorts of people to hell

The hard lot of the pro-ver-bi-al-ist

consider the plight of the harried exploiters who, in order to exploit a man, must sell him an electric refrigerator, a deep freeze, a washing machine, a television set, a new automobile before his old one wears out, a trip to Florida, a ton of magazines, etc., etc.,—and that's not all

Freud's theory of the father-kill may not be true of all, but it does seem true of Freudians

if they were getting along so well, why did one harp on the theme of killing rats, and why did the other keep spitting?

the shepherd to his flock: "Don't you worry, my shorn darlings. For every one of you thus a-shiver on a bare hill in the winter wind, there is a wool-clad over-stuffed fathead even now miserably sweltering in some over-heated city apartment."

They also serve, who only sit and are waited on

WAS AFRAID TO TREAT THEM WITH RESPECT, LEST THEY CEASE TO RESPECT HIM

the toppling headstones, in

he could not read of an unsolved crime without feeling a strong desire to "confess" that he was the criminal; perhaps because the criminal was "wanted," and he wanted to be wanted

as he lay half awake in the bedroom, the sound of jays in the garden was like the scraping of carrots in the kitchen

THEY SAY ALCOHOL REVEALS OUR TRUE SELVES—BUT WHICH OF OUR SELVES IS THAT?

they were so keen on standardization, their women had interchangeable parts

an old decrepit cemetery itself near death ★ it is dangerous to cross raging torrents and

SEEING HOW HE TURNED HIS ENVY OF OTHERS INTO PRAISE OF THE LORD, YOU UNDERSTOOD WHY HE THOUGHT THE LORD WAS SO EAGER TO BE PRAISED BY THE LIKES OF HIM.

THE CURE FOR DIGGING IN THE DIRT IS AN IDEA; THE CURE FOR ANY IDEA IS MORE IDEAS; AND THE CURE FOR ALL IDEAS IS DIGGING IN THE DIRT.

BUCK UP! PUT ON YOUR PANTS. GO OUT FOR A WALK.

THINGS AREN'T SO BAD. PUT IN YOUR TEETH AND

ALONE, WITH STARS AND HORIZON, BY A HERMIT ROCK, OR WIDE WATER, OR A BIG BARE TREE — & ALL SET TO THINK PUBLIC THOUGHTS

*every time you resolved to love him, you found out all over again he was just something to take notes on*

he felt it was alright to do like the others, if only he did it with a bad conscience.

Where many people might say, "It's six of one and half a dozen of the other," he would say, "It's either three biscuits or two triscuits."

wearing her hat trimmed with mistletoe and spikes

The only civilized tempests are tempests in a teapot, like Shakespeare's

"Small craft warnings"—that's for YOU

going up stream down stream might seem all your life to be going out of step

If a critic attacks you stupidly, give him a chance to forget it.

Draw out the time.

hold up your head, and not too high,

will help you read rightly, good books,

*An ecstatic snowstorm -- a grand dumping of pure white filth that made the whole countryside clean*

*He began by hoping to be heard, and ended by fearing to be overheard.*

learn not to take umbrage, just penumbrage

*tragedy helps us pity those we might otherwise envy or fear.*

*all sitting pretty, in an ugly sort of way*

it's not the snowfalls, however heavy — It's the drifts

you say "criticism of criticism," and they hear "ideas on fleas"

Three stages of universal history:
(1) "Be generous, let me in."
(2) They let him in.
(3) "Be picky, keep the others out."

*"Be as straight as a die." Now, in the Hemming Way, "Be as straight as a die."*

he held that poets were made for critics, just as sick people are made for doctors.

the trouble with raising unanswerable objections is that people won't answer you

*it's hard to remember : but often all we need do is nothing*

THOUGH HE DESPISED ALL MANKIND, HE DEARLY LOVED AN AUDIENCE

, he said.

And echo answered,

what next!

"What Next!"

around I know my know how I know, my know how I...

AFTER FIFTY, ONE FURTHER THING TO LEARN: HOW RIPEN WITHOUT ROTTING?

EACH YEAR, MORE ACQUAINTANCES FEWER FRIENDS

Inherited several million dollars, plus Original Sin

94

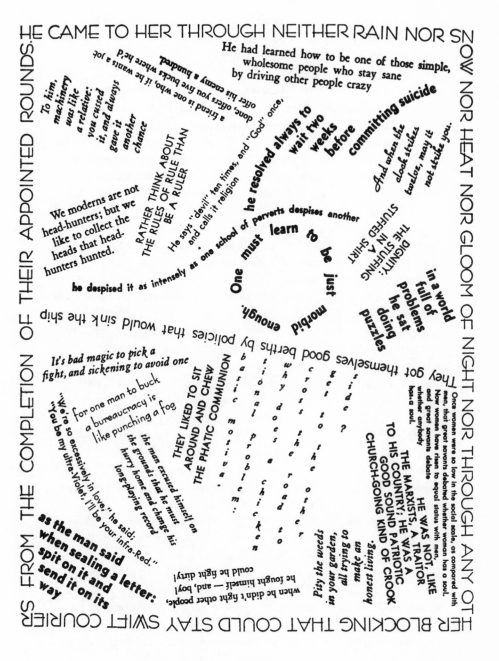

He had learned how to be one of those simple, wholesome people who stay sane by driving other people crazy

To him, machinery was like a relative: you cussed it, and always gave it another chance

a friend is one who, if he wants a jot, don't — offers you five bucks where he'd offer his enemy a hundred

he resolved always to wait two weeks before committing suicide

And when the clock strikes twelve, may it not strike you.

We moderns are not head-hunters; but we like to collect the heads that head-hunters hunted.

RATHER THINK ABOUT THE RULES OF RULE THAN BE A RULER

He says "devil" ten times, and "God" once, and calls it religion

One must learn to be just morbid enough.

he despised it as intensely as one school of perverts despises another

DIGNITY: THE STUFFING IN A STUFFED SHIRT

in a world full of problems he sat doing puzzles

They got themselves good berths by policies that would sink the ship

It's bad magic to pick a fight, and sickening to avoid one

for one man to buck a bureaucracy is like punching a fog

"We're so excessively in love," he said: "You be my ultra-Violet, I'll be your infra-Red."

THEY LIKED TO SIT AROUND AND CHEW THE PHATIC COMMUNION

the man excused himself on the grounds that he must hurry home and change his long-playing record

basic motiva-tional problem: why does the chicken cross the road to get to the other side?

Once women were so low in the social scale, as compared with men, that great savants debated whether woman has a soul. Now women have risen to equal status with men, and great savants debate whether anybody has a soul.

HE WAS NOT, LIKE THE MARXISTS, A TRAITOR TO HIS COUNTRY; HE WAS A GOOD SOUND PATRIOTIC CHURCH-GOING KIND OF CROOK

Pity the weeds in your garden, all trying to make an honest living.

as the man said when sealing a letter: spit on it and send it on its way

when he didn't fight other people, he fought himself — and, boy! could he fight dirty!

95

These appear in a book of poems but clearly belong to the middle ground between prose and poetry we have seen Cage and Sterne staking out. Here the visual metaphors for prose style can all be literalized, and in constructions so full of puns as those are, we are clearly invited to do so. A symmetrical prose? Parallelism? Running style? Pointed style? Curt style? All are *literally* represented here. And the play with type styles emphasizes type's tremendous evocative power. What happens when you print "Beware the Ides of March" in Olde English type? Or use boldface, caps, or all the other variations here? Type styles, too, represent an area of expressivity prose usually throws away unnoticed. So too with the other aspects of book design. Burke, like Cage, reminds us of an area of potential expressivity which *both* poetry and prose typography have given up. He adds game and play to prose's resolute purpose. Like Cage and Sterne, he does it with a light and punning heart, but the didacticism stands out clearly enough. Visual conventions of design and presentation still can, and usually do, tell us whether we have to do with a scholarly book or a popular one, a school book (remember the big print, boldface headings, obvious illustrations?), a scientific treatise (all those charts and diagrams), a Victorian book or a Renaissance one. And these are important clues, major guides to interpretation. We haven't—and can't—discard all the stylistic clues prose presents to the eye. But we have discarded as many as we can, moved steadily toward a prose typographical convention that allows the eye to help very little.

It was not always so. Look at the following page from a fourteenth-century Italian treatise on marriage. In its basic cruciform pattern, it looks like one of Burke's Flowerishes. The whole illuminated manuscript tradition testifies to just the urge I've been trying to describe, the urge to help out prose style with *visual* coordinates, to complement its symbolic with an iconic meaning. Next is a page from a fifteenth-century Italian breviary to make the point (see p. 98).

Book design, like prose style, has since the Renaissance become ever more transparent, ever less noticed. We look *through* it rather than *at* it. But this conventional self-denial of visual reinforcement has been the exception, not the rule, since the beginning of writing, and perhaps will not last forever. However hard we try to abolish the visual allegory, it forever sneaks back in when we are not looking. Here's a trivial but revealing instance of how it does so.

Robert Townsend was the businessman who made the Avis car-rental

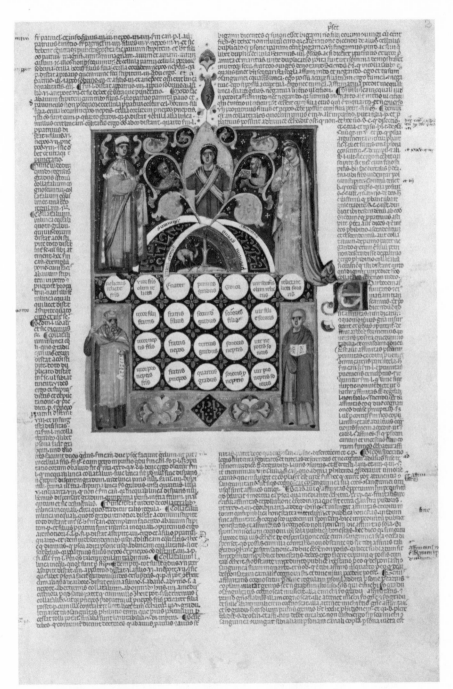

Summa de Sponsalibus et Matrimoniis. Arbor Consanguinitatis et Affinitatis, *Johannes Andreae, Bologna, first half of the fourteenth century. (The Pierpont Morgan Library Manuscript M.715.) Reprinted by permission.*

*Breviary (Roman Usage), Ferrara, ca. 1470.* (Illuminated and Calligraphic Manuscripts, *Harvard College Library, Cambridge, Mass., 1955; by permission of the Houghton Library, Harvard University.*)

company rich and famous. After he had worked his miracle, he wrote, in
the Horatio Alger tradition, a small book of advice to those who would follow in his footsteps. Called *Up the Organization* (New York: Knopf, 1970),
it was printed in an odd way. Here are a few excerpts:

### TRAINING

The only way I know to get somebody trained is on the job.
The first time I learned this was by accident. I'd laboriously
recruited an assistant (note: not an assistant-to). By the
time I'd offered the job and he'd accepted I was pretty sure
I had a good man. But the earliest he could come to work
was the day I left for vacation. Turmoil! Should I go?
For the wrong reasons I went.

Thrown in the deep end, he learned some plain and fancy
swimming while I was away. And he developed some
valuable relationships in those three weeks that might
never have developed if I'd been there. He got in the habit
of growing and has never stopped.

If you have more than one possible successor, *never*
anoint a favorite. You'll stop the healthy competition for
your job and paint a bull's-eye on your heir's shirt-front.
I did it once, and the organization tore him to shreds. Better
to keep an open-minded show-me attitude toward all
contenders.

### PROMOTION, FROM WITHIN

Most managements complain about the lack of able
people and go outside to fill key positions. Nonsense.
Nobody inside an organization ever looked ready to move
into a bigger job.

I use the rule of 50 per cent. Try to find somebody inside
the company with a record of success (in any area) and
with an appetite for the job. If he lookes like 50 per
cent of what you need, give him the job. In six months
he'll have grown the other 50 per cent and everybody will
be satisfied.

How to do it wrong: go outside and get some expensive
guy* who looks like 110 per cent of what you want and a

*Like Bunky Knudsen or Bo Polk

> year later, after having raised salaries all around him,
> you'll still be teaching him the business. The people
> around him will be frustrated and ineffective.
>
> One of the keys is to pick someone within the company
> who has a well-deserved reputation as a winner. Not
> someone who looks to you like a *potential* winner but
> doesn't happen to be fitting in very well where he is.
>
> The organization will rally around an accepted winner
> even when he's temporarily over his head, because in
> their eyes he deserves the chance. The phony who conned
> you into giving him the job will go down for the third
> time and pull down everybody else he can reach.

The prose—plain, direct, colloquial—doesn't tell us much about Townsend but the typography does. The paragraphs are presented as discrete units, brief self-contained nuggets of wisdom like the Beatitudes in the Sermon on the Mount. That is, in fact, what they amount to, Business Beatitudes. This typographical convention has long been common for the inspired and oracular wisdom of great teachers. You can see it in books as widely separated as the *Thoughts of Chairman Mao* (at least in the English translation) and Wittgenstein's *Tractatus*.

A wise saying, then a visual pause while we ponder its wisdom. So with Townsend's Business Beatitudes. To underline this suggestion of oracular wisdom, the paragraphs have no indentation. And yet the suggestion is made subtly, because this kind of itemized division is also characteristic of business list-making. Townsend comes across not only as guru but as a crisp, no-nonsense list-maker who, by crackey, has met some payrolls. The structure of the book, series of chapters keyed alphabetically A–Z, testifies to both effects. The old improvisational tradition of inventing something—a proverbial saying, folksong verse, whatever, for each letter of the alphabet—here finds a new use. A nugget of business wisdom for each letter of the alphabet. (The use of key letters—"P" for "People," reminds you of medieval manuscript illumination's "key-letter" technique of decoration, doesn't it?) Yet what more directly businesslike, more hearty in its abjuration of all fancy, "artistic" structured planning than this alphabetical list?

Nothing in Townsend's text required this kind of organization. He could have organized the book under much more conventional headings, printed it with conventional paragraph indentation and spacing, and altered not a single word. But he would have had to *say* what here he lets the eye find out for itself: "I'm at the Top, a Business Guru, yet no airs, just one of the boys." You can see the same split in how he footnotes—on the one hand scholarly footnotes to "Theory X" in the bibliography, and on the other, familiar references to those famous 110-percenters Bunky Knudsen and Bo Polk, just folks like Townsend but Big Business Gurus too. Townsend, by uniting his two approaches, becomes just one of the gang, but in a gang of Gurus like himself.

I'm not knocking Townsend's presentation of self, or his book either, which really does offer wit and wisdom, but trying to show that the dimension of visual expressivity for prose which we've pushed out the front door keeps trying to sneak in the back. And, as we shall see, the same thing happens to verbal style. The more transparent and unself-conscious we try to make it, the more pressure builds up for self-conscious ornament. The eye and the ear work on even the most transparent style. They are, in fact, more necessary to a transparent style than to a literary one, because when we cease to see and to hear prose, we've thrown away two major tools for meaning. If a writer has ceased to see or hear his prose, he'll get no help from these two powerful organizational senses in his reader. And readers sensitive to shape and sound will be continually put off. This happens in modern prose style again and again. Shapeless and caco-rhythmic, it shows what happens when prose ceases to see and hear. Here's an example from *The Development of Writing Abilities* by James Britton (1978)—a book on teaching children how to write!

> Smith's work may suggest ways in which we might be able to make writing less difficult. It is possible that much of the advice normally given to children about how to write effectively would, if taken, increase the difficulties. Suppose for instance that a teacher has been to some pains to get the process going by engaging the interest of his pupils in a topic to the point where the ideas are flowing freely. If he then makes precise stylistic demands, grammatical prohibitions and admonitions, and insists, for instance, on the looking up in the dictionary of all words where the writer is in doubt, he may bring the conscious choosing and the mediated processes of the writer so much into the forefront of his mind that the production of ideas is interrupted to the point where it dries up. Fortunately children are very good at ignoring such stylistic advice and getting on with the job.
>
> This is not to suggest that it is wrong to try to influence how children write,

but merely to say that direct advice during writing is seldom helpful. Whatever influence can be exerted should come to the writer in other ways and at other times—at times when he is not actually engaged in writing. It is perhaps too much to suggest that we learn to write by reading and talking—and by writing.

This kind of prose resists visual sorting or vocal stress, smears emphasis across the entire sentence so that the voice has no place to rise or fall. Look at the first sentence:

Smith's work may suggest ways in which we might be able to make writing less difficult.

Do we accent "may"? Or "suggest"? And how read the "may . . . might . . . make" sequence? Which verb contains the predominant action? Or, to anticipate the next chapter, what can the voice do with the inadvertent sound resemblances, the "*may* suggest *ways*" and "*in*sists, for *in*stance"? They jingle at the back of the mind, inviting us to put together words that really don't belong together. Sentences in a prose like this are simply squeezed out like tomato paste. Look at sentence three as a final example:

Suppose for instance that a teacher has been to some pains to get the process going by engaging the interest of his pupils in a topic to the point where the ideas are flowing freely.

Let me try revising it:

Suppose that a teacher has gotten his students really thinking about a topic. The ideas are flowing freely.

Nobody would give this more than a $C^+$ but at least it allows both eye and ear to stress "thinking" and "flowing" and group the rest of the utterance around them. Or look at the sentence which begins "If he then makes precise stylistic demands. . . ." Try to diagram its shape. You'll end up rewriting it into something like a periodic sentence. As written, it's simply a maze. This prose offers no vertical coordinates at all, and no horizontal ones, either. It forbids the eye to help the mind. And in a mild irony, it recommends, as an educational technique, just the stylistic blindness which creates this kind of prose in the first place.

Modern prose typographical conventions have made many things easier. Just take an early printed text and transcribe it into modern spelling, punctuation, and line-separation for speakers, and see how much easier it is to read. But the ease comes at a price. If we cease to look *at* the prose, we lose the visual organization so many styles depend on. And if we cease, at the same time, to read prose aloud, we lose the emphasis and tonal control the voice supplies. The example above has lost both its eyes and its ears. The whole weight these two powers formerly supported now falls on a style's purely symbolic force. If, as we have done nowadays, we insist at the same time that prose use no ornaments that even suggest sight or sound, then we have weakened prose to the point of collapse. Dehumanized it, in fact, for it is human to see and hear. When we regain a full and sensible view of human verbal expression, the willingness with which modern prose allowed its eyes to be put out and its ears cut off will seem remarkable. The penalties exacted for the blindness of typographical convention, the kind of expressive power forsworn, I've tried to suggest in this chapter. In the next, we'll see the price silent reading has exacted.

# V

# Voiced and Unvoiced Styles

Perhaps the most famous moment in the history of prose comes when St. Augustine describes, with wonder, the reading habits of St. Ambrose: "When he read, he ran his eyes over the pages and searched out the sense, but his tongue and voice remained silent" (*Confessions,* VI. iii). Nobody knows, of course, how many other silent readers lurked in their closets during the late fourth century after Christ, or when they came out. But it must have seemed for everyone, as for St. Augustine, a stunning event. We stand so far from it now, silent reading so long a universal norm, that we seldom ponder this basic change. We think it a great milestone of progress, a putting away of childish things. And in many ways it has been. We couldn't function without silent reading. Not only libraries but offices, subways, waiting rooms would turn into madhouses. Reading is a private, not a social act. We can't conceive it otherwise.

Yet it helps, when analyzing prose, to try. For what has happened to prose style since it lost its voice can often be understood as an effort to regain voice by other means, to create a voiceless voice. And the prose which has not tried to regain voice has tried to abolish it, not simply to ignore voice but to speed-read it off the board. I've learned a lot by asking American college students to read something—anything—aloud. They hate to. It embarrasses them. Reading is a private act. You don't do it in public. If a sadistic professor forces you, you duck your face low, cover your head with a monotone, and mumble as fast as you can. You may have to move your lips but, by God, you won't *read aloud.* The reluctance seems to lie beyond shyness. Something more serious stands at issue. What? What happens when we suspend Ambrose's revolution and read aloud?

We socialize our behavior for a start. And this means taking an attitude toward it. We don't walk around in our daily lives totally neutral, like zombies. We take attitudes, always in one mood or another. Things, people, help us out or get in the way. Really neutral behavior comes across as hostile—"impersonal," "unfeeling." Try acting through any human relation without expressing *any* emotion. You can't do it. That absence of emotion will be received as implied hostility. Overt hostility is less hostile; we know where we are. These emotional range-findings supply our primary social radar, show us our way through the world. When asked to read a text aloud, we must take a stand, convey our feelings through tone of voice. So the students' dislike. Taking a stand may show that they have not understood the text or, worse, disagree with the professor about it.

We communicate an extraordinary range of meanings just through tone of voice. Listen to yourself talk to listeners—babies, dogs, cats—who can't understand concepts but who respond to intonation. You are talking a language of pure attitude, of love, reassurance, frustration, fatigue. This emotional overdubbing can color any event, make a laughingstock of the most sublime poetry, salvage the most banal cliché. It can tell you to seek out dirty innuendo or launder your mind. The distance between the line on the page and the line read represents precisely the distance between the play in the book and the play in the theater. To read prose aloud is to perform it, literally bring it to life. And life is no neutral place.

So St. Ambrose made a big decision. He had, as much as he could, taken prose out of society. The silent reader need not color his text with his own emotion, hate it, caress it, make it part of himself by reenacting it. He lives in a different world. He can ignore emotional signals without offending the writer, take information and let feeling go. He can stand outside, neutral and unendangered. And so can the writer who writes for such an audience. Prose writers have, since the Ambrosian revolution, had to make a fundamental choice. Would they court this neutrality or try to subvert it? Neutrality is lonely; it takes work for a writer to keep reading silent. People have done it, written a characteristic unvoiced range of styles; and, recently, modern speed-reading techniques have carried the Ambrosian revolution a step further by abolishing both voice and smaller-scale visual patterns as well. But this revolution has never fully succeeded. We are incorrigibly social. And so prose style, since it lost its voice, has suffered repeated invasions of its private reading-space by social voices. Forbidden to read aloud, we still seek a voice, recreate a society. Talking about "voice" in prose becomes confusing, since we are talking about style itself, about all the ways our social impulses, our feelings, declare themselves in the reading silence.

And we make it harder for ourselves by mixing up the criteria for voiced with those for unvoiced prose. In the canonical trio of judgmental terms for prose—clarity, brevity, and sincerity—the first two point to an unvoiced style while the third emerges only with voice. We want the best of both worlds, to share in society but not in its dangers. We want, for everyday, what only literary experience at its best can give us, something which, as C. S. Lewis put it, "heals the wound, without undermining the privilege, of individuality."

But if the distinction between voiced and unvoiced gets confusing in the abstract, the extremes come clear in examples. I'm imprisoned here, of course, by what I'm talking about, describing voice in a voiceless medium. No way to change this but there are ways around it. Let's start with a piece of genuinely voiceless prose. It comes from the *Federal Register,* a compendium that collects all the Federal Government's official proclamations. In the *Register,* vol. 42, no. 139 (July 20, 1970) appeared some rule changes proposed by the Federal Communications Commission for licensing citizens band radio service. The original version of "95.421—Who may sign applications":

> (a) Except as provided in paragraph (b) of this section, applications, amendments thereto, and related statements of fact required by the Commission shall be personally signed by the applicant, if the applicant is an individual; by one of the partners, if the applicant is a partnership; by an officer, if the applicant is a corporation; or by a member who is an officer, if the applicant is an unincorporated association. Applications, amendments, and related statements of fact filed on behalf of eligible government entities, such as states and territories of the United States and political subdivisions thereof, the District of Columbia, and units of local government, including incorporated municipalities, shall be signed by such duly elected or appointed officials as may be competent to do so under the laws of the applicable jurisdiction.
>
> (b) Applications, amendments thereto, and related statements of fact required by the Commission may be signed by the applicant's attorney in case of the applicant's physical disability or of his absence from the United States. The attorney shall in that event separately set forth the reason why the appli-

cation is not signed by the applicant. In addition if any matter is stated on the basis of the attorney's belief only (rather than his knowledge), he shall separately set forth his reasons for believing that such statements are true.

(c) Only the original of applications, amendments, or related statements of fact need be signed: copies may be conformed.

(d) Applications, amendments, and related statements of the fact need not be signed under oath. Willful false statements made therein, however, are punishable by fine and imprisonment, U.S. Code, Title 18, section 1001, and by appropriate administrative sanctions, including revocation of station license pursuant to section 312(a)(1) of the Communications Act of 1934, as amended.

Read this aloud. Not just mumbling your way through but with feeling. *Con amore.* Color it with your voice. Hate it! Love it! Let your voice ooze emotion, like a TV announcer giving his all in a dog food commercial. You burst out laughing. You can color almost anything by a voice-over, but not this stuff. You feel ridiculous trying to add a voice. Because none was intended, the voice has no place to go. Pitch finds no natural rise or fall, no obvious loud or soft, no performance instructions at all—purely conceptual prose, all cortex and no limbic system.

The author of this regulation will come back with a sensible gripe. Voice, feeling, has no place. Just what is *not* wanted. Impersonality is required here, pure denotative clarity. Oddly enough, though, this argument is disproved by the revision suggested for this original wording. For so popular has CB radio become that the regulations really did need to be clear. The revised version, now already famous in legal circles for its clarity and precision, aimed for a general audience. How? *By adding voice.* The reader is addressed directly. The original, by its very impersonality, puts us off. We tune out, don't want to understand it. Look how differently we respond to the revision:

### §95.425. How do I sign my CB license application?

(a) If you are an individual, you must sign your own application personally.

(b) If the applicant is not an individual, the signature on an application must be made as follows:

| Type of applicant | Signature of applicant |
|---|---|
| Partnership _ _ _ _ _ _ One of the partners. | |
| Corporation _ _ _ _ _ _ Officer. | |
| Association_ _ _ _ _ _ _Member who is an officer. | |
| Governmental Unit_ _ _Appropriate elected or appointed official. | |

(c) If the FCC requires you to submit additional information, you must sign it in the same way you signed your application.

(d) If you willfully make a false statement on your application, you may be punished by fine, imprisonment and revocation of your station license.

### Explanation

*Editorial changes.* This section has been redrafted in greatly simplified language to ensure that an applicant for a CB license knows how to sign his or her application. Paragraph (b) of existing §95.421 has been deleted as duplicative of §1.913 (b) of the Commission's Rules. Paragraph (c) of existing §95.421 has been deleted as unnecessary.

Plenty of other changes here, of course; some information tabulated, some simplified, some left out. But what strikes you first is the regained voice. The prose has again become social. The "you" has given the reader his sociality back. The passage has been "clarified," but maybe "socialized" would be closer to the truth. Try reading the revision aloud. Even the table has become readable. The voice has pegs to hang emphasis on: "If you are an *individual,* you must sign your application *personally.*" In section (d) there is even a (for a dedicated CBer) climactic structure—"fine, imprisonment and revocation of your station license." And it climaxes a sentence which allows, on "willfully," a natural opening stress. These rules may not be declaimed in Washington's echoing marble halls, but that they can be voiced makes a difference. Truly unspeakable prose frightens.

Maybe this is why the neglect of voice seldom leads to the clarity it seeks. The speed-reading route, the simplification of St. Ambrose's simplification, sometimes proves self-confounding. The more unspeakable the prose the more urgently we want to speed-read it out of existence. The very need for speed-reading testifies to the power of St. Ambrose's choice. What else has generated all those words written only to be skipped over, sped through, never to be reenacted? Voice in prose means comfort, social reassurance. We want to linger rather than skim. Silent reading presents two choices, then: try to put voice back in "silently" or get rid of it entirely. The second choice has proved a dead end. Genuinely voiceless prose proves unworkable. The many dyslogistic epithets it carries—jargon, gobbledegook, bureaucratese—point to a single kind of failure, a social failure. We don't really have a choice. We can decide not *if* prose should be voiced but only *how* it should speak. What, this amounts to asking, does it mean to call prose style "voiced"?

"Voiced" suggests simply a transcription of speech, but raw conversation makes disastrous prose. The stops and starts, the "uh" fillers, the backpedalings and instant replays, the flat banalities floating on a sea of shrugs and grunts, make grotesque reading. No one taught this lesson more pertinaciously than the late Dwight D. Eisenhower. Under the pressure of great affairs he often spoke *ex tempore* and these improvisations, when frozen by print, made him sound like everyone's favorite dimwitted uncle. Excerpt from an Eisenhower press conference:

### The President's News Conference of July 8, 1953

THE PRESIDENT. One or two items, ladies and gentlemen, of possible interest. We have had a committee, as you know, called the Jackson Committee, studying the whole field that has been called by many names, but popularly known by the name of psychological warfare. Its report, of course, is largely confidential, but at my direction they have made a summary of the report which will be handed out by Mr. Hagerty around noon today, probably around 12 o'clock.

It is very interesting; and, of course, it is trying to draw together into one place in the Federal Government responsibility for all this kind of action.

In Korea, as you know, the Communists have accepted our suggestion that the talks be resumed looking toward the consummation of a truce.

Now, I just want to make it clear again: everybody in the United States, I believe, understands the aspirations of President Rhee and has a very warm spot in their hearts for what South Korea has done in this whole business. We must never lose sight of the fact that this is an incident in a great ideological struggle, as well as a struggle just by arms.

We look forward to a reunification of Korea by peaceful means and intend to work for it.

The question, though, of carrying on hostilities and trying to accomplish objectives by warfare in this world of today is something, of course, that you have to weigh against the future and the success of the United Nations, for which we all hope that there will be a great success.

On Germany, I received a telegram signed by the president of the AFL and the president of the CIO. They are over there as members—in Stockholm, they are actually meeting—they are over there as American representatives of a great union of labor organizations, free labor organizations from the free countries. . . .

Q. Charles T. Luccy, Scripps-Howard Newspapers: Did you discuss the Pennsylvania governorship with Senator Duff, and have you urged him to run for the governorship next year?

THE PRESIDENT. I don't participate in the kind of detail which you intimate in local political questions.

I have talked of many things, including listening very carefully to Senator Duff, but I have urged him to do nothing. I merely talked on this basis, that we, locally and federally, as a party, are trying to establish a record that gains the admiration and respect of the American people. That is what I am talking about. They will have to decide their local questions themselves.

Q. D. Harold Oliver, Associated Press: Does that go for Virginia, too?

THE PRESIDENT. Virginia?

Q. Mr. Oliver: Yes, the governorship race. I was asked to have you go on record about that.

THE PRESIDENT. Actually, yes, the same observation applies. I don't consider it my function to interfere in the local and State elections. After all, there are certain responsibilities placed upon the President of the United States. There are certain attitudes I think that he is expected normally to observe. I hope to do that.

Now, my own contention is this: the only worthwhile political program, particularly for the party in power, is to present at each new election, to the people of the United States, an accomplishment, a worthwhile progress that earns approbation. I can see no other way of approaching this thing, and I don't see how the President could interfere or attempt to interfere appropriately in the local political struggles—city, county, State, or anything of that kind. (*Public Papers of the Presidents of the United States, Dwight D. Eisenhower, 1953*)

Well, yes, a voice, all right. And it does help. No glacial bureaucratic chill. But what happens when it is read aloud? You will, remember, be recreating a real voice. First, it is hard to stress anything. A bland parataxis hovers over the passage. Look at the first sentence. "One or two items/ladies and gentlemen/of possible general interest." The order of these three like-sized elements almost doesn't matter. And the first paragraph continues in the same way—fillers ("as you know"), mindless amplifications ("the whole field that has been called by many names, but popularly known by the name of psychological warfare"), pointless replays ("around noon today, probably around 12 o'clock"). All these fillers, "it is very interestings," "of courses," and "as you knows," insure that no rhythm ever gets started. No climaxes can build. He'll start to come down hard on a point and then trail off:

Now, I just want to make it clear again . . .

or

everybody in the United States, I believe . . .

The "I believe" lets air out of a tire already going flat. Then a warm spot in our hearts for President Rhee, a balloon filler ("in this whole business") and finally a sentence of pure flaccid flummery:

We must never lose sight of the fact that this is an incident in a great ideological struggle as well as a struggle just by arms.

Read this sentence aloud again, as emphatically as you can. See the problem? The important elements—"lose sight" and the contrast between *ideological struggle* and *struggle by arms*—are separated by so much filler that the voice can't preserve its tension, build a climax. Try it again.

> We must NEVER LOSE SIGHT of the fact that
> this is an incident in a great IDEOLOGICAL
> struggle as well as a struggle just BY ARMS.

We want to glue "ideological" and "by arms" together because the power of the assertion lurks in making that contrast tight. The compared elements ought to be alike—either ideological struggle/armed struggle or by ideology/by arms. The difference between the two, like the da da *dum* fillers in between the major elements, prevents the voice from recreating any drama. The prose, as we say, falls flat.

He's talking about great issues, life and death. In July of 1953 we were, as he tells us, just about to make peace in Korea. Yet he speaks more like a man who remembers on Saturday morning that he should clean out the garage but decides to play golf instead.

We look forward to a reunification of Korea by peaceful means and intend to work for it.

Look at what happens to the *action* in this sentence. What's going on? 1) looking forward; 2) reunifying; 3) working for it. The force leaches into too many planes. "We intend to reunify Korea peacefully," would have given the voice something to hit hard—*peacefully*. But his style never allows that. It smoothes out differences. The next sentence. I'll voice-over its effect on us:

<blockquote>
<pre>
                                      uh uh  uh uh uh uh
The question though, of carrying on hostilities and trying to accomplish

uh uh uh uh uh  uh uh  uh uh    uh              uh uh
objectives by warfare in this world of today is something, of course,

that you have to weigh against the future and the success of the United

        uh   uh  uh uh uh   uh   uh  uh uh uh uh uh   uh
Nations, for which we all hope that there will be a great success.
</pre>
</blockquote>

We want to yell, "Spit it out, you mumbly, woolly-minded, garrulous old nitwit!" Sometimes, as when the dependable Sarah McClendon asks him what the government can do about the drought, the great statesman seems all cloud:

> I don't think you can prevent the effect, because drought is a meteorological condition that even the most powerful governments seem to be helpless in front of.
>   Now what they can do is this: plan for help, alleviation of distress, and so on—in other words, the old theory of prevention of disaster to great bodies of our citizens, particularly when that disaster could not be foreseen. Actually, I believe that the Governors of that whole region are to meet soon, again, to discuss these things. From them, I would expect worthwhile suggestions. We have moved only a little bit at a time, but certainly we hope to do what an enlightened and humanitarian America would expect us to do with respect to a whole area like that, that is so stricken.

Yet we're standing here in the presence not only of a great statesman but of great art, of a prose that recreates in life what Jane Austen's Mr. Woodhouse and George Eliot's Mr. Brooke reenact in fiction, the archetypical kindly-but-muddle-headed old man. It is easy to see how Eisenhower fell into this archetype. As a general, he was the resolver of allied disputes, the Great Coordinator. He was terrific at *smoothing out differences.* The prose reflects, indeed caricatures, that habit of mind. He saw no reason, as President, to change the pacifying habits of a lifetime.

But, reading the transcript, we don't think of that. We read it as literature. We can't help it. It is no accident that Eisenhower the *ex tempore* speaker was so parodied. His literary appeal made it inevitable. And so our impulses to rewrite the prose, to have him "Get on with it, My God!" are all wrong. For political purposes, Eisenhower had found, in the unstudied but kindly old uncle, a perfect voice. The intellectuals didn't like it but it worked.

Voice, then, obviously means personality. It points to one central truth— the inevitable *literary* ingredient in all prose. Even when you leave personality out, as in unvoiced prose, you have contrived a literary effect by the act of omission.

Now a different Eisenhower, writing during World War II to his commander, the austere Chief of Staff, General George C. Marshall:

ALGIERS                                    *September 6, 1943*
   *Dear General:* First, I will take up the subject of the permanent list referred to in your telegram #6595.

   Speaking generally, I think you are doing a very gracious and wise thing and, moreover, I must agree in general with the list as you have made it up.

   Concerning Stilwell, there can be no shadow of doubt about him. He took a very unattractive looking job, has carried on in the most discouraging kind of circumstances, and has apparently kept his head and done his share in preserving a workable team in that region. He seems self-effacing and effective.

   With respect to Patton, I do not see how you could possibly submit a list for permanent Major Generals, on combat performance to date, and omit his name. His job of rehabilitating the Second Corps in Tunisia was quickly and magnificently done. Beyond this, his leadership of the Seventh Army was close to the best of our classic examples. It is possible that in the future some ill-advised action of his might cause you to regret his promotion. You know his weaknesses as well as his strength, but I am confident that I have eliminated some of the former. His intense loyalty to you and to me makes it possible for me to treat him much more roughly than I could any other senior commander, unless my action were followed immediately by the individual's relief. In the last campaign he, under stress it is true, indulged his temper in certain instances toward individual subordinates who, in General Patton's opinion of the moment, were guilty of malingering. I took immediate and drastic measures, and I am quite certain this sort of thing will never happen again. You have in him a truly aggressive commander and, moreover, one with sufficient brains to do his work in splendid fashion. So I repeat that on the basis of performance to date, I concur completely. Incidentally, I think he will show up even better in an exclusively American theater than in an allied one.

As a last item, let me say that notice of your reappointment as Chief of Staff came to me as a bit of a shock, for the simple reason that I had not realized that your first four-year term was near its end. Time certainly goes by on speedy wings. My only other thought in connection therewith was that at least here was one action that no one in this world could question. I wouldn't even know how to proceed here if I didn't have the assurance of your firm backing and your complete understanding behind me every minute of the day.

I apologize for this long letter and add only my best wishes for your continued health. Very sincerely

(Alfred D. Chandler, Jr., ed., *Papers of Dwight David Eisenhower: The War Years,* 5 vols. [Baltimore: Johns Hopkins University Press, 1970])

Different man. Not simply ten years younger, but living in a different world, playing a different part, speaking a different voice. No folksy down-home act for General Marshall. A straightforward commentary, item by item. It is not speech. Official military phrases recur: "indulged his temper in certain instances toward individual subordinates who, in General Patton's opinion of the moment, were guilty of malingering." But a prose that can be voiced, performed. Eisenhower was never a self-conscious stylist and it shows here, as in all those nonmilitary "general"s in a letter about promoting military generals:

> Speaking *generally,* I think you are doing a very gracious and wise thing and, moreover, I must agree in *general* with the list as you have made it up.

But the voice can stress central words—"gracious" and "wise." Ike loved a cliché ("there can be no shadow of doubt," "kept his head," "time goes by on speedy wings") but they don't obscure his stable, shrewd judgment of men. And when he wants emphasis, he knows how to create it. Look at the end-stress in "So I repeat that on the basis of performance to date, *I concur completely*." Or earlier, "His job of rehabilitating the Second Corps in Tunisia was *quickly and magnificently done*."

The next-to-last paragraph provides a good lesson in voice. Not very well written, wordy and arrhythmical; it makes a schoolteacher's red pencil quiver. But look what happens when we let that pencil go to work.

> ~~As a last item, let me say that~~ notice of your reappointment as Chief of Staff came to me as ~~a bit of~~ a shock~~.~~ ~~for the simple reason that~~ I had not realized ~~that~~ your first four-year term was near its end. ~~Time certainly goes by on speedy wings.~~ ~~My only other thought in connection therewith was that~~ (at least) here was one action ~~that~~ no one ~~in this world~~ could question. I wouldn't ~~even~~ know how to proceed here if I didn't have ~~the assurance of~~ your firm backing and ~~your~~ complete understanding behind me every minute of the day.

REVISION

Notice of your reappointment as Chief of Staff came to me as a shock. I had not realized your first four-year term was near its end. Here at least was one action no one could question. I wouldn't know how to proceed here if I didn't have your firm backing and complete understanding behind me every minute of the day.

We've gotten rid of the wordy garrulity but the voice has gone with it. The occasional stilted official phrase ("in connection therewith") fits a general in circumstances like this. And the "in connection therewith" shades the letter a little toward formality, and this protects him from too close a social distance for what is to follow—compliment and thanks. Both are intensified by the awkward garrulity, not weakened. General Marshall was a very formal man. He awed even Dean Acheson. He was unlikely to be fooled by flattery or thanks. The *un*polished elements in the last paragraph keep Eisenhower from being misread. Both compliment and thanks came from the heart, as this chapter of the war attests, but the heart comes out through a prose voice a little off-balance, and nervously chatty. My refurbishment destroys precisely this nicely poised social relationship.

So voicing in prose can mean two things: prose that permits a natural rhythm and stress, and prose that seems to come from a believable human personality. And these two things finally amount to the same thing, a believable voice. To revise voice into prose means bringing it back into society, constructing a credible personality. If the revision does so, as in the CB regulations, it moves in the right direction. If it weakens or changes the voice, as does my diet version of Eisenhower's paragraph, it has gone wrong. No rules will tell you when you start to go wrong. Judging voice in prose is like judging the human personality which voice represents. You need to pay attention to the situation and you need experience. The two together add up to a trained intuition that comes only from wide reading. The wider the better—no substitute, finally, for knowing your native literature—but you can accumulate the right feeling even in the most prosaic everyday detail. A payroll clerk will develop a feel for the wrong kind of payroll history. It will "strike him a little funny."

Voice, then, amounts to style-plus-behavior. The list of descriptive attributes is endless. Voice will vary as widely as behavior—infinitely. We can only point to specific instances. Here are two diverse ones. The first opens a law textbook, David Mellinkoff's *The Conscience of A Lawyer* (St. Paul, Minn.: West Publishing Co., 1973):

### Love all the Lawyers—an Introduction

Forgive us our trangressions. . . . And love all the lawyers, for we know not what they do . . .

Lord love a lawyer? He must, you know. Who else does? Lord love a lawyer, indeed. How else explain the mystery of survival, surrounded by so many natural enemies?

To hear the lawyers tell it, the fact that they are not universally loved can only be attributed to some innate human perversity possibly related to original sin. Lawyers like to recall that they are members of an old elite, one of the three learned professions—medicine, theology, the law. Alike they share an ancient dedication to learning. Each ministers to a common psychic need for outside help. Taken together they encompass the most basic concerns of men everywhere—life, death, justice. It's a beautiful embroidery. And it is a constant sorrow if not a surprise to lawyers that their own estimate of the profession's worth is not shared by the rest of mankind.

Those who aren't lawyers agree with the lawyers only a little bit. Sure, the law is the third oldest profession all right, in close order after whoring and pimping.

What a law book! Written in the easy conversational prose which since the seventeenth century we've thought both the hardest and best to write, it encourages us to read aloud. Not simply the colloquial phrasing ("To hear the lawyers tell it") and the rhetorical questions but the rhythm tie it to speech. Just look at the first paragraph. Notice the dynamic range—the distance between loudest and softest sounds. Plenty of room for maneuver. And the voice wants to vary pitch, too. Prose has no accepted way to mark for rhythm, pitch, stress, or length but we can make do. Here's pitch marked with simple contour lines.

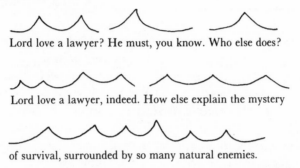

Lord love a lawyer? He must, you know. Who else does?

Lord love a lawyer, indeed. How else explain the mystery

of survival, surrounded by so many natural enemies.

This is not stress but pitch, high or low tone of voice. Americans tend to speak—and especially to read aloud—in a monotone. (The English use pitch-change much more. Listen to an English actor and then an American one.) But prose like this encourages pitch variation. It is a naturally dramatic prose because drama demands a wide dynamic range, from pianissimo whispering to full rant. The wide range allows an actor to suit voice to gesture. Shorn first of gesture, and then of voice, prose tries to preserve an echo of this expressivity through a broad dynamic range.

Actors use pauses carefully too, of course. So does this prose. Notice how much longer the pauses between sentences should take in the first paragraph than in the first half of the second? Mellinkoff uses at least four lengths of rest to heighten the drama, sharpen the voice, of his prose. Another rough-and-ready chart:

Lord love a lawyer?//// He must, you know.// Who else does?/// Lord love a lawyer, indeed.//// How else explain the mystery of survival, surrounded by so many natural enemies?//

To hear the lawyers tell it, the fact that they are not universally loved can only be attributed to some innate perversion possibly related to original sin./ Lawyers like to recall that they are members of an old elite, one of the three learned professions—medicine, theology, the law./// Alike they share an ancient dedication to learning.// Each ministers to a common psychic need for outside help./ Taken together they encompass the most basic concerns of men everywhere—life, death, justice.// It's a beautiful embroidery.//// And it is a constant sorrow if not a surprise to lawyers that their own estimate of the profession's worth is not shared by the rest of mankind.//

Those who aren't lawyers agree with the lawyers only a little bit./ Sure, the law is the third oldest profession all right, in close order after whoring and pimping.////

Again, voice permitted a broad working range. A short, climactic sentence like "It's a beautiful embroidery" invites a long following pause. So, too, "medicine, theology, the law" and its counterpart below, "whoring and pimping." Prose like this takes the CB regulation revision several steps further into society. We enter a conversation learned and unpretentious but dramatic.

Now an unexpected voice, a report in the publication *Variety* of how much money movies have made in Chicago during one week:

### 'CUCKOO' Stirring Chi Nabes with Fantastic 170G.

Chicago, Feb. 18—Mild weather and *some fresh product* have picked things up for Windy City deluxers, with the season's most consistent Near North winner working its magic in outlyers.

"One Flew Over the Cuckoo's Nest," which is just now starting to fade in its last week at the Esquire (pulling an adequate $18,000), is teeing off at eight nabes to a loud $170,000. Replacing "Cuckoo" at the Esquire this weekend is "The Man Who Would Be King," finally opening in Chicago.

"No Deposit, No Return" is preeming to a solid $200,000 at 15 outlyers and a nice $10,000 at the Loop.

"The Devil Within Her" is bowing to a hefty $52,000 at the Chicago.

"The Story of Adele H." is debuting to a combined $67,000 at Marina Cinemas 2 and 3—sunny biz.

"Dog Day Afternoon" is opening at the State-Lake (its first downtown exposure) to a slick $24,000.

"Goodbye Bruce Lee" has faded badly, pulling $21,000 at the Roosevelt after $50,000-plus total last sesh.

Combo of "Cooley High" and "Cornbread, Earl & Me" is drawing a crisp $28,000 in second glide at the Oriental.

"The Premonition" is down to a light $9500 in third at the Woods.

"Hester Street" is nabbing a spunky $11,000 in second canto at the Cinema.

"Sherlock Holmes' Smarter Brother" is pulling a nice $8200 in ninth round at the Carnegie. "Swept Away" is next.

Subrun of "Naked Came the Stranger" is opening to a fine $20,000 at the Cinestage.

"Lucky Lady" is drawing a trim $36,000 at seven nabes.

"Barry Lyndon" is grabbing a thin $30,000 at four spots in eighth sesh.

Charlie Chaplin festival at the Playboy is tallying a so-so $5000.

A voice of a different color. Easy enough to read once you get the hang of it. ("Nabes" = neighborhood movie houses; "deluxers" = deluxe movie houses; "sesh" = session; "second canto" and "second glide" = second runs.) The opposite of Professor Mellinkoff's voice, it presents a particular society rather than a general one but succeeds too in being social. The passage resembles, like much prose at base, a *list*. It could just as easily be presented as a table. But the neutral list would leave out the society making it, and the spirit in which it is made. It would leave out the pressure to dream up something new, here represented by all those neologisms: "deluxers," "outlyers," "nabes," "preeming," "sesh," "glide," "canto." It would leave out show biz's long love affair with the cliché: "Windy City," "working its magic." It would leave out the hair-down, let-it-all-hang-out informality: "teeing off," "sunny biz," "some fresh product." What if they had said "some fresh product*s*"? Putting the communal effort at movie-making into a collective singular, "fresh product"—more endless feet of homogeneous celluloid—tells how, in what spirit, all that money is being made. The product exists for the money, *Variety's* style tells us, and not vice versa. And so the list becomes variations on *epitheton,* descriptive epithet:

| | | |
|---|---|---|
| an adequate | $18,000 | |
| a loud | $170,000 | |
| a solid | $200,000 | |
| a nice | $10,000 | |
| a hefty | $52,000 | |
| a combined | $6,700 | —sunny biz |
| a slick | $24,000 | |
| a crisp | $28,000 | |
| a light | $9,500 | |
| a spunky | $10,000 | |
| a nice | $8,200 | |
| a fine | $20,000 | |

| a trim | $36,000 |
|--------|---------|
| a thin | $30,000 |
| a so-so | $5,000 |

Here voice operates at a basic level; emotion works hard to infuse quantity, translate it into its feeling equivalent, humanize it. Here, given the circumstances, is what all those figures ought to *feel like*. The verbs used for cash flow work the same way: "pulling," "teeing off," "starting to fade," "preeming," "bowing," "debuting," "opening," "drawing," "nabbing," "tallying." A frantic finding of new words for the eternal plus or minus, but it works. It creates a society, a place where its audience feels at home.

If *Variety's* mock-efficient poetic diction is a "voiced" style, we've obviously come a long way from simply reading aloud. We've had to. Silent reading, as a convention, is literally a radical convention. It cuts to the root of things. Like the prose/poetry typographical choice, it omits much and changes more. And, like the typographical either/or choice of poetry or prose, it has become so uniform a convention that we seldom notice how strong a force it exerts. But it works everywhere. If you abjure voicing, push silent reading to its logical extreme, the unreadable style, this is immediately felt as an antisocial act. A silent "voice" leaves us genuinely at sea. Something is known of voice physiology which hints at what reading aloud means in social terms. One scholar, David Abercrombie, has argued that reading aloud someone else's writing makes us, if we perform it carefully, actually imitate the original writer's breathing patterns. If the central contention here is true, it means that the more fully you perform prose, the closer you will get to identity with the writer. A native speaker, if the passage was written to be performed, will breathe in the same rhythm, the musculature tense or relax as the writer's did. Reading will be turned by the prose into an act of social oneness.

The actor's becoming the part he plays constitutes an egregious instance of this and so does religious chant and jazz music. They tune us together, blend us into a social harmony. Before the Ambrosian silent-reading revolution, reading's overlap with music was obvious and pronounced. This overlap continues, less obvious and less pronounced, for silent reading. Other techniques take over, techniques not yet adequately described. They blend quickly into "style" in general, so that the great philosopher of style, Kenneth Burke, could say simply that "style is ingratiation." We are here tracing a single thread of this ingratiation, this unstated invitation to join a comforting, shared world.

The difference between voiced and unvoiced styles is easy to see. Read them aloud. The many unreadable modern styles stick out. The voiced styles are another matter. They move, in silent reading, all the way from a base in physiology to a base in character, and yet provide a single thing—the emotional information, the behavioral clues we seek in a human voice. Reading aloud did not really die out until this century, and may not be dead even now. It's too much fun. The human voice says too much. The deep and asocial silence of today's unreadable prose amounts to a temporary extreme. Voice puts prose, any prose, in a new light. Reading aloud should be less a specialized investigative technique than a daily practice. It will then feed back into our daily speaking patterns, as it should and could do. The relation of speech to writing will then draw closer instead of, as it tends to now, separating ever more into a bureaucratic, unvoiced, asocial official style and an ever-changing and shapeless shrug-and-slang; all concept on the one side, all gesture on the other. Prose needs to be embodied but that body needs a head. When the two work together, prose takes on a voice.

# VI

# Tacit Persuasion Patterns

Some social situations seem to carry within themselves a kind of natural persuasiveness, suggest by their very shape a "logical" or "just" outcome. The game theorists who have studied these shapes have christened them "tacit bargaining" patterns, patterns which tacitly suggest a certain outcome. Assume, for example, that you and I are paratroopers dropped behind enemy lines. We become separated during the descent and, since we carelessly failed to plan for such an eventuality, we don't know where to meet. We do, though, have the same map:

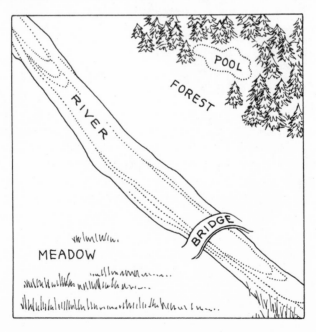

I land in the meadow. You, though I don't know it, come down in the forest. Where would you guess I would guess you might guess that we might "logically" meet? Most people say the bridge. Why? It is not in the center of the map. And if it were, would that make a difference? Obviously, because the center provides a natural focus. And so, though off center, does the bridge. It comes as close to a crossroads, a natural meeting point, as this map affords. If we had both grown up in this area, and spent many a long summer's afternoon at the forest pool, it would be a different story. Or suppose, instead, that a red army entered the mapped area from the wooded side and a white army from the meadow. Each had orders to occupy as much territory as possible without actively engaging the enemy. Chances are they'd both stop at the river. These tacit bargaining situations occur all the time. Their "logic," though, often seems hidden and seldom really logical. If you are the boss and I ask for a raise from $5 to $6 per hour you might say you'll "meet me halfway" at $5.50 per hour. It somehow "seems fair." Actually my going rate may be $6.50 and so $5.50 will not be "logical," that is to say commonly thought fair, at all: If so, I ought to have asked for a raise from $5 to $8 per hour so that the tacit bargaining logic would operate with real "logic"—at least from my point of view—to suggest $6.50 per hour.

Something analogous to these tacit bargaining patterns occurs in verbal style. Shapes, either sound patterns or sight patterns, often seem to bring with them their own kind of illogical persuasion. We might call them "tacit persuasion" patterns. For the most part, we simply don't know why they affect us as they do. It must come from how the brain processes information but that doesn't really tell us anything. To answer the question properly, we would need to ask how the visual cortex processes visual patterns and then apply that information to chiasmus, say, or isocolon. I'm not competent to do this kind of analysis, even if we had time for it here. We don't. We can offer only a general caution: shape makes a lot of difference in prose. A great deal of persuasion occurs in this way and most of it remains tacit, unacknowledged. Some shapes seem to carry their own persuasiveness, irrespective of their content. A few examples of how such tacit persuading works may alert you to these subcutaneous strategies, even if none of us is quite sure how they work.

We have always—Aristotle started it—restricted the most obvious tacit bargaining shapes to poetry, but the restriction has never worked. Even the most obvious tacit bargaining shape—rhyme—comes into prose all the time. We reach for it every time we want to seem cunning or memorable, as when the first New England Lodge rejoined to a member of the rival family, "It's their habit, Cabot." Here the rhyme (it *is* a rhyme in Lodge-and-Cabot Land) works just for fun, but sound resemblance can yoke meaning, too, as when a politician never hesitates to "fight for the right" but remains "deft with the left." This kind of capitalizing on the chance resemblances of language occurs all the time. Do it too much, of course, and people get annoyed. You've moved over from clever prose stylist to third-rate versifier. And so prose more often uses rhyme's kissing cousins than rhyme itself. Thus a lapidary phrase-maker might use *polyptoton* (repetition of a word with the same root but a different ending). Lord Randolph Churchill was fond of saying that "The duty of an Opposition is to oppose," and Disraeli of urging that "Adventures are to the adventurous." This neat trick offers a lot of put-down mileage, especially in the "Law is too important to leave to the lawyers" form, filling in for "Law" whatever activity you want to disparage. Or you vary the form by using a synonym instead of the same root word, as when George Bernard Shaw sighed "How wonderful is youth: why must it be wasted on children?" Such a pattern becomes a kind of mold for thought, or machinery for generating it.

Or we can use a homonymic pun *(paronomasia)*, as in "If life is a gamble, make it also a gambol." No *etymological* logic galvanizes this capitalization on linguistic chance. "Gambol" comes from the Italian word *gamba* (leg) and "gamble" from the Anglo-Saxon word for game, *gamen*. But the near-rhyme invites us to a tacit bargain: yes, gamble and gambol ought to be equivalent in something besides sound. Chance should lead to pleasure.

Even the most dedicated opponents of pleasure and language play have been tempted by the near-rhyme polyptotonic habit. The very hammer of the rhetors, Socrates, says (albeit ironically) when he is accused of dressing up to go to Agathon's house: καλὸς παρὰ καλόν—"one must be beautiful when going to visit the beautiful." Proverbs, in the European languages at least, use polyptotonic techniques all the time. "*Homo proponit sed Deus disponit*—Man proposes but God disposes." Why does it work so well? What itch does it scratch? If I say of a now-faded classical beauty, "She is but a shadow of her faded middle-aged self," ho-hum. But, "She has faded long since to the shadow of a shade," seems to echo time itself. Why do we want to become Rabelaisian word-spinners, take a word and conjugate or decline its essence out? The tacit power here seems to flow from conjugatability itself, from the transforming power exercised when we use one part of speech for another (the rhetorical term for this is *anthimeria*) or change form or case. The root word exudes a power the whole range of tacit persuasion patterns can draw upon.

Polyptoton is often reinforced by another tacit persuasion pattern—alliteration. Churchill writes "We shall not flag or fail." An Elizabethan storyteller calls Helen of Troy "a piece of price." The liberated puritan calls a misfortune "Sad as Sunday." Clichés pickle themselves in a similar alliterative form: "cool, calm, and collected," "fast and furious," "flight of fancy," "forbidden fruit," "top to toe," "enough to make your blood boil." Why do we find this alliterative, "following the letter" form of tacit persuasion so attractive? No one knows for sure. Clearly the pleasure is childlike and harks, as Freud argued, back to babbling, to the fun we had with sounds before they were disciplined by meaning. But this doesn't go far in explaining how alliteration works in mature prose. Alliteration, after all only a kind of front rhyme, poses the same fundamental question. Why do we like it? The simpler question—how does it work?—involves tacit persuasion at its most obvious. In the map illustration we began with, there just happened to be a bridge across the river. We met there by capitalizing on that chance. Alliteration, or front rhyme, has been traditionally more acceptable in prose than end-rhyme but both do the same thing—capitalize on chance. They can do it just for fun, as in the clichés I've just listed. Or they can underscore other tacit persuasion patterns, chiasmus, isocolon, or climax, for example. This powerful glue can connect elements without logical relationship. Because alliteration does work so well, because we acknowledge the "rightness" of "fate's fickle finger" with a part of our mind not under logical control, people have always resented alliteration and tried to outlaw it. It has no right to work as well as it does.

Language is full of these chance resemblances of sound and spelling and prose stylists have always capitalized on them, used them to suggest a natural affinity between objects or concepts which logically possessed none. Such plays on words, because they please us so, persuade us more than their logical content merits. And there are shapes of phrasing which do the same thing. Antithesis provides perhaps the best example of this second kind of tacit persuasion magic. As a habit of mind, antithesis may well be intrinsic to how we think, part of the brain's now-familiar right and left hemisphericality. And, beginning with Darwin (in *The Expression of the Emotions in Man and Animals*), it has been argued that human gesture, too, seems to operate on antithetical principles. If a dog stands erect and bristles its hair as an evolutionary gesture of defiance, then flat hair and a lowly, cringing posture may develop by antithesis—as a formal rather than an evolutionary posture. However persuasive these long-range explanations, clearly antithesis taps a deep power somewhere; its use as a tacit bargaining pattern occurs far too often to be caused by chance. And again, not only powerful but dead easy to work. The root pattern is called *chiasmus* because, diagrammed, it forms an "X" and the Greek word for X is *chi*. When John Kennedy constructed his famous bromide "Ask not what your country can do for you but what you can do for your country," he went to the Well of Antithesis for his active ingredient. Where does the "X" power come from?

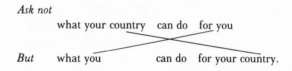

*Ask not*
    what your country can do for you

*But*  what you    can do for your country.

Obviously a kind of judo works here. By keeping the phrase but inverting its meaning we use our opponent's own power to overcome him, just as a judo expert does. So a scholar remarked of another's theory, "Cannon entertains that theory because that theory entertains Cannon." The pun on "entertain" complicates the chiasmus here, but the judo still prevails—Cannon is playing with the power of his own mind rather than figuring out the secrets of the universe.

  The New Testament uses chiasmus repeatedly to suggest the fundamental reciprocity of human ethics, the tacit bargain that we ignore at our peril. Just think about how much New Testament wisdom comes in this form. Not only "Do unto others as you would have them do unto you," but:

    The first shall be last and
    the last shall be first.

    Judge not, that ye be not judged.

    For with what judgment ye judge,
    ye shall be judged.

And with what measure ye mete
it shall be measured to you again.

He that findeth his life shall lose it; and
he that loseth his life for my sake shall find it.

For judgment I am come into this world,
that they which see not might see,
and that they which see might be blind.

Such a persistent pattern can suggest balance and inversion of all kinds. Here it points insistently to the absolute inversion of worldly values which Christian ethics implies, a 180 degree reversal which literally makes the last into the first.

The X-pattern sometimes almost *defines* words. Professional football players, for example, use a chiasmus proverb to think about injuries:

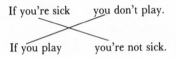

What's going on here? The X seems to establish two different, mutually exclusive roles. It excludes, *by its form,* the temptation to stand in the middle—play, but if you don't play well, blame it on being sick. The X-form provides precisely the diagrammatic force a player needs, the force to separate experience into two mutually exclusive camps. The player makes a tacit bargain with himself. Pattern supplies reassurance.

Winston Churchill used the X-form differently, but still for reassurance, in his famous Mansion House speech in November of 1942. He said, of the African campaign, "This is not the end. It is not even the beginning of the end. But it is perhaps, the end of the beginning." Not *cheap* reassurance. Don't get your hopes up, mistake the first chapter for the last. But, still, yes, get your long-term hopes up, because I've imposed a pattern on the war: beginning-end of beginning-beginning of end-end. The AB→BA flip-flop suggests a reversal of fortune by its very shape. You know where you are, and the *logic of the pattern* will ultimately carry you to victory, because the end of the beginning leads—by the X-form logic—to the beginning of the end. As always, Churchill takes pleasure in verbal pattern for its own sake, and this too consoles us. Only strong men can enjoy word games while in grave danger. It demonstrates an ultimate cool.

Now a less awesome X. Cleveland Amory, in *The Last Resorts,* comments on the changing length of women's skirts: "The granddaughter of the girl who wouldn't show her instep now shows her step-ins." No need, so clear the reversal, even to gloss "step-ins." The chiasmus brings not consolation (maybe, for men, not *only* consolation) but surprise. It has yoked a part of the body with one of its clothes but the two don't fit and thus the reversal gains power from the droll indecorum. It also bestows power, by showing that fashion moves not only widely but suddenly, by flip-flops, like the X-pattern itself.

We might, as a last instance of this most obvious tacit bargaining pattern, instance former Attorney General John Mitchell's stirring words about the Watergate disaster: "When the going gets tough, the tough get going." Sounds great, huh? Hard times bring out the greatness in the great. Alas, as John Dean saw when he passed this apothegm on from Mitchell to posterity, the reversal-logic here suggests another and opposite meaning: "When the going gets tough, sensible people take the first train out." Dean's suggested redefinition was cleverly turned but it only reemphasizes the tacit-persuasion logic chiasmus always buys: the second half of the assertion seems to follow inevitably from the first because the shape of the phrasing says so. The two senses of Mitchell's proverb are diametrically opposed, but both depend on the same tacit-persuasion power that chiasmus, by the nature of its symmetrical geometry, seems to create.

Repetition works almost as strongly as X inversion. Instead of ABBA, we get ABAB. I open the *Viking Book of Aphorisms* at random and find:

| | | | |
|---|---|---|---|
| To be engaged | | in opposing wrong | |
| affords but slender guarantee | | for being right. | |

| | | | |
|---|---|---|---|
| Let not thy will | | roar | |
| when thy power | can but | whisper. | |

| | | | |
|---|---|---|---|
| The more you are | | talked about | |
| the less powerful | | you are. | |

| | | | |
|---|---|---|---|
| A man who | could not | seduce | men |
| | cannot | save | them either. |

Antithesis still works here, but in the words alone. The pattern is ABAB, the sense ABBA. The ABAB parallelism draws the opposing poles of meaning so close together that magnetic force can flow between them. This magnetic pattern is often the basic form for aphorism. So here. The aphorist piles "opposing wrong" on top of "being right" and "be engaged" on top of "affords slender guarantee." Often, as here, one of the pairs, A or B, generates more electricity than the other. But not always.

Let not   *thy will*               *roar*
when     *thy power*   can but *whisper.*

Here A and B work with equal strength. Sometimes this equal kind of pattern seems too pat, a little cute. Unequal pairs seem to work better.

Where does the tacit persuasion come from here? Well, somehow from those horizontal and vertical visual coordinates considered earlier. From here flows the periodic sentence's power, or at least half of it. The isocolon in these aphorisms operates with brute simplicity: equal length = equal entity. Then put two of them in parallel but make the sense an X-pattern, and the paradoxical electricity which galvanizes aphorism begins to flow. The terms may not really be so antithetical as the pattern implies, but the energetic quickness of the play hides this.

Patterns like these become templates for thinking; they both frame thinking and, by their formal "logic," urge certain thoughts upon us. To take a trivial instance, I just now got up from my desk to get a drink of water. I've been writing all morning and my hand has fallen asleep from cramp. As I was drinking the water my subconscious mind must have been thinking "I have written too much. I should stop for lunch." But this thought came *as an aphorism:*

Your hand can go to sleep   from writing too much
as well as   from writing too little.

The pattern somehow had prompted as well as formed the thought. This formal back-pressure works on several levels. Every argument has two sides, we like to say, but it may have seven or eight. It "has two sides" because for many reasons it proves convenient to give it two sides. The formal pressure manifest in tacit persuasion never lets up.

Two basic tacit persuasion patterns have now emerged, inversion and repetition, **ABBA** and **ABAB**. In this kind of visual geometry, there can be only one more, climax/anticlimax, an extension of the **ABAB** pattern either up or down. Since the aphorism reveals this geometry so clearly (since that clear geometry is what defines an aphorism!) let's stay with this form. Churchill said about the Battle of Britain pilots: "Never in the field of human conflict was so much owed by so many to so few." First, a simple root expansion,

A   B   A′  B′   A″ B″
ABABAB—so much/so many/so few/.

But with complications. "Much" and "many" are alike (and so yoked by alliteration) but "few" stands opposite to them. A′ repeats A but A″ stands as an antithetical climax to it. "So much" and "so many" lead us to expect a third repetition instead of the antithesis. A climax strategy but based on an antithetical pattern.

We've seen *anaphora* (similar opening patterns) at work before. In the next example, Churchill uses it to build a straightforward climax, a repetition that grows but does not reverse itself:

> We shall not flag or fail. We shall fight in France, we shall fight on the seas and oceans, we shall fight with growing confidence and growing strength in the air, we shall defend our island, whatever the cost may be, we shall fight on the beaches, we shall fight on the landing grounds, we shall fight in the fields and in the streets, we shall fight in the hills; we shall never surrender. (Randolph S. Churchill, comp., *Into Battle: Speeches by the Right Honourable Winston S. Churchill* [London: Cassell, 1941)]

The climactic progression stands out.

> We shall not flag or fail.
> We shall fight in France,
> we shall fight on the seas and oceans,
> we shall fight with growing confidence and growing strength in the air,
> we shall defend our island, whatever the cost may be,
> we shall fight on the beaches,
> we shall fight on the landing grounds,
> we shall fight in the fields and in the streets,
> we shall fight in the hills;
> we shall never surrender.

Nice symmetry, for a start. The "f" alliteration set up with "*f*lag or *f*ail" continues through "fight" to the climactic "we shall never surrender" with only one slight break in the middle, where "we shall de*f*end" defers the alliteration to the second syllable. This break states the general theme whose particulars are itemized before and after. *Before,* a survey of offensive fighting—in France, at sea, in the air; *after,* a survey of where the fighting will occur if the enemy does invade—on the beaches and on the landing grounds (stage one), then fields and streets (stage two), then in the hills (stage three), and finally the climax—"we shall never surrender." The whole pattern equalizes two kinds of statements: 1) where Britain will fight; 2) that she will defend the island, whatever the cost, will never surrender. The equalizing is done by the list and the list is paced by the summary comment ("we shall defend our island") halfway through and climaxed by "we shall never surrender." The form welds both processes into a chain of certainties. By our tacit agreement, Churchill's assertion becomes a proleptic fact. And, oddly enough, a kind of reversal occurs here too, for we are so sure the "no surrender" spirit prevails that we refuse to believe the invasion will succeed, the backward steps from landing ground to field to street to hills will be taken.

The *locus classicus* for the tacit persuasion patterns we have been discussing is a linguistically lunatic Elizabethan short novel, John Lyly's *Euphues.* Lyly came down to London from Oxford in the 1570s determined to make a splash. This otherwise commendable resolve issued in the publication of *Euphues, The Anatomy of Wit* (1578). Euphues is a prodigal-son type who goes to Naples, steals his best friend's girl, and after she jilts him, comes home to repent. Not much happens in the silly and sketchy plot, and if we read *Euphues* for the plot we really will hang ourselves. But when we read it for the style we're tempted to do the same thing. The book consists mostly of moralizing speeches, couched in a style so full of antithesis, isocolon, climax, and alliteration that it comes to be *about* tacit persuasion patterns. A typical sentence-paragraph:

> When parents have more care how to leave their children wealthy than wise, and are more desirous to have them maintain the name than the nature of a gentleman; when they put gold into the hands of youth where they should put a rod under their girdle; when instead of awe they make them past grace and leave them rich executors of goods and poor executors of godliness—then it is no marvel that the son, being left rich by his father's will, becomes retchless by his own will.

Maybe a chart will help (see p. 133).

The italicized alliteration only begins the game. It is intensified by word repetition ("executors ... executors"/"will ... will"—this repetition is called *diacope*). The isocolon, stacking up phrases equal in length and structure, jumps off the chart. And there is hidden rhyme like the m*ai*ntain/n*a*me/n*a*ture patterns. Antithetical words are pulled closer together by the alliteration: "wealthy/wise; name/nature; goods/godliness." The goods/godliness pairing creates a kind of sight-and-sound slant pun. Good and God both sound and look somewhat alike, *as if* they might be different forms of the same root word. The ABAB isocolons sometimes omit the second A:

> leave their children wealthy than
> (leave their children) wise

> leave them rich executors of goods and
> (leave them) poor executors of godliness.

But even here sometimes a smaller full ABAB pattern lurks:

| A | B |
|---|---|
| rich executors | of goods |
| A | B |
| poor executors | of godliness |

And the last pair of parallel phrases generates a Chinese box effect:

| A | B |
|---|---|
| being left rich | by his father's will |
| becomes retchless | by his own will |

Fair enough, but look at the chiasmus hidden in the A side:

When parents have more care how    to leave their    children

and    are    more desirous    to have    them maintain

the *name* than the *nature*

of a gentleman;

when they put gold into the hands of youth

where they should put a rod under their *girdle*

when    instead of awe

they make them past *grace*    and leave them    rich executors of    *goods* and

poor executors of    *godliness*

then    it is no marvel that the son    *being* left    *rich* by his father's will

*becomes*    *r*etchless by his own will.

A self-generating dynamic operates between chiasmus and the double-iso-colon (ABAB), each threatening to turn into, or overlay, the other. It begins to work in the goods/godliness contrast:

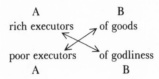

Straightforward double-isocolon, but a reader of Lyly is so conditioned to antitheses that he starts to make them at the least suggestion. Chiasmus as well as double-isocolon has become a *way of perceiving*. So we start to cross them here:

*rich* executors      *goods*
*poor* executors      *god*liness

And out pops the central moral of this relentless moralizing: people poor in goods are rich in godliness and vice versa. Not always true? The proverbial wisdom disagrees and the tacit persuasion patterns have been enlisted to help convince us.

The sentence, with its "when . . . when . . . where . . . when . . . THEN" periodic suspension, constitutes a climactic syllogism which expresses the central theme of Lyly's prodigal son tale—prodigal sons are made, not born. They are the sons of prodigal fathers. A sensible point but stale. But look at it from Lyly's point of view. He didn't have anything new to say. In his moral world, nothing new was left to say. How make a splash, then? You let the tacit persuasion patterns generate the meaning for you. Finding your-self with nothing to say, you deliver yourself methodically into the arms of chance. Since you make a splash by being extreme, he does this extremely. And so *Euphues,* whatever help it may provide for prodigal sons, comes to be about tacit persuasion patterns. We see better illustrated here than in any other text I know the back-pressure form exerts on thought. Vernon Lee, an acute student of English style, once called syntax "the cast left by long repeated acts of thought." Lyly turned this observation on its head, thought becoming the cast left by infinitely repeated tacit persuasion patterns.

Prose like this stands at the typographical interface between prose and poetry. Lyly maximizes the tension between horizontal and vertical coordinates which verse typography allows but prose typography does not. Lyly's prose wants to be diagrammed. Its pronounced visual coordinates allegorize a search for moral ones, form a geometrical analogue for the proverbial wisdom it heaps upon us.

One more tacit persuasion pattern—the list. It creates a world of equal integers which permits systematic search and arrangement. It underlies more prose than we usually realize. Lyly uses it all the time:

| | | |
|---|---|---|
| If I be | in Crete | I can lie |
| if | in Greece | I can shift |
| if | in Italy | I can court it. |

| | |
|---|---|
| I can carouse | with Alexander |
| abstain | with Romulus |
| eat | with the epicure |
| fast | with the Stoic |
| sleep | with Endymion |
| watch | with Chrysippus |

The aim is to exhaust the riches of the universe, to have been everywhere and to have done everything. The list is based on fraudulent conversion from numerical extension to infinity, from quantity to quality. List enough items and you'll have grasped the essence, generalized, grasped intuitively. It's not true, but it seems so. The basic tacit persuasion patterns—the antithesis and balance of the "X" and "double-Isocolon" patterns, the climax often built upon them, and the iterative listing as alternate to climax—often develop into one another.

$$\text{lists} \longleftrightarrow \text{"X" and "double-I"} \longleftrightarrow \text{climax}$$

Taken together, they seem to represent all the basic patterns available. Not many styles are so compulsive as to be *about* these patterns—that is why *Euphues* is so valuable an illustration here—but many use them. For example, from the Declaration of Independence:

When in the Course of human events, it becomes necessary for one people to dissolve the political bands which have connected them with another, and to assume among the Powers of the earth, the separate and equal station to which the Laws of Nature and of Nature's God entitle them, a decent respect to the opinions of mankind requires that they should declare the causes which impel them to the separation.

Our old friend the "when-then" syllogism, the "then" being understood ("entitle them, *then* a decent . . .").

Then the lists start:

> We hold these truths to be self-evident:
>     that all men are created equal
>     that they are endowed by their Creator with certain unalienable Rights
>     That among these are Life, Liberty and the Pursuit of Happiness
>     that to secure these rights . . .
>     that whenever any form of Government . . .

The list form is stressed by the repeated "that"s. Take them out and the tacit-persuasion list pattern submerges:

> We hold several truths to be self-evident. All men have been created equal and endowed with certain unalienable Rights, by their Creator. These rights include Life, Liberty and the Pursuit of Happiness. To secure these rights Men institute governments which derive their just powers from the consent of the governed. Whenever any form of Government . . .

Notice how the climax ("Life, Liberty and the Pursuit of Happiness") loses power without the listing to play off against? You can deflate the whole document simply by subtracting the anaphora. Try it:

> He has refused his Assent to Laws, the most wholesome and necessary for the public good.
> He has forbidden his Governors to pass Laws of immediate and pressing importance, unless suspended in their operation till his Assent should be obtained . . .
> He has refused to pass other Laws for the accommodation of large districts of people, unless those people would relinquish the right of Representation in the Legislature . . .
> He has called together legislative bodies at places unusual, uncomfortable and distant from the depository of their Public Records . . .
> He has dissolved Representative Houses repeatedly, for opposing with manly firmness his invasions on the rights of the people.

He has refused for a long time, after such dissolutions, to cause others to be elected . . .

He has endeavoured to prevent the population of these States; for that purpose obstructing the Laws of Naturalization of Foreigners; refusing to pass others to encourage their migration hither, and raising the conditions of new Appropriations of Lands.

He has obstructed the Administration of Justice, by refusing his Assent to Laws for establishing Judiciary Powers.

He has made Judges dependent on his Will alone, for the tenure of their offices, and the amount and payment of their salaries.

He has erected a multitude of New Offices, and sent hither swarms of Officers to harass our People, and eat out their substance.

He has kept among us, in times of peace, Standing Armies without the Consent of our legislature.

He has affected to render the Military independent of and superior to the Civil Power.

He has combined with others to subject us to a jurisdiction foreign to our constitution, and unacknowledged by our laws; giving his Assent to their acts of pretended legislation:

For quartering large bodies of armed troops among us:

For protecting them, by a mock Trial, from Punishment for any Murders which they should commit on the Inhabitants of these States:

For cutting off our Trade with all parts of the world:

For imposing taxes on us without our Consent:

For depriving us in many cases, of the benefits of Trial by Jury:

For transporting us beyond Seas to be tried for pretended offences:

And so on, through several more repetitions. Exhausting but exhaustive, a damning list as reductively egalitarian as the political philosophy it argues for—all these sins equal, all equally sinful.

The double-I patterns emerge here as a direct formal implication of the anaphora–list-making.

| A | B |
|---|---|
| He has refused his Assent to Laws, | the most wholesome and necessary |
| A′ | B′ |
| He has forbidden his Governors to pass laws | of immediate and pressing importance |
| A | B |
| He has dissolved Representative Houses | for opposing |
| A′ | B′ |
| He has refused | after such dissolutions |

A suggestion of chiasmus:

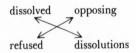

The two lines of the X differ in kind: polyptoton creates the "dissolved" axis synonym but not the "opposing-refused" one. A double-I pattern lurks below the surface in other places, too. For example:

| A | B |
|---|---|
| unless suspended in their operation | till his Assent |
| **A′** | **B′** |
| when so suspended he has utterly neglected | to attend to them. |

And *tricolon*, three-element climax, occurs as well, here reinforced by *anaphora* through *homoioteleuton* (similar endings):

> He has endeavored to prevent the population of these States;
> for that purpose
>   obstructing the Laws of Naturalization of Foreigners:
>   refusing to pass others to encourage their migration hither and
>   raising the conditions of new Appropriations of Lands.

The chiasmus here more often than not hesitates on the brink of self-consciousness:

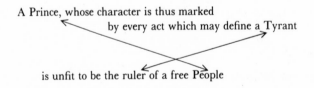

Or happening on a scale too large to notice:

| A | B |
|---|---|
| He has combined with others to subject us | and unacknowledged |
| to a jurisdiction foreign to our constitution, | by our Laws |

|                    A′                    |                   B′                   |
| :--------------------------------------: | :------------------------------------: |
|       giving his assent to their acts       |        of pretended legislation        |

A and A′ are yoked by his *combining* and his *assenting;* B and B′ by "laws" and "legislation." And isn't there an X-pattern suggested too?

The whole document moves from list-making through the parallelism, balance, and antithesis that come from chiasmus and isocolon to the resolution of tricolon climax. The balance and antithesis patterns don't declare themselves; the list pattern blows a trumpet. And so, at the end, does the resonating *tricolon:*

> we mutually pledge to each other
> > our Lives
> > our Fortunes and
> > our sacred Honor.

How could anyone resist this? And that is what the tacit persuasion patterns are all about, forming the path of least resistance. In their ideal form they have the nice symmetry we have seen: list ↔ X and double-I ↔ climax. They constitute, in fact, as we can now see, the basic beginning ↔ middle ↔ ending strategies for sentences. Put them to work in actual prose and they grow so complex that, like the other exploratory patterns we've been examining in these chapters, they become less a component of style than style itself, the inevitability that revolutions seek in events themselves and find so often only in the words used to describe them.

# VII

# Two Lemon Squeezers

Each of the previous chapters has taken a single way into prose analysis, followed one thread to see what happened. And in every case the same thing happened. The single thread led to the whole cloth, a specific stylistic feature gradually implied all the rest. Now we reverse that direction, start with everything rather than one thing, and see what patterns emerge. "Lemon squeezer" is not a classical term. It was T. S. Eliot, I think, who used it to describe the minute rhetorical analysis for which the New Criticism was famous. A modern term, then, for an old-fashioned exercise—exhaustive rhetorical description. Find every verbal pattern you can in a given text. (I've appended a basic glossary to this volume. For a fuller listing, see my *A Handlist of Rhetorical Terms* [Berkeley: University of California Press, 1968].) Since people often think classical rhetorical description fits only classical texts, perhaps we might squeeze a modern lemon instead, Tom Wolfe's essay "The Saturday Route" from *The Kandy-Kolored Tangerine-Flake Streamline Baby* (New York: Farrar, Straus and Giroux, 1965):

1.  Is that Joan Morse, the fabulous dressmaker, over there on the curb? With that fabulous Claude-yellow heath coat, those knee-high Rolls-Royce-maroon-boots and the biggest sunglasses since Audrey Hepburn sunbathed on a cantilevered terrace in the Swiss Alps? Well, it *has* to be Joan Morse.
    "Joan!"

2.  And there at Madison Avenue and 74th Street Joan Morse, owner of A La Carte, which ranks in fabulosity with Mainbocher, swings around and yells:

3.    "Freddie! I saw you in Paris, but what happened to you in London?"

4.    One is not to find out immediately, because the light has just changed. Joan is doing the Saturday Route *down* Madison Avenue. Freddie is doing the Saturday Route *up* Madison Avenue. But they keep on walking because they know they will meet sooner or later at Parke-Bernet and catch up on London. Or if not there, at the Wildenstein Gallery, the Emmerich or Duveen's or Castelli's or one of those places.

5.    And so will Greta Garbo and her old friend, George Schlee—nothing retiring about Greta Garbo on the Saturday Route, no Garbo glasses, no peekaboo Ulster collar. And so will lovely Mimi Russell and her sister Serena and Nick Villiers—Mimi is not giving up the Saturday Route just because the newspapers run headlines such as "Indicted Deb Denies All."

6.    And so will Herbert Lehman, Kirk Douglas, Norman Norell, August Heckscher, Emmett Hughes, Jan Mitchell, Pierre Scapula, Kenneth J. Lane, Alfred Barr, Dorothy Miller, Ted Peckham, and, well, you know, everybody.

7.    The thing is, any old boy from the loblolly flatlands of Georgia knows how Saturday is supposed to work out in the United States. All the old people drive down to the railroad station and park alongside the tracks and rare back and socialize on the car fenders until the main event, which is the Seaboard sleeper barreling through to New York City. And the young people drive in from all over and park along the street near the Rexall and neck under the Bright Lights stimulation of the street lamps.

8.    But what about New York City? Just because one lives in New York and is Greta Garbo, there is no need to give the whole business up. Never mind the charisma of the Seaboard sleeper. In New York there is the new religion, Art. And none of your parking alongside the tracks. In New York there is a route from 57th Street to 86th Street through the art galleries that line Madison Avenue and the streets just off it. And, naturally, no necking under the arc lights. In New York, on the Saturday Route, they give each other New York's newest grace, the Social Kiss.

9.    As the sound of the wet smack begins ricocheting between the charming buildings of upper Madison Avenue, about noon, everyone knows the Saturday Route is on. Babs Simpson of *Vogue Magazine* lives up on East 83rd Street, so she starts out near the 86th Street end, walks down as far as 78th Street to Schrafft's for brunch, and then moves on down Madison Avenue. She meets "hundreds" of people she knows. So does Jan Mitchell, the owner of Luchow's, and his wife, the gorgeous, demure-looking blonde, who start out from 57th Street. So does everybody, because everybody is starting out from one end or the other.

10.    "Martha!" "Tony!" "Edmond!" "Jennifer!" "Sarah!" "Bryce!" And Tony and Martha embrace and he pastes a Social Kiss on her cheek, and she pastes one on his cheek, and Edmond pastes one on Jennifer, and Jennifer pastes one on Edmond, and then Tony and Martha trade them and Bryce and Jennifer and Sarah and Martha and Martha and Jennifer.

11.    Irresistibly, this promenade of socialites, stars, literati, and culturati begins to attract a train of vergers, beadles and hierophants of fashion. One whole set is called "Seventh Avenue"—as in, "Her? That's Marilyn. She's Seventh Avenue"—designers, manufacturers' agents, who want to know what They are wearing on the Saturday Route. Also a vast crowd of interior decorators, both young and foppish and old and earnest. And jewelry makers, young museum curators and curates, antique dealers, furniture designers, fashion journalists, art journalists, press agents, social climbers, culture climbers, moochers, oglers, duns and young men who have had pairs of leather slacks made or young women in black stretch nylon pants and alligator coat outfits who have been looking all week for somewhere to wear them. So by 2:30 P.M. the promenade is roaring up and down Madison Avenue like a comet with the little stars trailing out like dust at the end.

12.    At the Wildenstein Gallery on East 64th Street, Greta Garbo, a turban hat on her head and a vicuna coat over her shoulders, is standing in a corner before the Wildenstein's inevitable velvet-draped walls, between two drawings, a Tchelitchev and a Prendergast. She is with a smashingly well turned-out woman, who is no decoy, however. All around people are starting the business with the elbows, nudging, saying, "That's Greta Garbo, Greta Garbo, Garbo, Garbo, Garbo, Garbo." Everyone sort of falls back, except Marilyn, who is trying to peek around to the front to see what is under the vicuna.

13.    "What's that?" Marilyn says to Lila, who is also Seventh Avenue, as they say. "It looks like one of those Pucci knit things."
      "Oh, for crying out loud, relax," says Lila. "She can't be in the corner forever."

14.    Downstairs, by the door, where the ironwork rises up, inspired, in filigrees, is Pierre Scapula, the interior decorator. He is wearing a leather overcoat with a sash belt and talking in French to one of Mr. Wildenstein's people and in English to a friend: "It's the most marvelous place. Seven French sofas, and the minute you . . ."

15.    Four blocks away, at 68th Street, Mimi Russell is walking down Madison Avenue in the direction of T. Anthony's, the leather goods shop. Mimi, of 1 Sutton Place, granddaughter of the Duke of Marlborough, daughter of the publisher of *Vogue,* is the one girl among 14 young per-

sons of good blood, good bone, indicted by the Suffolk County Grand Jury, accused of taking part in the big smashup at the Ladd house after Fernanda Wetherill's coming-out ball. Right now, though, on Mimi that story, like good memoir material, is wearing as well as a checked coat, which she has on. Right now, on the Saturday Route, she looks like a million dollars, flanked by good-looking kids, her sister Serena, for one, and Nick Villiers.

16.     On the other side of the street, the fellow with the trench coat and the two little girls is Mindy Wager, the actor.

But up at 77th Street, on the corner near Parke-Bernet, the big fellow with the gray plaid shirt and the striped gray tie and the plaid sport jacket is an artist, Mark Rothko. How did he get out here? Well, he is heading for the Rauschenberg show at the Castelli gallery, 4 East 77th Street, where, later, Marilyn will say, "Well, some of the small ones would be nice," and Lila says, "Oh, for God's sake, Marilyn, you're not buying lingerie."

17.     Rothko is standing out in the midst of the incredible comet and saying he usually doesn't go near the Saturday Route with a ten-foot pole. "Yes, I go to openings," he says, "the openings of my friends. I am an old man and I have a lot of friends. This time I just happened to be in the neighborhood."

18.     To the beautiful people on the Saturday Route, however, it does not matter in the least that artists, and serious collectors, look down on the promenade as a social and, therefore, not very hip spectacle. The fact is, the Route through the art galleries bears approximately the same relation to Art as church-going currently bears to the Church. Formerly, Saturday was the big day for the collectors. Now they come around knowingly Tuesday through Friday, avoiding "the mob"—although at this moment at Wildenstein's the Charles Wrightsmans are in that room of port-colored velvet and, as always, a single painting is up on an easel by the north light, and two others, never more, are propped up against the wall nearby.

19.     "I love it," says J_____, a customer and admirer. "It's like a game of yellow dog. Two down and one up."

But never mind Art in the abstract. It is almost 3 P.M. and the whole comet seems to be veering toward Parke-Bernet. August Heckscher has just finished up at the Kootz (Raymond Parker's hard-edge abstracts) and the Staempfli (the wild things by Jorge Piqueras) and is heading for Parke-Bernet. The fellow in the black Chesterfield, across from Parke-Bernet, near Stark's is John Loeb of the Loeb & Loeb Loebs, grandson of Arthur Lehman. All the Lehmans seem to be out on the Saturday Route. Robert Lehman has just left Wildenstein's. Herbert Lehman, the

Governor, the Senator, the 88-year old patriarch, is already up in the great meeting place, the third floor at Parke-Bernet. The two big gallery rooms are, as always, a profusion of antiques that will be auctioned off next week, all numbered and set out for inspection: beechwood Louis XVI chairs of mustard yellow plush, Zonsei armchairs of vermilion lacquer inlaid with the playing card faces of Chinese aristocrats, draped bronze maidens holding fluted cornucopiae out of which sprout light fixtures, a Kulah prayer rug, a curved cigarette holder of Cloisonné enamel, malachite Easter eggs, a pair of gilded palm trees about 8½ feet high, bibelots, silver creamers, snuff boxes, low tables, chandeliers, napkin rings and all the assorted tabourets, bibelots and marquetry inlays of bygone Czars, noblemen, Mayfair jousters and isolated West of England gentry.

20. On the walls—more velvet—is a crashingly forthright assortment of 19th century paintings, all condemned forty years ago by the avant-gardeists of Paris as "literary," "academic" and "soppy," but now rather fiercely, if sometimes perversely, "in"—Messonier, von Bremen, Vibert, Millet, Ridgway Knight.

21. Off to the left is the auction hall where porters in green uniforms are lugging Adam settees, pedestal desks, dwarf cabinets and other formidable objects out onto the stage while John Marion of Parke-Bernet chants in his pulpit. But everybody is waiting for the *pièces de résistance,* two serpentine-front Chippendale commodes with splayed feet.

22. G———, the young man who is selling commodes, looks a little anxious, but his wife, a blonde, is looking beautiful mainly, and his friends are not going to let this be too serious an occasion.

"G———, where are you going? You look so cross."

"I'm going to see Marion," he says. That would be Louis J. Marion, the president of Parke-Bernet.

"Well, I'm glad you're not hunting for me, looking so cross."

23. Meantime, the comet is going full force, around and around the gallery rooms and in and out of the auction hall. Governor Lehman is looking at the Rousseau—that is Pierre Etienne Theodore Rousseau—the picture of the cows moseying around the marsh puddle. Jan Mitchell and his wife are looking at a sketch Gainsborough did for some gal's portrait. Norman Norell, the dress designer, is walking into the auction hall. August Heckscher is sitting in the back row. Mrs. Edmund Lynch, whose husband is Lynch, as in Merrill Lynch, is walking out. Emmett Hughes is looking in through the back door.

24. "It seems to me that in the last year this place has become *very* social," says Emmett Hughes. "It's a little like those little cafes on the Via Veneto used to be."

Society, the bright young people, the celebrities, Seventh Avenue, the vergers, the beadles, the hierophants are bubbling up on all sides.

25. "Darling, don't keep telling me you're not going to *buy* anything. Go buy a malachite *egg* or something."

"Of course, I know what to do with two eight-foot-high palm trees. You just put gas jets in the top and . . ."

" . . . Oh, go to Hell. I think you read that some place . . ."

" . . . the thing is, I was in his studio. But *too* blinding . . ."

" . . . *Smart* set? Everybody is from Kew Gardens . . ."

"Good Lord, the *gall*eries . . ."

" . . . This place is getting to be the coffee break . . ."

"Tony!"

"Martha!"

"Edmond!"

Wet smack!

26. Then—pow—the second of two commodes is sold, for $10,000, just like the first. And everybody feels it, even those who paid no attention at all. When the last of the heavy business is over at Parke-Bernet, it is like the warning bell at the Metropolitan, and everyone starts to wind up the Saturday Route. It is as if someone let the magic out.

August Heckscher is out by the elevators.

"Do you have change for a quarter?" he says.

Then he heads off to the telephone booth.

27. Of course, it is not all over yet. Ted Peckham and about 19 others have headed down to the Parke-Bernet garage for the auctioning of the last item on the list, No. 403, a Mercedes-Benz limousine, built three years ago for $16,000, with Naugahyde inside and on the roof, and a roll-up glass partition and portholes. The garage is rather *basic*-looking, you know, for Parke-Bernet. The door is up and it is already dark outside.

28. Ted Peckham smiles arcanely all through the chanting and picks up the Mercedes for $3,800.

Somehow it seems like an awesome acquisition.

"Ted, boy, can I be your chauffeur?"

"Sure," says Ted, "In fact, you can buy it. It's for sale if you want to buy it."

29. Outside, on Madison Avenue, G——— and his wife—she has on a plain suede coat lined like mad with sable—are smoking and breathing easier. They now have a small entourage in their magnetic field.

30. Across 77th Street, Kenneth J. Lane, the jewelry designer, is walking up Madison Avenue with his hands in his pockets and his tweed coattails flying out like wings.

31.    Up at Staempfli's, Phillip Bruno is winding up the Piqueras show. He says goodby to Paula Johnson of the Osborne Gallery—she hasn't been able to get up to see Piqueras until now—with the proper Social Kiss. It is really getting black outside now, and colder, but he still has some kid in his office who is looking at about a dozen pieces of jade-green sculpture resting on a pile carpet.

32.    "Looks sort of like the ruins of Karnak," says the kid, who has the biggest black Borsalino hat on Madison Avenue.
    Mr. Bruno suppresses a few immediate responses.
    "Well, they won't look like that on Tuesday."

33.    Tuesday—another opening! And four days from then, Saturday, like filaments skidding towards the mother lode, all the old people and all the young people will stride down to the Avenue and race back alongside the pedestals and socialize until the main event, which will probably be another prodigious serpentine-front commode with splayed feet at Parke-Bernet, and get the wet smacks echoing between the limestone fronts, while Joan Morse finds out, to be sure, just what *did* happen to everybody else during the warm season in London.

Not what you would consider "rhetorical" prose, is it? It does not knock you over with its verbal patterns. They are there, though. How do they work?

Wolfe starts out with a rhetorical question: "Is that Joan Morse ... ?" This is *aporia,* true or feigned doubt about an issue. Also a kind of *apostrophe,* breaking off discourse to address a person or thing present or absent. Beginning with this abrupt question implies a previous discourse one has interrupted, and this is exactly what Wolfe wants us to think—that we've just walked into an animated conversation. He then answers his own question: "Well, it *has* to be Joan Morse." This asking and answering of questions is called *anthypophora.* Wolfe uses it later, too: "But what about New York City? . . . In New York there is . . ." (par. 8). And in paragraph 16, "Mark Rothko. How did he get out here? Well, he is heading. . . ." Wolfe's characters ask a lot of questions too. Joan Morse at the beginning asks "Freddie! I saw you in Paris, but what happened to you in London?" (par. 3). At the end we're promised that next week "Joan Morse finds out, to be sure, just what did happen to everybody else during the warm season in London" (par. 33). And questions echo throughout: "Her? That's Marilyn" (par. 11). "'What's that?' Marilyn says to Lila . . ." (par. 13). Against these stated questions, Wolfe's essay comes to seem a series of answers to *our* questions: Who's that? What's that? Where's that? He acts as our tour guide. "Downstairs, by the door . . . is Pierre Scapula . . ." (par. 14); "Four blocks away, at 68th Street" (par. 15); " . . . the fellow with the trench coat . . . is Mindy Wager, the actor" (par. 16). "The fellow in the black Chesterfield . . . is John Loeb" (par. 19). "Off to the left is the auction hall . . ." (par. 21). "That would be Louis J. Marion" (par. 22). The many explicit questions render the whole passage a set of implicit questions and answers. We ask; the guide explains.

The first question, "Is that Joan Morse . . . ?" is answered by "It *has* to be Joan Morse," and by "Joan!" and in "Joan Morse, owner of A La Carte" in the next line. Repetition of a word with other words intervening is called *diacope*. Wolfe often uses this and other patterns of repetition, especially *anaphora:*

| (par. 4) | Joan is doing |
| | Freddie is doing |
| | |
| (par. 5) | And so will Greta Garbo |
| | And so will lovely Mimi Russell |
| (par. 6) | And so will Herbert Lehman |
| | |
| (par. 8) | In New York there is a new religion |
| | In New York there is a route |
| | In New York, on the Saturday Route |
| | |
| (par. 9) | So she starts out |
| | So does Jan Mitchell |
| | So does everybody |
| | |
| (par. 10) | he pastes a Social Kiss on her cheek |
| | she pastes one on his cheek |
| | Edmund pastes one |
| | Jennifer pastes one |

Sometimes the word recurs without any break *(epizeuxis):* "Greta Garbo, Greta Garbo, Garbo, Garbo, Garbo, Garbo" (par. 12). Sometimes the repetition forms part of an isocolon reinforced by alliteration: "*good blood, good bone*" (par. 15). Sometimes the repetition is exact and close together:

Right now, though, on Mimi that story, like good memoir material, is wearing as well as a checked coat, which she has on. Right now ... (par. 15)

Sometimes it is widely separated and varied.

> The fellow with the trench coat (par. 16)
> The fellow in the black Chesterfield (par. 19)

Several words recur throughout—"comet," "promenade," "Route" and "Saturday Route," and others. And some are varied by *polyptoton* (same root word, different form) like "fabulous" and "fabulous" (par. 1), becoming "fabulosity" (par. 3), or "curators and curates" (par. 11). Or repetition becomes part of an incantatory name game: "John Loeb of the Loeb and Loeb Loebs" (par. 19); "Arthur Lehman, All the Lehmans ... Robert Lehman ... Herbert Lehman" (par. 19); "Mrs. Edmund Lynch, whose husband is Lynch, as in Merrill Lynch" (par. 23). Sometimes the verbal echo pulls together thematically related elements. The Georgia hicks "rare back and socialize on the car fenders until the main event" (par. 7); New Yorkers on the Saturday Route "race back alongside the pedestals and socialize until the main event" (par. 33). Sometimes it seems simply a refrain: "And so will lovely Mimi Russell and her sister Serena and Nick Villiers" (par. 5), "and Mimi Russell ... her sister Serena, for one, and Nick Villiers" (par. 15).

What stands out in the first paragraph, though, are the epithets (the formal name is *epitheton*):

> Joan Morse, the fabulous dressmaker
> that fabulous Claude-yellow heath coat
> those knee-high Rolls-Royce-maroon boots.

I don't know what a "heath coat" is but "Claude" refers to the misty yellow in Claude Lorrain's landscape paintings. The boots remind one of A. E. Housman's parody of a Greek tragedy:

> O suitably-attired-in-leather-boots
> Head of a traveller, wherefore seeking whom
> Whence by what way how purposed art thou come
> To this well-nightingaled vicinity?

Housman is making fun of the Greek habit of epitheton and, in a way, Wolfe does the same thing. Epithets run through the essay from beginning to end.

|  |  |
|---|---|
| (par. 5) | Saturday Route |
|  | Garbo glasses |
|  | peekaboo Ulster collar |
|  | lovely Mimi Russell |
| (par. 7) | loblolly flatlands |
| (par. 12) | velvet-draped walls |
| (par. 18) | beautiful people |
|  | port-colored velvet |
| (par. 21) | serpentine-front Chippendale commodes |
| (par. 25) | eight-foot high palm trees |

The epithets, though, are dwarfed by the names—celebrity names, plain names, brand names, style names, business names, objet d'art names, artists' names, clothes names.

**BRAND NAMES**

Rolls-Royce (par. 1)
Seaboard sleeper (par. 7)
*Vogue Magazine* (par. 9)
Pucci knit things (par. 13)
Mercedes-Benz (par. 27)
Naugahyde (par. 27)
Borsalino hat (par. 32)

**PLACE NAMES**

Paris, London, New York, Georgia, Via Veneto, Kew Gardens, Karnak, Swiss Alps, Madison Avenue

**BUSINESS NAMES**

A La Carte, Mainbocher, Wildenstein, Emmerich, Duveen's, Castelli's, Rexall, Luchow's, Schrafft's, Kootz, Stark's, Parke-Bernet, Staempfli's, T. Anthony's

CELEBRITY NAMES

Joan Morse, Greta Garbo, George Schlee, Mimi Russell, Herbert Lehman, Kirk Douglas, Norman Norell, August Heckscher, Emmett Hughes, Jan Mitchell, Pierre Scapula, Kenneth J. Lane, Alfred Barr, Dorothy Miller, Ted Peckham, Suffolk County Grand Jury (!), Fernanda Wetherill, Mindy Wager, the Charles Wrightsmans, John Loeb, Mrs. Edmund Lynch, John Marion, Louis J. Marion, Babs Simpson, Phillip Bruno, Paula Johnson, Kenneth J. Lane

FIRST NAMES (ANONYMITIES AND NONENTITIES)

Freddie, any old boy, all the old people, the young people, Martha!, Tony!, Edmund!, Jennifer!, Sarah!, Bryce!, Marilyn, Lila, sister Serena, G_____ ("the young man who is selling commodes"), and his wife, the kid in the Borsalino hat

ARTISTS' NAMES

Mark Rothko, Rauschenberg, Raymond Parker, Jorge Piqueras, Messonier, von Bremen, Vibert, Millet, Ridgway Knight, Gainsborough

OBJETS D'ART NAMES

Seven French Sofas, Two serpentine-front Chippendale commodes with splayed feet, beechwood Louis XIV chairs of mustard yellow plush, Zonsei armchairs, a Kulah paper rug, Adam settees—and others too numerous to mention

The sheer weight of *names* threatens to turn essay into list, a blasphemous recitation of the New York art world's sacred names. Just, in fact, what it is. Wolfe's central thesis argues that art provides the new religion. If so, the names form a pantheon of fashionable saints, churchmen, and relics. Sometimes, as with "Garbo, Garbo, Garbo, Garbo," they are chanted, as in an Eastern religion. Or, in the "curators . . . curates" polyptoton, he'll derive an art term and a religious one from the same root word. So the two religions are equated in a telling asyndeton: "Society, the bright young people, the celebrities, Seventh Avenue, the vergers, the hierophants are bubbling up on all sides" (par. 24). (A verger is an attendant on a bishop or, alternately, the custodian of a church; a beadle, a lower church official too; a hierophant, an expositor of sacred mysteries.) Wolfe energizes the same equalizing gesture through metaphor when he makes the Parke-Bernet auctioneer "chant" "in his pulpit." And the same kind of extravagant metaphor (it is called *catachresis*) occurs in the mock-heroic comparison of the Saturday Route group as a "comet," with the awesome portentousness such an appearance brings:

> So by 2:30 P.M. the promenade is roaring up and down Madison Avenue like a comet with the little stars trailing out like dust at the end. (par. 11)
>
> Rothko is standing out in the midst of the incredible comet. (par. 17)
>
> It is almost 3 P.M. and the whole comet seems to be veering toward Parke-Bernet. (par. 19)
>
> Meantime, the comet is going full force, around and around the gallery rooms ... (par. 23)

An extravagant, hyperbolic metaphor, then, a catachresis which describes a New York crowd as a shower of stars. But since, with the pun on "stars," the crowd is exactly that, if we read "stars" metaphorically, the catachresis isn't far-fetched at all but a literal description. Rhetoric has several terms for fancy set-piece descriptions:

> of trees—dendrographia
> of nations—chorographia
> of faces or persons—prosopographia
> of places—topographia

The Greek word for star is ἀστήρ (aster). Why not astrographia—a description of stars—for Wolfe's essay?

Several rhetorical terms refer to belittling or mock-heroic comparison. *Hyperbole* (extravagant comparison) can work this way, as when the Saturday Route Social Kisses are described as "ricocheting between the charming little buildings of upper Madison Avenue" (par. 9). Kiss = bullet. *Tapinosis* is the use of undignified language as belittling description. "The Saturday Route" abounds with it. The Social Kiss is a "wet smack" and you don't bestow it on someone, you "paste" it on:

> . . . he pastes a Social Kiss on her cheek, and she pastes one on his cheek, and Edmond pastes one on Jennifer, and Jennifer pastes one on Edmond.

And "pow" is used, in comic book-ese, for the blow of the auctioneer's hammer:

> Then—pow—the second of two commodes is sold, for $10,000, just like the first.

Notice, as well as the *tapinosis,* the use of *polysyndeton* as a kind of belittling gesture. All those "ands" reduce the art of kissing to a meaningless ritual. Another term for belittling comparison is *meiosis,* as if you called a Rolls-Royce a child's toy. The essay's title is obviously meiostic in this sense—The Saturday *Route,* rather than pageant, parade, spectacle, whatever. And "Route" allows Wolfe to pun on the obsolescent "rout," meaning a mob, as well as the more current sense of "a complete defeat." And the synonym for the Saturday Route is another meiosis, "the main event," a phrase from prize fighting (pars. 7 and 33).

The standard rhetorical term for the head-to-toe description of a heroine is *effictio.* Wolfe uses this device in a belittling way too, in the first paragraph, when Joan Morse gets itemized from coat to Audrey Hepburn sunglasses. And we also find the description of ancestry a romance heroine requires:

> Mimi, of 1 Sutton Place, granddaughter of the Duke of Marlborough, daughter of the publisher of *Vogue* . . .

but what follows?

> is the one girl among 14 younger persons of good blood, good bone indicted by the Suffolk County Grand Jury . . .

And the "good blood, good bone" epic formula suggests a further mock-heroic note. And so, repeatedly, does the diction, as when Gainsborough did a sketch "for some gal's portrait" (par. 23), or when bygone Czars and noblemen are lined up with "Mayfair jousters" (par. 19). (Mayfair is a fashionable residential district in London.) Wolfe also uses *hypocrisis,* mocking the speech patterns of an opponent, as in the italicizing in paragraph 25 or in the "Martha! Edmond! Wet smack!" (par. 25) sequence. He also does this by capitalizing certain words: Art, Bright Lights, Stimulation, Social Kiss, Saturday Route, They, the Church. The capitalization equates, as they are equated in the fashionable mind, Art and the Church.

One of the basic rhetorical terms is *metonymy* (substitution of cause for effect, or vice versa, proper name for quality, or vice versa). Wolfe uses this kind of displacement all the time: "Seventh Avenue," all the store names, "his wife, a blonde" and so on. Everything and everybody seem described in terms of something else, some attendant circumstance. Rhetoric has a term, *systrophe,* which means piling up descriptions of an object without really defining it. In a way, "The Saturday Route" seems one huge systrophe. Everything is described as something else. Nothing has any essence. Instead of *definition* we are offered only metonymic description. People are What They Do:

> Babs Simpson of *Vogue*
> Jan Mitchell, owner of Luchow's
> John Loeb of the Loeb and Loeb Loebs
> Mrs. Edmund Lynch, whose husband is Lynch, as in Merrill Lynch
> Kenneth J. Lane, the jewelry designer
> Norman Norell, the dress designer

Or, above all, What They Wear:

> The fellow with the trench coat
> the fellow in the black Chesterfield
> the woman with "a plain suede coat lined like mad with sable"
> Kenneth J. Lane "walking up Madison Avenue . . . his tweed coattails flying out like wings"
> the kid with "the biggest black Borsalino hat on Madison Avenue"
> Pierre Scapula "wearing a leather overcoat with a sash belt"
> Mimi Russell "wearing . . . a checked coat"
> Mark Rothko, "the big fellow with the gray plaid shirt and the striped gray tie and the plaid sport jacket"
> porters in green uniforms
> Greta Garbo in "a turban hat" and "a vicuna coat"

You could compile similar lists by Where You Come From or Who You Know. They all parody high style, with its epithets and categories. Direct catalog parodies do in fact occur, as for example the parody-catalog of names in paragraph 6, or the catalog of objects (the rhetorical term for this is *energia* or *descriptio*—clear and vivid description) in paragraph 19, or the formulaic repetition of the "he pastes one/she pastes one" in paragraph 10, or the catalog of social types in paragraph 11. All these mock-heroic elements work at least two ways. They belittle The Saturday Route world and they suggest that it is all surface and accident, no centrality or essence.

We can describe the essay on a larger scale, too. It is obviously built on two basic meiostic comparisons, for a start: religion is compared with art and New York City with a small town in Georgia. But the first comparison works in a standard mock-heroic way; the second deflates art differently. It equates New York and Georgia. Since both Georgia and New York display a Saturday Route, art becomes equal to the Seaboard sleeper, an excuse for social display rather than a profound spiritual experience. The two meiostic comparisons together suggest a reversal not unlike that operating in Lyly's *Euphues,* a world in which surface has become center.

The rhetorical term *ethopoeia* also provides a larger view. *Ethopoeia* can mean character portrayal generally or, more specifically, a description of natural propensities, of characteristic vices and virtues. Again this fits the whole essay. Or all the individual descriptions—by job, name, clothes, friends, etc. Or we might use it to explore the narrator's character. Many aspects of the essay converge on such a *persona,* as this voice is usually called. We've discussed already‘ the frequent repeating of questions and phrases. The term for this when repeated is *epimone.* Or we could consider the phrasings that intensify this question-and-answer colloquiality: "Well, it *has* to be Joan Morse" (par. 1); "The thing is, any old boy" (par. 7); "And none of *your* parking alongside the tracks" (par. 8—emphasis mine); "And, naturally, no necking . . ." (par. 8); "Well, you know, everybody" (par. 6); "Never mind the charisma . . ." (par. 8); "Then—pow—the second of two commodes is sold" (par. 26). The colloquiality comes out often in the syntax, too. It can be either polysyndetic or asyndetic. The polysyndeton of all those "And so will" constructions in paragraphs 5 and 6 creates a voice but so does an asyndetic parenthetical aside like "On the walls—more velvet—is a crashingly forthright assortment . . ." (par. 20). The syntax seems often so loose as to follow the mob as they go their rounds. Look at how the prepositions work, for example, especially in paragraph 23 or in 9. The narrator plays a part in the Saturday Route yet distances himself from it; alike in voice, set apart by the distance all those mock-heroic comparisons create.

The essay is obviously intensely voiced—but try reading it aloud. Not as easy as it looks. Wolfe demands agility if the reader's voice is to reflect all those mock-heroic colorations. How much hyperbole do you let your voice show, for example, when you read aloud a line like "Rothko is standing out in the midst of the incredible comet . . ." (par. 17)? Or in presenting a formula like "good blood, good bone" (par. 15)? Or "That's Greta Garbo, Greta Garbo, Garbo, Garbo, Garbo, Garbo" (par. 12)? Do you do a straight imitation of star-struck adolescent gush? Or exaggerate it yet further into irony? The essay obviously uses the high style/low style oscillation and ironic juxtaposition characteristic of mock-heroic, but a good deal of rehearsal is needed to get it right.

What conclusions emerge from this analysis? This *kind* of analysis? Well, to start, a miscellaneous pulling of first one thread then another, a random description, quickly starts building a coherent whole. The epitheton, the catalogs, the formulae, the anaphora and other repetitive patterns, all cohere into a central mock-heroic strategy. The many patterns that make up the voice, both of satirist and satirized, build a single conversational ethos very quickly. "The Saturday Route" offers an extraordinarily coherent style. And it grows out of an equally coherent double-paired structure of art/religion and New York/Georgia. Style and structure interpenetrate perfectly. Style makes on a small scale the same point narrative and theme offer on the larger one. For a prose as coherent as Wolfe's, the lemon squeezer's random blanket description shows up basic patterns very soon.

The second conclusion stands equally clear: This kind of analysis could go on forever. There seems no natural, logical place to stop. You could easily find three times as many patterns as I've found. Where do you stop? Just where we did. When you see the basic patterns, the basic relationship of style to structure. Lemon-squeezing is a qualitative analysis finally, not a quantitative one. You won't necessarily find out how Wolfe uses anaphora by counting them. You use the lemon squeezer as a generalized search technique that gradually exposes the fundamental shapes a prose is composed of. As you come to see these, they will determine which kinds of patterns you continue to seek and which terms—of the many overlapping ones, large scale and small—you choose as essentially descriptive.

With this procedure in mind, let's try a second, shorter lemon squeezer. Wolfe's essay is not "rhetorical" prose. Neither is the following brief passage, usually considered a masterpiece of spontaneous and unprepared clarity, brevity, and sincerity.

**Abraham Lincoln**
**Address**
**at the Dedication of the Gettysburg National Cemetery,**
**November 19, 1863**

| | |
|---|---|
| 1 | Fourscore and seven years ago our fathers brought forth on this |
| 2 | continent a new nation, conceived in liberty, and dedicated to the |
| 3 | proposition that all men are created equal. |
| 4 | Now we are engaged in a great civil war, testing whether that |
| 5 | nation, or any nation so conceived and so dedicated, can long endure. |
| 6 | We are met on a great battlefield of that war. We have come to ded- |
| 7 | icate a portion of that field as a final resting-place for those who here |
| 8 | gave their lives that that nation might live. It is altogether fitting and |
| 9 | proper that we should do this. |
| 10 | But in a larger sense, we cannot dedicate—we cannot consecrate— |
| 11 | we cannot hallow this ground. The brave men, living and dead, who |
| 12 | struggled here, have consecrated it far beyond our poor power to add |
| 13 | or detract. The world will little note nor long remember what we say |
| 14 | here, but it can never forget what they did here. It is for us, the living, |
| 15 | rather, to be dedicated here to the unfinished work which they who |
| 16 | fought here have thus far so nobly advanced. It is rather for us to be |
| 17 | here dedicated to the great task remaining before us—that from these |
| 18 | honored dead we take increased devotion to that cause for which they |
| 19 | gave the last full measure of devotion; that we here highly resolve that |
| 20 | these dead shall not have died in vain; that this nation, under God, |
| 21 | shall have a new birth of freedom; and that government of the people, |
| 22 | by the people, for the people, shall not perish from the earth. |

The first thing we notice, perhaps, is the alliteration:

| | |
|---|---|
| (line 1) | *f*our *s*core and *s*even years ago our *f*athers |
| | brought *f*orth |
| (line 2) | *c*ontinent a *n*ew *n*ation *c*onceived |
| (line 7) | that *f*ield as a *f*inal resting place |
| (line 12) | our *p*oor *p*ower |
| (line 13) | the *w*orld *w*ill *l*ittle *n*ote *n*or *l*ong remember |
| (line 19) | we *h*ere *h*ighly resolve |

And the patterns of repetition. (*Diacope,* remember, repeats a word with a few words in between; *polyptoton* repeats a word with the same root but different form or ending.)

| (line 2) | a new nation |
| (line 5) | any nation |
| (line 8) | that nation |
| (line 20) | this nation |

| (line 2) | conceived and dedicated |
| (line 5) | conceived and dedicated |
| (line 6) | dedicate |
| (line 10) | dedicate—consecrate |
| (line 12) | consecrated |
| (line 15) | to be dedicated |
| (lines 16–17) | to be here dedicated |
| (line 18) | devotion |
| (line 19) | devotion |

| (line 20) | shall not |
| (line 21) | shall have |
| (line 22) | shall not |

| (line 8) | lives—live |
| (line 11) | living |
| (line 14) | living |

| (line 11) | dead |
| (line 18) | dead |
| (line 20) | dead—died |
| (lines 21–22) | people—people—people |

| (line 7) | here |
| (line 12) | here |
| (line 14) | here—here |
| (line 15) | here |
| (line 16) | here |
| (line 17) | here |
| (line 19) | here |

The *anaphora* is also striking:

| (line 4) | we are engaged |
| (line 6) | we are met |
| | we have come |
| (line 9) | we should do |
| (line 10) | we cannot dedicate |
| | we cannot consecrate |
| (line 11) | we cannot hallow |

| (lines 13–14) | we say here |
| (line 18) | we take increased devotion |
| (line 19) | we here highly resolve |
| | |
| (line 5) | so conceived and so dedicated |
| | |
| (line 14) | It is for us |
| (line 16) | It is rather for us |
| | |
| (line 17) | that from these |
| (line 19) | that we here |
| (line 20) | that this nation |
| (line 21) | that government |

And Lincoln loves doublets, usually antithetical. The largest one supplies an antithetical encapsulation of the whole speech:

> our fathers *brought forth* (line 1)
> shall not *perish* (line 22)

Within this envelope-antithesis other pairings occur: "living and dead" (line 11), "we take ... they gave" (lines 18–19), "dead shall not have died ... new birth" (lines 20–21), "little note nor long remember" (line 13), "we say here ... they did here" (line 14). In addition to this antithetical balance, tricolon climax is used twice:

> we cannot dedicate
> we cannot consecrate
> we cannot hallow (lines 10–11)
>
> of the people
> by the people
> for the people (lines 21–22)

And tetracolon (4-member) climax once:

> that from these honored dead
> that we here highly resolve
> that this nation
> and that government (lines 17– 21)

The first tricolon also exemplified *hypozeuxis,* a construction in which every clause in a sentence has its own subject and verb, here all three governing the same direct object. And the second exemplifies yet another figure, *antistrophe* (repeating a closing word or words at the end of several successive clauses or sentences). This figure occurs several times—"what we say here/ what they did here," for example.

With so much elaborate patterning we might expect chiasmus as well. There are two instances, to start on a small scale, in the alliteration:

> A        B     B        A
> *c*ontinent a *n*ew *n*ation, *c*onceived (line 2)

> A    B    B    A
> *l*ittle *n*ote *n*or *l*ong (line 13)

And, on a larger scale:

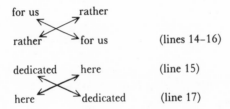

    dedicated    here        (line 15)

    here        dedicated    (line 17)

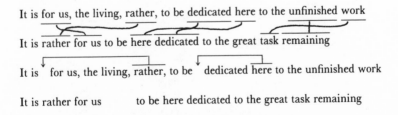

Lincoln, working variations on a very strict parallelism, creates the double-X patterns by a seemingly easy and yet infinitely skillful sideways gliding.

What do these patterns add up to? Repetition at the beginning of phrases, in the middle, at the end; isocolonic balance and antithesis; chiasmus; and a pronounced alliteration which often reinforces these patterns? Prose with pronounced horizontal and especially vertical coordinates. Charting brings this out:

PARAGRAPH 1

```
Fourscore and seven years ago
  our fathers brought forth on this    continent a new nation
                                       conceived in liberty
                              and dedicated to the proposition that
               all men       are , created      equal.
```

Here the diagram runs a little ahead of our first reading. I've followed patterns, not fully established until later, that a first reading does not notice. I've rearranged the sentence/paragraph so that equivalent elements are ranked vertically one over the other. Sometimes the vertical cement is alliteration:

```
        fourscore              continent
        fathers                conceived
                               created
```

Sometimes it is *homoioteleuton,* a similar sound pattern at the end of the words rather than at the beginning.

```
        conceived              nation
        dedicated              proposition
        created
```

Sometimes the sense relates the words:

```
        fathers                nation
        all men                liberty
                               proposition
                               equal
```

Still, we feel, this is a pattern imposed on the text as much as one inherent in it. We *can* thus rearrange but how strongly are we *invited* to? The invitation gets stronger in the second paragraph (see p. 161). Here the vertical

## PARAGRAPH 2

Now we are engaged   in a great civil       *war*

testing whether   *that nation*

or     *any nation*   *so conceived* and

*so dedicated*   can long endure.

We are met   on a great battle-   *field* of that    *war*

We have come to dedicate a portion of that   *field* as a final resting-place

for those who   *here* gave their   *lives*

that *this nation*     might *live*.

It is altogether fitting and proper that
*we should do this.*

coordinate which creates what we call parallelism becomes more pronounced. The "we are" anaphora begins a pattern of repetition on the horizontal axis that creates the vertical patterns here. So when we read downward:

<pre>
        great civil war      civil war
        great battlefield    that war
                     field
           here      so concerned
        that nation so dedicated
        any nation
        this nation          lives
                             live
</pre>

This chart shows how dominant repetition can be as a stylistic pattern and how it works. It creates a vertical pattern. The charted prose looks like verse which has suffered slight sideways displacement and rearrangement. Just so. The iterative patterns can, as we have seen, move in either of two directions: toward everyday lists or toward ritualistic repetition, scriptural lists like the Ten Commandments or the Beatitudes. This second aim Lincoln pursues here. But, as with the triple chiasmus pattern seen earlier, he breaks up the exact parallelism of ritualistic prayer by sideways displacement and substitution. Thus, although the passage makes us feel prayerful, indeed feels like a prayer, it doesn't look like one. It has, in fact, from the day it was delivered been taken as the model of heartfelt simplicity, without design and ceremony.

In the third paragraph this technique becomes so complex that we might almost call it fugal, so strongly climactic is it in developing the pattern nascent in paragraph 1 and emergent in 2 (see p. 163).

See how the patterns of repetition and antithetical doublets form part of the same overall plan of vertical orientation? The verbal patterns, especially the central one, include repetition and antithesis, both enforced by beginning-sound resemblance (alliteration) and end-sound resemblance (homoioteleuton). It begins with the tricolon climax:

<pre>
        we cannot  dedicate
        we cannot  consecrate
        we cannot  hallow
</pre>

But   in a larger sense   we cannot   dedicate
                          we cannot   consecrate
                          we cannot   hallow   this   ground.

The brave men,   living and dead, who struggled here, have consecrated   it   far beyond our power to add or
                                                                                                           detract.

The world will little note   nor long remember what we say here but
it                           can never forget   what they did here.
It is   for us; the living, rather to be   dedicated   here
                                                        they who have fought   to the unfinished work which
It is rather for us        to be here       dedicated   here have thus far so nobly advanced.
                                                        to the great task remaining

        before us—
that from   these honored dead we take   increased devotion   to that cause for which
                                         they gave
                            the last   full measure of devotion

that we here highly resolve that
            these dead   shall not   have died in vain,
that this nation under God   shall   have a new birth of freedom and
that government   of the people
                  by the people and
                  for the people shall not perish from the earth.

163

have   consecrated
dedicated
dedicated
devotion
devotion
died
a new birth
shall not perish

The rest of the paragraph is hung on this as from a backbone.

What we say here
what they did here
they who fought here
to the great task remaining
to that cause for which
living and dead
for us the living
these honored dead
these dead

Surely here random search-and-name procedure has uncovered the basic pattern underlying Lincoln's famous speech. The vertical coordinates tell us visually what we already feel—that the speech is really a prayer, and very nearly a verse prayer. Yet it gains strength by stopping short of both the prayer form and the verse form. The speaker before Lincoln at this ceremony spoke for two hours, giving Lincoln's famous brevity a little support from behind, as it were, made it sound even more restrained, controlled, unsentimental. But the refusal to sentimentalize inheres in the form, in its movement to the verge of verse prayer but not beyond. This is what generates the sense of strong feeling under yet stronger control readers have so often felt. (The *written* form intensifies the sense of control, of course. In this sense, the Address works better for us than it did on the battlefield.)

With the basic territory mapped, we can continue our search for applicable terms, our nomenclatural game, but we'll have some idea of how to apply the terms, *on what scale* they fit the text. And we will also know when to stop. Thus clearly the Gettysburg Address exemplifies a *chorographia* (description of a nation) which depends on *anamnesis* (a recalling of the past). The speaker tries to measure the reason for his controlled feelings—the immense distance between the event and what anyone can say about the event—by an *occupatio* (seeming to pass over what he really goes on to say) ("the world will little note nor long remember"). Yet—here is what I mean about scale—the speech doesn't really include an instance of occupatio ("I will not mention that General X has won four medals of honor, three silver stars, two bronze stars, and a purple heart"), so much as reflect that to say anything inevitably will be an occupatio, will mention what, given the distance between words and deeds here, between life and death, ought to be passed over. *Occupatio* becomes a key term here, but only when we see how it fits, and we can see that only when we see the overall rhetorical strategy.

So again we see the basic oscillation that makes a lemon squeezer a useful technique for understanding prose. The random description eventually exposes a pattern which then allows us to use the terminology in a specific and specifically useful way, use it to explain the text rather than, as when we began, to use the text as an excuse for parading all the terms. The nomenclatural game, kind of fun in itself, leads to a critical understanding which in its turn reclarifies and redefines the nomenclature. No wonder this kind of description is the oldest technique for prose analysis we have. Creaky and awkward though it can be, it works.

# VIII

# High, Middle, and Low Styles

The oldest set of categories for prose style is the division into high and low. It starts with Aristotle and continues to the present day. It turns up everywhere, and people are forever translating from high style to low, formal to informal, and back again without reflecting much about it. Boswell's *Life* catches Johnson in the act, apropos "The Rehearsal":

> "It has not wit enough to keep it sweet." This was easy:—he therefore caught himself and pronounced a more rounded sentence: "It has not vitality enough to preserve it from putrefaction."

Here the shift simply changes an Anglo-Saxon to a Latinate diction, with a little alliteration ("*P*reserve ... a *p*utrefaction"). For English speakers, Latinate words have always seemed high-class—longer, more mouth-filling and impressive, full of Roman gravitas-by-association, showing that you have studied Latin at school—while Anglo-Saxon words have been for more common, everyday use. Even people who would have been hard-pressed for an instant etymology could play with this difference. Fats Waller, for example, halfway through his classic send-up, "Your Feet's Too Big," sends up the send-up with, "Honey, your pedal extremities really are enormous." It's a schoolchild's trick originally, this kind of translation, prompted by studying Latin. From "feet" by simple translation you synthesize an intellectual Twinkie like "pedal extremities." In our time, first the social scientists and then the bureaucrats have picked up this habit and fashioned from it a new formal style which we can call The Official Style. Thus a psychologist does not say that more people think of suicide at Christmas than at other times

166

of the year. He says "There is an upsurge in suicidal ideation for some." (Yes, this is a real quotation.) And a building owner does not say "The air conditioning is wearing out and it has the superintendent worried," but "The continuing deterioration of the ventilation system is generating a considerable amount of ongoing concern to the superintendent of the facility." (Yes, real too.) Or you take a bunch of Latinate words and string them together into a noun compound: "the estimated within regression coefficient structural model," for example. And the habit then falls back into the popular culture with something like "The Second Unofficial Annual Miss Las Vegas Showgirl Fashion Beauty Pageant Contest." We all yearn for the high style. Even the matter-of-fact geologist, with not only his feet on the ground but maybe his hands and knees too, will write "arenaceous deposit" instead of "sand," "intense placation" instead of "close folding," and from "the overlying bed is limestone" will synthesize "the superincumbent material consists of a stratum of calcareous composition." (I've taken these pairings from George Otis Smith, "Plain Geology," *Economic Geology* [1922], vol. 17.)

We all want to put on the style. It is part of presenting our public self, like getting dressed up for a party. Often, when we actually get to the party all gussied-up, we'll take great pains not to act that way, to show that the high style hasn't really changed us, that we're still just folks. Americans have always had a hard time with the high style. It is not so much that it is undemocratic—though it is that—as that it implies a difference between the public and private self that our egalitarian social philosophy has always pretended doesn't exist. We are, we like to think, what we are, whether in public or in private. No back-stage/front-stage difference divides our lives. This is an illusion but we cherish it. If someone writes in the high style, he is a fake, putting on the dog, insincere. Such persistent golden-age sincerity was H. L. Mencken's target when he parodied the Declaration of Independence:

> When things get so balled up that the people of a country got to cut loose from some other country, and go it on their own hook, without asking no permission from nobody, excepting maybe God Almighty, then they ought to let everybody know why they done it, so that everybody can see they are not trying to put nothing over on nobody. (*The American Language*, 3rd ed. [New York: Knopf, 1923])

And the same fond illusion—down home, plain, folksy, colloquial, ungrammatical = REAL AND SINCERE—energizes the humor in Oliver Jensen's equally famous parody of the Gettysburg Address in "Eisenhowerese":

> I haven't checked these figures but 87 years ago I think it was, a number of individuals organized a governmental set-up here in this country, I believe it covered certain Eastern areas, with this idea they were following up based on a sort of national independence arrangement and the program that every individual is just as good as every other individual. (Dwight Macdonald, *Parodies* [London: Faber and Faber, 1960])

The comedy comes from a time-warp. The America that could applaud, that could generate, Lincoln's eloquence is no longer the America beguiled by Eisenhower's calculated uncalculation. If Ike had had to dedicate Gettysburg rather than simply farm it, no doubt he would have done it the Jensen way. It would sound more "sincere."

But Americans are not the only people who have trouble keeping the high style and the low in balance. This stylistic relationship forms part of a larger one, the relation of front stage and back stage in human life, of balancing public life and private. Sometimes you can surprise a style at work in this balancing act. Here is a clear example, a passage from A. E. Housman's "Introductory Lecture" for the 1892 academic year of University College, London:

> Perhaps it will be objected that we see, every day of our lives, plenty of people who exhibit no pleasure in learning and experience no desire to know; people, as Plato agreeably put it, who wallow in ignorance with the complacency of a brutal hog. We do; and here is the reason. If the cravings of hunger and thirst are denied satisfaction, if a man is kept from food and drink, the man starves to death, and there is an end of him. This is a result which arrests the attention of even the least observant mind; so it is generally recognized that hunger and thirst cannot be neglected with impunity, that a man ought to eat and drink. But if the craving for knowledge is denied satisfaction, the result which follows is not so striking to the eye. The man, worse luck, does not starve to death. He still preserves the aspect and motions of a living human being; so people think that the hunger and thirst for knowledge can be neglected with impunity. And yet, though the man does not die altogether, part of him dies, part of him starves to death: as Plato says, he never attains completeness and health, but walks lame to the end of his life and returns imperfect and good for nothing to the world below.

But the desire of knowledge, stifle it though you may, is none the less originally born with every man; and nature does not implant desires in us for
nothing, nor endow us with faculties in vain. "Sure," says Hamlet,

> Sure, He that made us with such large discourse,
> Looking before and after, gave us not
> That capability and godlike reason
> To fust in us unused.

The faculty of learning is ours that we may find in its exercise that delight
which arises from the unimpeded activity of any energy in the groove nature
meant it to run in. Let a man acquire knowledge not for this or that external
and incidental good which may chance to result from it, but for itself; not
because it is useful or ornamental, but because it is knowledge, and therefore
good for man to acquire. "Brothers," says Ulysses in Dante, when with his
old and tardy companions he had left Seville on the right hand and Ceuta on
the other, and was come to that narrow pass where Hercules assigned his
landmarks to hinder man from venturing farther: "Brothers, who through a
hundred thousand dangers have reached the West, deny not, to this brief vigil
of your senses that remains, experience of the unpeopled world behind the
sunset. Consider of what seed ye are sprung: ye were not formed to live like
brutes, but to follow virtue and knowledge." For knowledge resembles virtue
in this, and differs in this from other possessions, that it is not merely a means
of procuring good, but is good in itself simply: it is not a coin which we pay
down to purchase happiness, but has happiness indissolubly bound up with
it. Fortitude and continence and honesty are not commanded to us on the
ground that they conduce, as on the whole they do conduce, to material success, nor yet on the ground that they will be rewarded hereafter: those whose
office it is to exhort mankind to virtue are ashamed to degrade the cause they
plead by proffering such lures as these. And let us too disdain to take lower
ground in commending knowledge: let us insist that the pursuit of knowledge,
like the pursuit of righteousness, is part of man's duty to himself; and remember the Scripture where it is written: "He that refuseth instruction despiseth
his own soul." (*Selected Prose,* John Carter, ed., [New York: Cambridge
University Press, 1962])

Housman alternates between a formal and a less formal, a higher and a
lower, a generally Latinate and a generally Anglo-Saxon style. He makes,
that is, a stylistic strategy from the Latinate translation Boswell observed in
Johnson and we saw in Fats Waller.

Everything here is said twice, first on one level and then on the other.
This surely fits a Latin professor, and it unfolds with such careful variation
that we scarcely notice it. It is not resolutely maintained, the basic antithet-

ical strategy taking other forms, a "not merely ... but" construction, for example, but the pattern stands out: noun style *vs.* verb style, passive *vs.* active, Latinate *vs.* Anglo-Saxon diction. Such a clear pattern invites us to make the translations for which Housman himself has supplied none. (I've done this in b and c.)

| | LATINATE AND FORMAL | ANGLO-SAXON AND INFORMAL |
|---|---|---|
| a) | If the cravings of hunger and thirst are denied satisfaction | if a man is kept from food and drink |
| b) | [starvation results finally in mortification and the individual's life is terminated] | the man starves to death, and there is an end of him. |
| c) | This is a result which arrests the attention of even the least observant mind. | [as any fool can see] |
| d) | hunger and thirst cannot be neglected with impunity | a man ought to eat and drink |
| e) | He still preserves the aspects and motions of a living human being | The man, worse luck, does not starve to death. |
| f) | He never attains completeness and health | but walks lame to the end of his life |
| g) | returns imperfect | and good for nothing |

If, as Edmund Burke once said, "a clear idea is another name for a little idea," then the three levels of style must be a very large idea. The middle style, though, is a little idea. It can be clearly and consistently defined as halfway between the high and low style, whatever we think those extremes to be. The "logic" of tacit bargaining has operated strongly here. A few theorists have wanted to add a fourth category—the Greek theorist Demetrius, for example, proposed "the forceful"—but none has caught on. And some, Aristotle for one, really distinguished only the two opposed extremes. But everyone soon came across a style that was, well, somewhere in between. And so the three-level definition has stuck around with the remarkable pertinacity reserved, probably, for categories based on tacit bargaining principles rather than on any clear, universally accepted content.

For, alas, a clear, universally accepted content is just what the high-middle-low division does not have. Defining high-middle-low styles is a game anyone can play. If the middle can be immediately determined by the extremes, choose two extremes and off you go. It has, in practice, been almost this capricious. The following criteria, in any order and combination, have been used to define the two:

| HIGH | LOW |
|---|---|
| rhetorical | logical |
| emotional | rational |
| persuasive | informational |
| ornamented | plain |
| opaque | transparent |
| Latinate | Anglo-Saxon |
| front-stage | back-stage |
| aristocratic | plebeian |
| serious | comic |
| affected | sincere |
| literary | conversational |
| hypotactic | paratactic |
| periodic | loose |
| dramatic | everyday |
| self-conscious | natural |

The situation, as nearly as I can make it out, stands thus: two basic oppositions, two strands of definition have twined about one another—the public life/private life distinction and the emotion/reason distinction. Sometimes, but not always, the verbal patterns which express these antitheses overlap. No use pretending that the situation is any clearer than it is. A good case could be made for junking the whole distinction, except that it would be speedily reinvented. And so we must make the best of it. Two ways to go: you can trace the history of the three styles as they are discussed by the rhetorical theoreticians, beginning with Aristotle; or, as the theorists themselves often do, you can depend on "touchstones," to use Matthew Arnold's term, examples which embody what theory cannot specify. You cannot, however, do both at once because the touchstones rarely agree with the theory. I've chosen the Arnoldian route: start with touchstones and see what emerges.

We're reading, remember, within a basic antithetical framework. The first extreme is social—our fondness for separating public occasion from private, front stage from back. The second is ethical—the distinction between language that describes the facts and language that elicits emotions. This second kind Aristotle called λόγος πρὸς τοὺς ἀκροωμένους, language which aims at its audience. The first kind, which aims at the events themselves, he called λόγος πρὸς τὰ πράγματα. From Aristotle onward, the style aimed at the facts has been applauded and the style aimed at the listeners suspected. It is the suspected style, the style aimed at the hearer's

emotions rather than the facts, which develops into the high style. The λόγος πρὸς τὰ πράγματα, the style which aims only to make the facts clear, has
developed into the low style. Yet from the beginning the style that has been
discussed, analyzed, marveled at, has been the high style. No surprise.
Ornamented, emotional, spotlighted, it was the style you could see. And the
style you could talk about. The transparent, neutral, unemotional style
could be applauded but there wasn't much to say about it. Ideally, it wasn't
there at all. You looked right through it to the facts beyond. And so from
Aristotle onward, Western rhetorical theorists have been condemned to
admire a style they could not talk about and to talk about one they could
not admire. This has confused people. The confusion persists in the modern
rhetoric course, "composition" as we usually call it, where the Clarity-Brevity-Sincerity cluster of low-style values leads us to a style, and hence a subject, logically not there at all. And so style is either dismissed—in favor of
discussing argumentation, the psychology of creativity, whatever—or the
high style is discussed only to be deplored as a "mistake."

A fundamental contradiction runs through the other basic distinction, too,
the front-stage/back-stage one. We continually want a public reality that
differs from the private one. We want to dress up, go to a party, give a
speech, march in a parade. And yet we want public and private world, front
and back stage, to agree. We don't want private truth and public charade.
The split makes us uncomfortable. And so we continually create a difference
we continually try to annul.

To these two basic confusions, let me add a third, and then we'll get on
with the analysis. In any human communication four elements exist besides
the words themselves: speaker, audience, subject, and situation. The public/
private distinction refers to situation. It can't leave out the other three, obviously, but they enter indirectly. The fact/emotion distinction refers to subject. Its "decorum," as we say, derives from the facts it discusses. The facts
call the tune. The other three elements, speaker, audience, and situation,
enter secondarily. This exclusivity of both basic antitheses has made for
much confusion. Most often when the three styles have been discussed, it
has not been clear whether the "decorum" which continually reappears
refers to situation, audience, subject, or speaker.

So, with the three basic minefields crudely mapped, let's look at some
examples of high, low, and middle. (Again the reasoning is necessarily circular—we must know what high and low mean before we choose the exam-

ples, but only examples can tell us what high and low mean. Can't be helped.) Let's start at the top. I'll use my favorite orator again, Winston Churchill, in his famous radio broadcast of May 19, 1940:

> I speak to you for the first time as Prime Minister in a solemn hour for the life of our country, of our empire, of our allies and above all of the cause of freedom.

1. A tremendous battle is raging in France and Flanders. The Germans by a remarkable combination of air bombing and heavily armoured tanks have broken through the French defenses north of the Maginot line and strong columns of their armoured vehicles are ravaging the open country which for the first day or two was without defenders. They have penetrated deeply and spread alarm and confusion in their tracks. Behind them there are now appearing infantry in lorries, and behind them again, the large masses are moving forward. The regroupment of the French armies to make head against and also to strike at this intruding wedge has been proceeding for several days largely assisted by the magnificent effort of the Royal Air Force.

2. We must not allow ourselves to be intimidated by the presence of these armoured vehicles in unexpected places behind our lines. If they are behind our front, the French are also at many points fighting actively behind theirs. Both sides are therefore in an extremely dangerous position. And if the French army and our own army are well handled, as I believe they will be, if the French retain their genius for recovery and counterattack for which they have so long been famous; and if the British show the dogged endurance and solid Viking power for which there have been so many examples in the past; then, a sudden transformation of the scene might spring into being.

3. It would be foolish, however, to disguise the gravity of the hour. It would be still more foolish to lose heart and courage or to suppose that well-trained, well-equipped armies numbering three or four millions of men can be overcome in the space of a few weeks, or even months, by a swoop or raid of mechanized vehicles, however formidable. We may look with confidence to the stabilization of the front in France and to general engagement of the masses, which will enable the qualities of the French and British soldiers to be matched squarely against those of their adversaries.

4. For myself, I have invincible confidence in the French army and its leaders. Only a small part of that splendid army has yet been engaged and only a very small part of France has yet been invaded. There is good

evidence to show that practically the whole of the specialized and mechanized forces of the enemy have been already thrown into the battle; and we know that very heavy losses have been inflicted upon them. No officer or man, no brigade or division, which grapples at close quarters with the enemy, wherever encountered, can fail to make a worthy contribution to the general results. The armies must cast away the idea of resisting attacks behind concrete lines or natural obstacles, and must realize that mastery can only be regained by furious and unrelenting assault. And this spirit must not only animate the high command but must inspire every fighting man.

5.    In the air, often at serious odds—often at odds hitherto thought overwhelming—we have been clawing down three or four to one of our enemies; and the relative balance of the British and German air forces is now considerably more favourable to us than at the beginning of the battle. In cutting down the German bombers we are fighting our own battle as well as that of France. My confidence in our ability to fight it out to the finish with the German air force has been strengthened by the fierce encounters which have taken place and are taking place. At the same time our heavy bombers are striking nightly at the tap-root of German mechanized power and have already inflicted serious damage upon the oil refineries on which the Nazi effort to dominate the world directly depends.

6.    We must expect that as soon as stability is reached on the western front, the bulk of that hideous apparatus of aggression which dashed Holland into ruin and slavery in a few days will be turned upon us. I am sure I speak for all when I say we are ready to face it, to endure it, and to retaliate against it to any extent that the unwritten laws of war permit. There will be many men and many women in this island who, when the ordeal comes upon them, as come it will, will feel comfort and even a pride that they are sharing the perils of our lads at the front— soldiers, sailors, and airmen, God bless them—and are drawing away from them a part at least of the onslaught they have to bear. Is not this the appointed time for all to make the utmost exertions in their power?

7.    If the battle is to be won, we must provide our men with ever-increasing quantities of the weapons and ammunition they need. We must have and have quickly more airplanes, more tanks, more shells, more guns. There is imperious need for these vital ammunitions. They increase our strength against the powerfully armed enemy. They replace the wastage of the obstinate struggle; and the knowledge the wastage will speedily be replaced enables us to draw more readily upon our reserves and throw them in now that everything counts so much.

8.    Our task is not only to win the battle—but to win the war. After this battle in France abates its force, there will come the battle for our island—for all that Britain is and all that Britain means. That will be the struggle. In that supreme emergency we shall not hesitate to take every step, even the most drastic, to call forth from our people the last ounce and last inch of effort of which we are capable. The interest of property, the hours of labour—now nothing compares to the struggle for life and honour, for right and freedom, to which we have vowed ourselves.

9.    I have received from the Chiefs of the French Republic, and in particular from its indomitable Prime Minister, M. Reynaud, the most sacred pledges that whatever happens they will fight to the end, be it bitter or be it glorious. Nay, if we fight to the end, it can only be glorious.

10.    Having received His Majesty's commission, I have formed an administration of men and women of every party and of almost every point of view. We have differed and quarreled in the past, but now one bond unites us all: to wage war until victory is won and never to surrender ourselves to servitude and shame, whatever the cost and the agony may be.

11.    If this is one of the most awe-striking periods in the long history of France and Britain, it is also beyond doubt the most sublime. Side by side, unaided except by their kith and kin in the great Dominions, and by the wide Empires which rest beneath their shield—side by side, the British and French people have advanced the rescue, not only of Europe, but of mankind from the foulest and most soul-destroying tyranny which has ever darkened and stained the pages of history. Behind them, behind the armies and fleets of Britain and France—gather a group of shattered states and bludgeoned races: the Czechs, the Poles, the Norwegians, the Danes, the Dutch, the Belgians—upon all of whom the long night of barbarism will descend unbroken even by a star of hope, unless we conquer, as conquer we must—as conquer we shall.

12.    Today is Trinity Sunday. Centuries ago words were written to be a call and a spur to the faithful servants of truth and justice. "Arm yourselves, and be ye men of valour, and be in readiness for the conflict; for it is better for us to perish in battle than to look upon the outrage of our nation and our altars. As the Will of God is in Heaven, even so, let it be." (Randolph S. Churchill, comp., *Into Battle: Speeches by the Right Honourable Winston S. Churchill* [London: Cassell, 1941])

What does "high style" mean here? Start with the first pair of antitheses, back and front stage. This is obviously a speech, a front-stage public occasion of ultimate importance. Yet Churchill is speaking not in the House of Commons but over the radio. And the radio, for the audience at home as well as for the speaker in the studio, remains a private medium. Television, a more public medium, has shown us that. If we can see the speaker, he can use the gestural language of the public man. Not so with radio. So the medium which Churchill uses blends the public and private worlds in a then-unique way. An enormous audience—all of England and much of the world—but all of them sitting at home. The front-stage/back-stage anti-thesis was potentially healed, the whole range spanned, before Churchill began to speak. He could either throw this advantage away or make the most of it. As we now know, over and over again he made the most of it, brought all Britain into a sublime unity where public and private worlds fused. It was a time, as Churchill wrote in *Their Finest Hour,* when "not only individual death, which is the universal experience, stood near, but, incomparably more commanding, the life of Britain, her message and her glory." Leadership, in such a time, means just this sublime fusion of public and private life. How does Churchill do it here?

With the pronouns, for a start. He speaks as if in conversation, "I speak to you for the first time . . ." but the "we" that speedily follows—such is the miracle of radio—is not only Churchill and you and I, but Churchill and all of Britain. Radio takes the "we" and expands it to all England without destroying its private You-and-I immediacy:

> "*We must not* allow ourselves to be intimidated . . ." (par. 2, my emphasis here and in what follows)
>
> "And if the French army and our own army are well handled, *as I believe they will be* . . ." (par. 2)
>
> "*We may look with confidence* to the stabilization of the front in France . . ." (par. 3)
>
> "*For myself,* I have invincible confidence in the French army and its leaders . . ." (par. 4)
>
> ". . . *we know that* very heavy losses have been inflicted upon them." (par. 4)
>
> "In the air, often at serious odds—often at odds hitherto thought overwhelming—*we have been* clawing down three or four to one of *our* enemies" (par. 5)
>
> ". . . *we are fighting our own* battle as well as that of France." (par. 5)
>
> "*My confidence in our ability* to fight it out to the finish . . ." (par. 5)
>
> "*We must expect* that as soon as stability is reached on the western front . . ." (par. 6)

"*I am sure* that *I speak for all* when *I say we are ready* to face it . . ." (par. 6)
" . . . they are sharing the perils of *our lads at the front—soldiers, sailors, and airmen, God bless them* . . ." (par. 6)
"*Our task is* not only to win the battle—but to win the war." (par. 8)

And so on throughout the speech. We are taken into a conversation. And yet the struggle is distanced too, described in the third person as well as the first, and in impersonal constructions, part of a public reality distinct from the private one.

"A tremendous battle is raging in France and Flanders." (par. 1)
"The French and British soldiers to be matched squarely against those of their adversaries" (par. 3)
"There is good evidence to show that . . ." (par. 4)
"No officer or man, no brigade or division . . ." (par. 4)
"If this is one of the most awe-striking periods in the long history of France and Britain, it is also beyond doubt the most sublime." (par. 11)

And, at times, the two constructions together:

"After this battle in France abates its force, there will come the battle for our island—for all that Britain is and all that Britain means." (par. 8)

Finally, at the end, comes the reference to "Trinity Sunday," to the ceremony of public worship which unites by its ritual the private and the public worlds.

Yet it is more than a conversation. The Churchillian climaxes come from the public-speaking occasion. His favorite tetracolon at the beginning, for example.

in a solemn hour for the life     of our country
                                  of our empire
                                  of our allies
                and above all of the cause of freedom (par. 1)

if the French army and our own army are well-handled . . .
if the French retain their genius for recovery and counterattack . . .
if the British show the dogged endurance . . .
then, a sudden transformation . . . (par. 2)

Or two and three element repetitive patterns:

It would be foolish, however, to disguise the gravity of the hour.
It would be still more foolish . . . (par. 3)

No officer or man,
no brigade or division . . . (par. 4)

we are ready    to face it
                to endure it
        and     to retaliate against it . . . (par. 6)

We must have
    and have quickly
                more airplanes
                more tanks
                more shells
                more guns. (par. 7)

Or the short climactic sentence:

        That will be the struggle. (par. 8)
        Today is Trinity Sunday. (par. 12)

Or the epic catalog in the next-to-last paragraph, with its alliterative formulae ("side by side," "kith and kin"), the emphatic alliteration ("gather a
group," "barbarism . . . unbroken," "shattered states") and the emphatic
epithets ("great Dominions," "wide Empire"). And look at the periodic
suspensions:

Side by side,
    unaided except by their kith and kin in the great Dominions
                and by the wide Empires which rest beneath their shield
side by side, the British and French people have advanced the rescue
                not only of Europe
                but of mankind
                    from the foulest
                    and most soul-destroying tyranny which has ever
                        darkened and
                        stained the pages of history.
Behind them,
behind the armies and fleets of Britain and France
    gather a group of shattered states and
                bludgeoned races:

the Czechs,
the Poles,
the Norwegians,
the Danes,
the Dutch,
the Belgians
upon all of whom the long night of barbarism will descend unbroken even by a
star of hope
unless we conquer
as conquer we must—
as conquer we shall.

And the metaphors which accompany these suspensions: "beneath their shield," "darkened and stained the pages of history," "the long night of barbarism," "star of hope."

Churchill, here, resolves the antithesis between front stage and back, uses the devices of both to make the public and private life one. What of the other basic contrast, between a neutral style loyal to fact and an emotional style loyal to audience? That antithesis seems hard to sustain, too. Churchill spoke not only in a solemn hour but in a dark one. Nobody knew what was going on in France and Flanders (even the alliteration was delivered to him ready made!) and everybody wanted to. Churchill had the audience a newscaster hungers for. And he satisfied it. He seems here more Ed Murrow during the Blitz than Shakespeare's Henry V on the eve of Agincourt:

> The Germans by a remarkable combination of air bombing and heavily armoured tanks have broken through the French defenses north of the Maginot line and strong columns of their armoured vehicles are ravaging the open country which for the first day or two was without defenders.

When you hear him read this—the speech was of course recorded—he sounds like a substitute announcer for the BBC, not very experienced but very earnest. And this earnestness runs right through the speech. The people want to know what is going on over there and he is telling them, briefly and without softening the news. You don't feel that he is making things out to be better than they are, covering things up with a pep talk.

And yet Churchill offers as much pep talk as information, maybe more. He no sooner lets us know that the German armored columns have broken through the lines, than (par. 2) he tells us that we ought not be intimidated by this intimidating news. He will not, he tells us, be foolish enough "to disguise the gravity of the hour." Yet, he reassures us, "it would be still more foolish to lose heart and courage or to suppose that well-trained, well-equipped armies numbering three or four millions of men can be overcome in the space of a few weeks . . . by a swoop or raid of mechanized vehicles, however formidable" (par. 3). Yet this was, in fact, exactly what was going on and Churchill suspected it. That it *could* happen he knew from Poland, where it *had* happened. It was an illustration of what he had for years been warning against and what for his whole life he counseled for his own side— the immense psychological advantage of the offensive.

The speech really wants less to inform us about France than to warn us about Britain:

> We must expect that as soon as stability is reached on the western front, the bulk of that hideous apparatus of aggression which dashed Holland into ruin and slavery in a few days will be turned on us. (par. 6)

Invasion! The next great peril to be faced. Germany could not invade England without conquering or at least neutralizing France. Churchill knew this, and did not think an invasion would succeed even then. But the gravity of the hour must not be over-stressed. Sufficient unto the day the trouble thereof. So he stage-manages the news. The passage obviously resorts again and again to emotional appeal, speaks with an overpowering sense of audience. A perfect example of the λόγος πρὸς τοὺς ἀκροωμένους, the speech addressed to the audience. It is from the audience, from the people of Britain, that Churchill draws his real optimism, not from the events in Flanders. The gravity of the hour must be measured by how people respond to it, and no neutral style can measure or express that. Emotion constitutes so much a part of this reporting anyway that the neutral style can't begin to attain the accuracy for which it renounces all else. Thus here again Churchill has created his sublimity, forged his high style, by uniting a pair of basic opposites.

What of the third area of confusion—situation, speaker, subject, audience? What claims to be high style here? All of them. The speaker? The Prime Minister. The controlling intelligence of the state. The prophet who had finally found honor in his own land. An *elder* statesman, we must remember, sixty-five years old, who had both fought and governed in the

First World War, and had been a romantic hero in the war before that—the Boer War at the beginning of the century—and who as a very young man had participated in the last great cavalry charge in military history, at Omdurman. But, too, the disgraced figure of the failed Dardanelles campaign, the man shut out of ministerial life, the private-citizen prophet of the dozen years before 1939. And, of course too, one of the most widely read journalists and political historians of his time, a famous biographer of his father, Lord Randolph, and of his great ancestor the Duke of Marlborough. Churchill, in his own person, healed the public/private split and the emotional/factual one, too. Here too he knew both sides, spanned the whole spectrum.

And the audience. They had been lied to and misguided since the 1914–1918 war. Now they wanted to know the full magnitude of their peril, the scope of needed sacrifice. "Blood, Sweat, Toil and Tears" was, at long last, what they wanted to hear. And yet how far from the audience of rational and unemotional men Aristotle postulated for the plain style, the style loyal only to facts, stands this audience unified by a surge of patriotism to defend the homeland. The subject, too. The war that would affect every moment of every life. And yet—again the desire to inform—full of ordinary detail. And the situation as well, the public speech entering as a private conversation into a private living room. Throughout, then, we find a unification of conflicting opposites.

We can see now why the rhetorical theorists have a hard time *defining* the high style and so often resort to *illustrating* it with Arnoldian touchstones. When it works, the high style transcends the categories by which we usually try to define it. It heals the psychological conflicts which made us want to divide the styles into levels in the first place. It is thus impossible to describe in terms of specific intrinsic elements. A high style often uses a Latinate diction but not always. And so, too, with the other traditional ingredients—suspended syntax, frequent or forceful metaphor, isocolon, chiasmus, and other devices of parallelism and balance, alliteration, patterns of word repetition, marked variation in sentence length, and so on. And conversely all these put together need not make a high style. The high style, in this meaning of sublime, awesome, grandly important, can be defined only by interpretation and thus only through touchstones, through significant examples. A high style will always resolve the basic antitheses but each style does so in its own way. There can be—how frustrating this has proved—no rules for manufacturing a high style. When Lear says, after the death of Cordelia, "Never, never, never, never, never" he leaves out, to put it mildly, the standard ingredients of the high style. Yet who would not call this sublime?

Are there, then, no intrinsic ingredients at all? If not, why do the same patterns so often recur in the high style? Two kinds of explanation seem possible: conventional and evolutionary. Latinate diction would best exemplify a conventional explanation. For the English-speaking peoples Latin has always been the learned language, the language of the Church and, if not of the aristocracy, at least of their clerks. Latin was the badge of an upper-class education. Simply by association, by custom, Latinate diction sounds ponderous and important, "enormous pedal extremities" more significant than "big feet." Any definition of high-middle-low that depends on an analogy to social class will work in the same way. A style will be "high" in this sense if it echoes the usages of a particular aristocracy, or "low" if it sounds low. There is nothing wrong with such definitions. They point to real and demonstrable stylistic particularities. But they change as society changes. All these high-middle-low definitions based on social analogies are likely to cut across one another, too. An upper-class speaker using upper-class slang will be using a high style in one sense (social *class*) but a low style in another (social *occasion*). A lower-class speaker trying to express deep feeling will be using the low style (class) but the high style (subject). And so on through the permutations. One suspects that the high-middle-low distinction has lasted so long precisely *because* it encourages this vague definition-by-social-analogy rather than in spite of it.

The second kind of "intrinsic" definition may be more intrinsic. The habit of raising our voice for emphasis, threat, or danger, can be given an evolutionary explanation. Threat displays and danger calls form part of the behavioral repertoire of many animals besides primates. It may be that the kinds of stylistic patterns that recur in the high style can be traced back to basic patterns of primate authority-display. This would provide a genuinely intrinsic explanation. Nobody, so far as I know, has ever tried to do it, but the current explosion of work in sociobiology and related disciplines may teach us how to begin. We may find that repetition patterns, for example, are sociobiological, act as intensifiers for communication in certain species including man. We certainly find ourselves using some of the high style devices—repetition, wide dynamic range of voice pitch and stress—even in talking to pets and babies. Maybe other such patterns somehow underlie the more obviously conventional associations like Latinate diction.

So when we call a style "high," "middle," or "low" we ought to remember what criteria we are using to do so. It's not really hard. We do it all the time. A pair of Gucci loafers or some snazzy French jeans would "fit" into social situations where the Sears Roebuck imitation would not and we register this without thinking. (Another example of our hunger for the high style, this apotheosis of blue jeans from barnyard to salon.) We need not worry. Our intuition will usually be sound. We just need to trace its sources, so far as we can. Here is a modern try at the high style which shows how the process works, an impassioned tract from the early days of feminism called *I, B.I.T.C.H., Have Had It,* by Caroline Hennesy (New York: Lancer Books, 1970).

A specter is haunting the Male Establishment—the specter of Feminism.

All the Powers of the Male Establishment have entered into a holy alliance to exorcise this specter: Priapus and Salesmanship, Mailer and TV Guide, Frenzied Radicals and General Motors.

It is high time that Feminists should openly, in the face of the whole sorry, Male-Manipulated World, publish their views, their aims, their tendencies, and meet the attacks on Feminism with a Manifesto of the Women's Liberation Movement itself.

### Oppressors and Oppressed

The history of all hitherto existing society is the history of Male Chauvinism, of exploitation and depersonalization of the female.

Freeman and slave, patrician and plebeian, lord and serf, guildmaster and journeyman, in a word, all males, have stood in constant opposition to the granting of human rights, of identity, to females.

Our present epoch possesses this distinctive feature: it has simplified the sexual antagonisms. Society as a whole is more or less splitting up into two great hostile camps, into two great classes directly facing each other: Male and Female.

The Male, historically, has played a most reactionary, repressive part. Obtaining the upper hand, it has ever put an end to equal and honorable relationships, torn asunder what naturally should be the mutual bonds between women and men, who conferred upon themselves the title of "natural superiors," and left no other nexus between man and woman than the naked self-interest of the former.

The Male has drowned the life-spark of the female in the icy water of egotistical calculation. The Male has resolved the personal worth of the Female into exchange value as an object and in place of numberless indefeasible chartered freedoms has set up that single, unconscionable freedom—the freedom to be completely submissive. In one word, for exploitation, veiled by religious and political illusions, it has substituted naked, shameless, direct, brutal exploitation.

Male Society suddenly finds itself put back—and why? Because there is too much civilization, too much means of subsistence, too much industry, too much commerce—and too much of an awakening among the oppressed. The forces at the disposal of the Male Society no longer tend to further the oppression of the subjugated females. On the contrary, the females have discovered themselves too powerful for the conditions by which they are fettered and as soon as they overcome these fetters, they will bring disorder into the whole of the Male Establishment and endanger the continued existence of Male Supremacy and Chauvinism.

Plenty of the standard "high" ingredients here. Diction: a "specter" which men must "exorcise," a male who in "our present epoch" has "torn asunder" mutual bonds and "drowned the life-spark of the female in the icy waters of egotistical calculation," and deprived woman of "numberless indefeasible chartered freedoms," and kept "subjugated females" "fettered." Anaphora and climax: "their views, their aims, their tendencies"; "too much civilization, too much means of subsistence, too much industry, too much commerce, and too much of an awakening among the oppressed." Isocolon: "Freeman and slave, patrician and plebeian, lord and serf, guildmaster and journeyman." Alliteration: "Male-Manipulated," "patrician and plebeian," "too much means," "nexus . . . naked," "indefeasible . . . freedoms." The epic catalog: "Priapus and Salesmanship, Mailer and TV Guide, Frenzied Radicals and General Motors." *Ploce* (word repetition): "numberless indefeasible chartered *freedoms* has set up that single, unconscionable *freedom*— the *freedom* to be exploited."

And yet the sublime note is sung off-key, isn't it? Clichés like "it is high time," "put back," and "obtaining the upper hand" deflate the heroic tone. And the climaxes prove to be anticlimaxes ("their views, their aims, their tendencies") or trip over their own feet, as in the too many "too much"s with their clumsy "too *m*uch *m*eans" alliteration. And the diction falls over from epic into the social science world of "shun" words like "exploitation" and "depersonalization." Ringing wholesale condemnations ("Society . . . is . . . splitting up into two great hostile camps") are deflated by meaningless qualification ("Society *as a whole*") and mealymouthed modification *("more or less* splitting up"). Swinging attacks are made with wooden daggers: as soon as women "overcome" "their fetters" they are going to "*bring disorder into* the whole of the Male Establishment." The women are not going to conquer, overwhelm, or even just plain whip, the men. Instead they will "endanger the continued existence of Male Supremacy and Chauvinism." Hennesy wants half the world to revolt against the other half, a high style subject surely, but she rallies them not with Joan of Arc's voice but like a sophomore sociology major in a snit because she got a B—. She's attacking the establishment with the establishment's own style. This vitiates her whole case. Once you adopt an enemy's style, you agree to his picture of the world.

What kinds of criteria have we used in a judgment like this? Well, other examples of the high style, for a start, and how climax, word repetition, and alliteration work there. And we involve our sense of the situation—the early days of the feminist movement and its characteristic strident tone. A feeling for the character of the speaker (ethos) that emerges from all kinds of detail—the error of idiom in "overcoming fetters," the sudden and inadvertent shifts from high to low style and back, the persistent overstatement, the "capital letters" identification of The Bad Guys, and The Good Girls. The passage vacillates from front stage to back, Joan of Arc to bitchy woman, and so confuses rather than unifies them. It confuses, that is, the second basic antithesis as well as the first. All kinds of judgments, then, have come together into the final judgment: a failed high style, a style finally neither high, low, nor an adequate middle.

Two criteria we have not used: the rest of the book from which the passage comes and the model for the passage, the beginning of Marx's *Communist Manifesto*. The rest of the book simply intensifies the ethos which emerges from this passage, makes the writer fall short more and more of her great subject. The overt model, though, operates in a more complex way. Here is how the *Manifesto* begins:

> The history of all hitherto existing society is the history of class struggles.
> Freeman and slave, patrician and plebeian, lord and serf, guild-master and journeyman, in a word, oppressor and oppressed, stood in constant opposition to one another, carried on an uninterrupted, now hidden, now open fight, a fight that each time ended either in a revolutionary reconstitution of society at large or in the common ruin of the contending classes.
> In the earlier epochs of history we find almost everywhere a complicated

arrangement of society into various orders, a manifold gradation of social rank. In ancient Rome we have patricians, knights, plebeians, slaves; in the Middle Ages, feudal lords, vassals, guild-masters, journeymen, apprentices, serfs; in almost all of these classes, again, subordinate gradations.

The modern bourgeois society that has sprouted from the ruins of feudal society has not done away with class antagonisms. It has but established new classes, new conditions of oppression, new forms of struggle in place of the old ones.

Our epoch, the epoch of the bourgeoisie, possesses, however, this distinctive feature: it has simplified the class antagonisms. Society as a whole is splitting up more and more into two great hostile camps, into two great classes directly facing each other: Bourgeoisie and Proletariat.

From the serfs of the Middle Ages sprang the chartered burghers of the earliest towns. From these burgesses the first elements of the bourgeoisie were developed. . . .

We see, therefore, how the modern bourgeoisie is itself the product of a long course of development, of a series of revolutions in the modes of production and of exchange.

Each step in the development of the bourgeoisie was accompanied by a corresponding political advance of that class. An oppressed class under the sway of the feudal nobility, an armed and self-governing association in the medieval commune; here independent urban republic (as in Italy and Germany), there taxable "third estate" of the monarchy (as in France), afterward, in the period of manufacture proper, serving either the semi-feudal or the absolute monarchy as a counterpoise against the nobility, and, in fact, cornerstone of the great monarchies in general, the bourgeoisie has at last, since the establishment of Modern Industry and of the world market, conquered for itself, in the modern representative State, exclusive political sway. The executive of the modern State is but a committee for managing the common affairs of the whole bourgeoisie.

The bourgeoisie, historically, has played a most revolutionary part.

The bourgeoisie, wherever it has got the upper hand, has put an end to all feudal, patriarchal, idyllic relations. It has pitilessly torn asunder the motley feudal ties that bound man to his "natural superiors," and has left remaining no other nexus between man and man than naked self-interest, than callous "cash payments. . . ."

Changes things, doesn't it? Both texts change. Poor Marx will never be the same and Hennesy's feminist manifesto exposes itself to a different kind of measurement. The intention stands clear enough: "The feminist revolution is an event as portentous as the communist revolution. I'll prove it to you by borrowing the rhetoric of the older revolution and applying it to the new."

But something goes wrong. The feminist revolution may be as important as the communist one—if Hennesy is right, it is *more* important—but it has not yet attained the same numinosity. The Marxist banner has indeed shaken the world; the feminist one has not yet done so. We're willing to give Marx the benefit of the doubt in a way we deny to Hennesy and, if we are Marxists at least, to read his *Manifesto* as history, as a *low* style that simply reports the facts, however shocking. And, too, Marx wrote in German, so we are reading a translation, and one still full of Germanisms. And, too, we read differently because we know that Marx, the obscure German refugee sitting in the British Museum day after day, was a very different person from Hennesy sitting in the Vassar College library. Too, the regiment of downtrodden American middle-class women reading Hennesy was different from the industrial slaves Marx described. Nor was Europe in 1848 America in the sixties.

These differing patterns of expectation change the texts themselves. Look at one instance:

Marx: Our epoch, the epoch of the bourgeoisie, possesses, however, this distinctive feature: it has simplified the class antagonisms. Society as a whole is splitting up more and more into two great hostile camps, into two great classes directly facing each other: Bourgeois and Proletariat.

Hennesy: Our present epoch possesses this distinctive feature: it has simplified the sexual antagonisms. Society as a whole is more or less splitting up into two hostile camps, into two great classes directly facing each other: Male and Female.

Marx doesn't sound like a revolutionary. This is the neutral style of social history, just telling us what has happened. And this neutrality continues throughout this section of the *Manifesto*. Its ardor is, here at least, banked by the constraints of responsible social history. The *Manifesto* of course has *become* a great rallying cry, but by being used as one. And so Hennesy assumes that it *is* written in the high style and begins to make little improvements that push it more obviously in that direction. The comparison provides a fascinating illustration of how speaker, audience, subject, and context all contend with the words on the page in our final judgment about stylistic level.

We've looked now at a successful and a less successful example of the high style. The first one managed to dissolve the basic antitheses, the second only to confuse them. Let's try a low style now. This is a description by an automotive journalist of what it feels like to drive a Cobra 427, a car with a light two-seater English body and a 500 h.p. American V-8 engine.

Door handle's on the inside. Careful, don't startle it. Slide your right leg in first, snake it under the wheel, then . . . plop. No room for your knees, right? Driving position reminds me of a prewar Alfa. Wood-rimmed wheel right up near your chin, hip-hugger bucket seat that fits only if you take your wallet out; pedals too close. And that long, red hood stretching . . . grasping . . . out in front. The top of the windshield cuts right across your line of vision, so you sit up extra tall and look over the glass, like driving an Invicta with Brooklands screens. Christ. Can't see a damn thing.

What's this? The tunnel is big enough to hold a driveshaft carved out of a telephone pole, and that curving gear lever has all the heft of a Louisville Slugger. The Cobra is not a, uhhh . . . dainty car. You know the minute you clamber in, it's going to take some muscle to move that shift bat from notch to notch, and the steering's gonna take two hands. No showing off. Even the clutch pedal might need two feet, and God only knows about the brake. Anyway, you get yourself all nicely settled in for a long spell. Survey that double row of white-on-black Stewart-Warner gauges—the very best. Kind of Aircraft. You know? Key's over there on the left, behind the wheel. Neutral? Waggle to make sure. Ready? Contact.

Holy Mother of God! Sheeut. No. It emphatically has *not* exploded. Those great rolling swells of noise, like the unrelenting Galveston surf, are what it's *supposed* to sound like. What? I can't hear you. What? It's okay. Oh. And the vibration. Honest, this is no exaggeration. Just sitting here at idle, the fenders are rocking maybe two full inches up and down in time to the engine. Hell, the whole *car* is rocking back and forth on the suspension like a crazy thing. *You're* rocking back and forth in time to the engine. That big 427 just sits there and *throbs,* right in cadence with your heart beat, like a Double-A Fueler. You can feel the motor right in behind your sternum—throb *throb* throb *throb* throb *throb.* Jeezus.

Lock your knee onto the clutch. Jam the old Roger Maris signature model into first. Eeaasee down on that throttle, gently upon the clutch and throb*throb*throb*throb* off we go in a faint squeal of tire smoke, just the slightest little twitch sidewise. And that's with no gas at *all.* Run it up to two grand in first. Get it all pointed nice and straight down the highway. All lined up. Now. Hold on tight, tense your back muscles and . . . *floor this sumbitch.* Yaaahoo/Shiiift. 4000–5000–6000. Shiift. 100 . . . 110 . . . 120 . . . Shiiift. Yaawoll. Ecstasy. You can't *hear* anything, and the vibration's so bad you can't *see* much and your eyes are pouring out tears past your ears, and the wind's whistling, and your goddamn knuckles are clenched so tight the wheel's gonna crush in your hands. That pounding V-8 plays up and up and up on the little nerves in the ends of your fingers and toes, and your pucker string is wound up so tight you won't be able to crap for a week. Jeezus.

The blood's all up in the back of your head, and your eyes are seeing little red dots swimming around like baby amoebas on your corneas and throb*throb*throb*throb* the blood is charging through your body like gas in a neon sign, maybe 5,000 volts. Hell, if it was dark out, you'd be goddamn lit up. Hooha. The trees are streaking by into a tight green tunnel with a black ribbon, narrow as hell, right at the bottom. And you're balanced on the black ribbon, yellow dots streaking under your ass. Hoohaa.

Your neck is already stiff from fighting the wind and the damn engine is just goin' on and on and on. This incredible, painful, tortuous, wonderful envelope of noise. Somewhere up around 160, it starts to feel a little wound up tight, a hard metallic clamor that seems like it would *have* to shatter *something*. Your eardrums, maybe. The glass on the instruments. Hell, the damn windshield.

Enough is enough. Take your foot off the gas and let it roll. And roll and roll. The bark from those big pipes comes sucking back in, crashing and booming. Touch, just *tooouch* the brakes. And whomph. Like running into a gigantic pillow. This huge Claes Oldenburg soft sculpture of a pillow comes down across the road, ten-foot-high lipstick stain in the corner, and you run right into it. Whomph. And there you are, feeling kinda foolish, sitting in the middle of the highway, perfectly still, with only the incessant throb*throb*throb*throb* battering its way through your senses. The key. KEY. Silence. Jeezus. This is it. I mean, this is IT. Right?

A 427 Cobra is the most incredible experience in the whole world of automobiles. (Rich Taylor, *Modern Classics: The Great Cars of the Postwar Era* [New York: Charles Scribner's Sons, 1978])

The front-stage/back-stage distinction works well enough here at least. This is back stage. The fact/emotion distinction, however, doesn't work at all. (It never does when you are trying to reflect faithfully, report about, an emotion rather than a fact.) Well, what makes this a low style? The colloquialism, obviously. All those articles and verbs omitted, to begin with.

(The) Door handle's on the inside.
(The) Driving position reminds me of a prewar Alfa.
(The) Wood-rimmed wheel (is) right up near your chin, (it has a)
hip-hugger bucket seat that fits only if you take your wallet out;
(and the) pedals too close

And the direct questions that pull us into the conversation, and into the car: "What's this?" "Neutral?"; "'Ready?'"; 'What? I can't hear you, what?" And the expletives undeleted: "Holy Mother of God! Sheeut," "Jeezus" and "Sumbitch." And the emphatic colloquial italics. And the colloquial repronunciations—"Shiiift" and "tooouch" and "Eeaasee." (If this figure has a name, I've not come across it. Name the baby yourself.) And the exclamations like "Yaaahoo!" and "Hoohaa" and the "throb *throb* throb *throb* onomatopoeia. And the colloquial asides like "Honest, this is no exaggeration." And the informal diction: 2000 rpm is "two grand"; "your pucker string is wound up so tight you won't be able to crap for a week"; "goddamn lit up"; "yellow dots streaking under your ass"; "kinda foolish"; "wheel's gonna crush."

A voice, for sure. Conversation, our side as well as his. And yet hardly a transparent, unnoticed style. Just the opposite. It is as mannered as Churchill, more so. Notice the similes and metaphors? Popular ones: the gear shift lever has "the heft of a Louisville Slugger," and later becomes "the old Roger Maris signature model," the engine throbs "like a Double-A fueler." Intellectual ones: "Touch, just tooouch the brakes. And Whomph. Like running into a gigantic pillow. This huge Claes Oldenburg soft sculpture of a pillow comes down across the road, ten-foot-high lipstick stain in the corner, and you run right into it." Learned ones: "The blood's all up in the back of your head, and your eyes are seeing little red dots swimming like baby amoebas on your corneas." And another: "The blood is charging through your body like gas in a neon sign, maybe 5000 volts." This last catachresis is far fetched enough to come from a metaphysical poet. In fact the whole description is intensely *literary,* conversation as it ought to be, fast, clever, climactically emphatic. Notice the wonderful changes of pace, the sudden stops and starts that imitate the flight of the car? If by "low style" we mean unadorned, or neutral, transparent, see-through, we're in the wrong ball park.

What kind of social-class-analogue judgment does this passage prompt? The high-low distinction doesn't offer much help here either, though we want to make it. "Double-A fueler" is a low-class image, reeks of the garage. The Claes Oldenburg pillow, on the other hand, is upper-class-sophisticated. (I mean, who would *ever* have thought of *that?*) No description of a dozen-years-old car that now sells for $50,000 and up can be meant, even as entertainment, for peons. But the class-analogue judgment makes no sense here. The power, if anything, flows the other way. The style of the passage tells us that a new social class has come into being, one that the style establishes as much as reflects. This class has, like all social classes, a special interest, but its special interest is cars. About cars it abounds not only with adolescent excitement but with encyclopedic fact. Here are the two paragraphs that follow the passage we've been discussing:

> There are a few—damn few—racing cars that will accelerate faster: Turbo Porsche 917s, Can-Am McLarens, top fuel dragsters and funny cars. But when it comes to street cars, this is it. This is the ultimate. Listen to the numbers. A Jaguar XK-120—*the* hot car of the early fifties—would do 0 to 100 in 25 seconds. A Ferrari 275 GTB/4 will do it in 15 seconds. A good— now I mean a really *sharp*—fuel-injected Corvette from 1964 or so would go from 0 to 100 in just about 14 seconds. Which is very, very quick, I promise you, too fast for most people to handle.
>
> Now listen carefully. A decent 427 Cobra—not the best, not the worst—a *decent* 427 Cobra will go from 0 to 100 mph and *back down again to 0* in less than 14 seconds. Think about it. A 427 Cobra will do 0 to 100 in less than 9 seconds. And 100 to 0 in less than 5. *Consistently,* time after time. Hell, all *day* and all *night* if you want it to. While that goddamn Ferrari is still struggling up to 100, the Cobra will already be sitting perfectly still, pipes crackling and brakes sizzling, having already been up to 100 and back down again.

Here is Aristotle's "style of information" but a little changed, infused with feeling. Taylor manages, as Churchill does, to span the whole spectrum from fact to feeling, to tell us how the facts feel. His audience is, as he is, informed but not stuffy about the information. And the style reflects the whole high-low range, from your "ass" to your "sternum." A see-through style can communicate a lot of emotion.

Up to now we've given the middle style short shrift. And, since it is generally agreed that the middle is *the* essential prose style, this cannot go on. There must be some way of defining what we mean by a middle style, of giving it some positive context. Let's start with an uncompromisingly workaday example, a military order from World War I:

### 13 OPERATION ORDER

XX CORPS OPERATION ORDER NO. **42.**

13TH SEPTEMBER **1918.**

1. On 'Z' day, the date of which will be notified later, the Army will take the offensive. The object is to inflict a decisive defeat on the enemy, and to

advance to the general line of the high ground Meshariq Nablus-Yasid (098.L.9)-Sh. Beiazid (098.K.9)-'Atara-Jebel Bir 'Asur (098.B.25)-Bala (098.A.22)-Yemma (083.N.26).2. (a) The main attack will be made by the XXI Corps with five divisions against the enemy's right between the foot-hills east of the railway and the sea. This attack will commence on Z day at an hour which will be known as 'XXI Corps Zero hour.'

(b) As soon as the crossings over the Nahr el Faliq are cleared of the enemy by the advance of the XXI Corps, the Desert Mounted Corps, passing round the left of the XXI Corps, will be directed on El 'Affule and Beisan with the object of cutting the enemy's railway communications and blocking his retreat in a northerly and north-easterly direction.

### STRATEGY AND TACTICS

Sect. vi

(c) As soon as the XXI Corps has gained the general line Three Bushes Hill (04/N.25)-High ground 03/K.14-Foot-hills east of Qualquilye-North-eastern edge of Et Tire (D.3/Y.13)-north bank of the Nahr el Faliq, it will move north-eastwards and advance to seize the high ground east of the railway between Deir Sheraf and 'Atara.

One division and a cavalry brigade will advance via Tul Karm on 'Atara; while two other divisions will advance up the El Funduq road on Deir Sheraf, and by Felamiye-Beit Lid on Mas'udye respectively.

The right division of the XXI Corps (54th Division) will not advance further east than an approximate north and south line through Bidya, unless required to assist the XX Corps.

(d) 'Chaytor's Force' will hold the present front in the Jordan Valley, and may be required later to advance as far as Jisr ed Damiye. . . .

No written orders of any description are to be taken into action; officers will mark immediate objectives only on their maps, inconspicuously.

11. The Artillery plan, Administrative instructions, and instructions on Signals, Co-operation with R.A.F., and for 'Watson's Force' are being issued separately.

12. Advance Corps Battle headquarters will be established at Ram Allah on 'Z' day.

13. Acknowledge.

      A. P. Wavell,

      Br.-General, General Staff, XX Corps.

Issued at 12.30 p.m.

Now, what can we say about a prose like this? First, that the occasion demands the most transparent, least distracting style possible. Action is all. We might remark on the basic command formula—"The X will Y to Z"—

or talk for a moment about the numbered paragraphing, but really in a style of this sort there is very little to talk about. A genuine, successful see-through. And here we have the only other way to define the middle style. It is either halfway between the two extremes of your choice or, as here, it disappears. And the second definition has ruled the day. The middle style is the style you don't notice, the style that does not show, ideal transparency.

This transparency can come just as well from our expectation as from the text. Look at this example from G. H. Mead's *Mind, Self and Society* (Chicago: University of Chicago Press, 1934):

> It is a difficult matter to state just what we mean by dividing up a certain situation between the organism and its environment. Certain objects come to exist for us because of the character of the organism. Take the case of food. If an animal that can digest grass, such as an ox, comes into the world, then grass becomes food. That object did not exist before, that is, grass as food. The advent of the ox brings in a new object. In that sense, organisms are responsible for the appearance of whole sets of objects that did not exist before. The distribution of meaning to the organism and the environment has its expression in the organism as well as in the thing, and that expression is not a matter of psychical or mental conditions. There is an expression of the reaction of the organized response of the organism to the environment, and that reaction is not simply a determination of the organism by the environment, since the organism determines the environment as fully as the environment determines the organism. The organic reaction is responsible for the appearance of a whole set of objects which did not exist before.

If the reader has been trained to notice the dominant patterns of the noun style—the "to be" verbs, the passive and nominalized verbal constructions, the strings of prepositional phrases—this style will be noticeable indeed. Unreadable, in fact, if taken in large chunks. But a card-carrying social scientist will notice nothing but the argument. The "middleness" of the middle style will lie, for such a reader, in the expectedness of the style. To define a style in this way, of course, means that we cannot talk about the style itself—the actual configuration of words on the page—at all. We must talk about the social substance surrounding it, the historical pattern of expectation which renders it transparent.

Here's a last example for our high-middle-low reconnaissance. Dick Francis, the ex-steeplechase jockey and now famous thriller novelist, is talking about a jockey's daily life on the English racecourse:

All through the winter months, and six days a week, except of course during the snow and frost, we were on the road, driving round the country from meeting to meeting. In a typical week we might go to Nottingham on Monday, return on Tuesday, go to Plumpton in Sussex and back on Wednesday, Wincanton in Somerset on Thursday, Doncaster on Friday, home again on Saturday, and on Monday morning the same sort of thing started again. We averaged roughly seven hundred miles a week, though sometimes less and sometimes much more.

I liked it. I like driving, and finding new and quieter roads to avoid traffic and towns. All the people whose business is racing travel these circuits too, so that one may say goodbye to one's friends in Kent one evening, and good morning to them the next day in Shropshire.

At each country meeting we got to know many of the people who lived there, and could look forward to seeing them again on our three or four yearly visits to their local course. It is very satisfactory when one's job not only allows but actually forces one to travel from friend to friend.

This nomadic life is one of great freedom. As long as a jockey arrives in good time to ride in a race, or to do some schooling, in the early morning, no one minds where he goes or what he does. There is no office to attend, no timeclock to be punched, no regular train to catch. Jockeys who have become trainers look back wistfully on the days when their work was finished with the last race and they did not have to hurry home to worry about the horses in their care. In the winter, when racing is very early because of the light, the day's work is often done by half-past three and one can relax until the next morning.

The real reason for my being a jockey, however, was not to be found in the freedom, the friendships or the travelling that I enjoyed, or even in the great satisfaction of winning races: and it was not in the means it gave me of earning a living either, for if I had been a millionaire I would still have been a jockey. The simple fact is that I liked riding horses, and I liked the speed and challenge of racing.

I cannot explain why all jockeys, amateurs as well as professionals, are happy to take pain, cold and disappointment in their stride as long as there are horses for them to race on. Why do people climb mountains, or swim the Channel? Why do people swing on trapezes, or explore potholes? Because they can, they want to and, in some obscure way, they feel they must. (*The Sport of Queens* [New York: Harper & Row, 1969])

A neutral, narrative, transparent style; not high certainly, but not markedly informal and conversational either. Yet wonderfully easy to read aloud. The voice has at every point natural places to rise and fall. And notice the acute sense of timing, the feeling for narrative suspense and climax? After the Nottingham-Plumpton-Wincanton-Doncaster catalogue of weekly driving comes the crisp "I liked it." Or the tidy and economical way that the previous argument is summarized in the penultimate paragraph: The real reason for being a jockey was not to be found

> in the freedom
> (in) the friendships or
> (in) the travelling . . . or even
> in the great satisfaction

And then a secondary climactic element in the series:

> and it was not in the means it gave me of earning a living either

And finally the climactic argument:

> The simple fact is that I liked riding horses . . .

And then the culminating reflection, in the last paragraph, on what motivates the life he has just been describing.

Although you don't notice them, Francis often uses isocolon, anaphora, and other devices of parallelism to reinforce his narrative timing:

> I liked it
> I like driving
>
> goodbye to one's friends in Kent one evening
> good morning to them the next day in Shropshire
>
> where he goes or
> what he does
>
> no office to attend
> no time clock to be punched
> no regular train to catch
>
> traffic and towns
> friend to friend

And the final tricolon climax:

> Because they can,
> they want to and, in some obscure way,
> they feel they must.

A style not self-conscious but not uncontrived, either; not "literary" but not "I mean, like, you know" conversational either; in no way heroic yet trying to dignify the deepest kind of human motive.

Maddening, isn't it? A positive definition of the middle style seems bound to elude us. Define it as halfway between two extremes of your choice and you've defined it negatively, derivatively, in terms of something else. But define it as transparency and you have defined it in terms of something else too. The second "positive" kind of definition turns out to be negative as well. And here the descriptive term turns into an evaluative one. The not-noticed prose style has become for us the ideal prose style. Yet you can *not notice* a style for a hundred different reasons that have nothing to do with the style itself.

Just here, I think, we surprise the boundary between description and evaluation. The high-middle-low distinction seems so easy and natural for us that we will continue to make it and to find it useful. But it will continue to confuse us too because at its heart lurks an evaluative judgment masquerading as a descriptive one. We want *rules* for the three styles and to an extent we can provide them. The high style is more likely to use a Latinate diction and suspended syntax than the lower, and so on. But beyond these simple and not very reliable rules lies the whole area of intuitive, interpretive judgments, and those are finally and necessarily value judgments. Here we will find that the crucial distinction is not a high-middle-low one but the simpler distinction that we have just seen emerging from it—the distinction between styles we notice and styles we don't, between, as I shall call them, opaque and transparent styles. To that distinction, and to the larger problem of value judgments which it implies, we must now turn.

# PART TWO

# Evaluative
# Analysis

# IX

# Opaque Styles
# and Transparent Styles

The debate over stylistic value judgments really begins with Book III of Aristotle's *Rhetoric*. There he argues for clarity as the dominant prose virtue: "Style to be good must be clear, as is proved by the fact that speech which fails to convey a plain meaning will fail to do just what speech has to do."* Clarity, he argues, comes from language which is appropriate (neither too high nor too low), familiar (neither cliché nor outré), and above all *natural*. "Naturalness is persuasive, artificiality is the contrary; for our hearers are prejudiced and think we have some design against them, as if we were mixing their wines for them." The words in Greek for "natural" and "artificial" are strong root words. The verb φύω (phuo) is the basic word for natural creation, "generate, beget, grow;" πλάσσω (plasso) is a basic word for the human power to form, mold, shape. Prose is better the more it seems to grow, rather than be formed by man.

Here starts the long-standing argument for styles that don't show, that are not noticed. For a style to be noticed *as a style* becomes here, and forever after, the primal crime. It puts the reader on his guard. We start patting our pockets to make sure the wallet is still there. Yet this demand for "naturalness," when you come to think of it, is not only self-contradictory but dishonest. Words don't grow like plants. Aristotle himself starts a backpedaling which has gone on ever since: "a writer must disguise his art and give the impression of speaking naturally and not artificially." The Greek

*I'm using here the W. Rhys Roberts translation.

199

word for "disguise" here, λανθάνω (lanthano), carries a strong sense of *hiding,* of *furtiveness.* There is nothing natural about this naturalness. And likewise with the not-noticed clarity: it must still be distinguished, noticeable albeit in a non-noticeable way.

What's going on with all this doubletalk? Well, first, it makes value judgments about prose impossibly difficult. These criteria all refer to the reader, not the text. "Clarity" can only indicate a reader's decision, for whatever reasons, to look *through* a style rather than *at* it, to concentrate on content and ignore style. And my reasons for doing this may not coincide with yours. My opacity may be your transparency. The whole apparatus depends entirely on a previous assumption of shared norms. We will agree on "clarity" only to the extent that we live in the same time, place, and world of values. The system of value judgments Aristotle bequeathed to us, then, *and that we have used without essential modification ever since,* does not describe verbal patterns. It describes a *process*—even, one might fairly say, the results of that process. The process aims at maximizing content and minimizing style, at minimizing our self-consciousness about words. Aristotle knew that you could not abolish words. But as much as possible that is what he wanted to do.

We have lived with this decision for so long we have forgotten that it was just that—*a decision.* It did not come from nature (πεφυκότως—pephukotos); it came from man (πεπλασμένος—peplasmenos). It was a system of value judgments that assumed—took as enabling premise—that facts matter but words do not. This assumption emerges clearly from Aristotle's discussion at the beginning of Book III: "We ought in fairness to fight our case with no help beyond the bare facts: nothing, therefore, should matter except the proof of those facts." But other things do matter, "owing to the defects of our hearers." See what is implied here? The natural, right, proper method of communication is direct communication of ideas from person to person. Words intervene because of "the defects of our hearers." For "defects" read "emotions."

> The arts of language cannot help having a small but real importance, whatever it is we have to expound to others: the way in which a thing is said does affect its intelligibility. Not however, so much as people think. All such arts are fanciful and meant to charm the hearer. Nobody uses fine language when teaching geometry.

The last sentence gives the game away. Geometry is pure ideational structure, "facts," "content" as it ideally should be. In teaching geometry we
don't need fine language and mostly don't need language at all. This kind
of teaching represents the ideal kind of communication.

Aristotle's system for value judgments then, and ours after him, is not
neutral. As a system, and before it makes a single judgment about a particular case, it is radically biased against words. It would like to abolish them.
Again, it needs to be said: this is not the way things are. It is the way Aristotle decided they are. He was not, as all the world knows, deciding for
himself. He was bequeathing to us Plato's view of language. And under that
view we have labored ever since. It has created a traditional discussion of
style riddled with self-contradictions. These do not come from the nature of
the case, from words themselves or how and why human beings use them.
They come from the initial, self-contradictory, Platonic assumption that
every discussion about words ought to nurse at its heart their abolition. All
our discussions under the Platonic-Aristotelian system work against themselves. They are bound to. They want to make words invisible, yet you cannot discuss or understand what you cannot see. Discussions of verbal style
in the West have always been notoriously unhelpful. They never give you
any advice you can really use, only vague clichés, the Aristotelian clichés, in
fact, warmed over. Now we see why. Rhetoricians in this tradition hated
their subject. They either hated it naturally, like Plato, or they loved it but
had to work within a system which assumed that they hated it.

There was, however, in Plato's Greece a group of people who offered a
different system of value judgments for verbal discourse. Not much of their
writing survives, and they have come into history only in the poison-pen
portraits which Plato drew of them in his dialogues. These were the "rhetoricians," the infamous Sophists who play the villain's role in Plato's discussion of language. They advanced a neutral theory of language, a value
judgments system which allowed a full range of utterance, from fully self-
conscious or "opaque" styles to the fully transparent ones Aristotle pleads
for. That their writings have been for the most part lost, and that they have
lived on only in Plato's caricature, has meant an enormous loss for our discussion of style. It has meant a tradition of double talk just like Aristotle's
and two-and-a-half millennia confused by it. I'll spend the remainder of this
book trying to correct this venerable historical problem, trying to suggest

what a neutral system of value judgments for verbal style might look like, how it might be used, and its importance for the political issues introduced by the social use of language. We badly need a neutral matrix for thinking about style, a system for making value judgments that in itself—not, of course, in the judgments it sponsors—works as we are accustomed to work when we make *descriptive* judgments. Only such a system can bridge the gap between the actual words on the page and the usual—and useless—pronouncements about clarity, brevity, and sincerity.

Its creators designed the Platonic-Aristotelian system not as a descriptive but rather as an ethical system, with judgments rigidly divided into only two categories: good and bad. As we have seen, this division resembled the transparent/opaque one, and the two together trapped subsequent writers about language in a fundamental problem. When they tried to describe—instead of merely evaluate—the basic verbal structures we examined earlier, they found they needed two words for any single pattern: one word to describe it when transparent, another when opaque. Rhetorical nomenclature thus became bifurcated into one list of stylistic "virtues" and another of unstylish "vices." The term "metaphor," for example, referred to a comparison which was o.k., decorous, striking without being visible. But when you noticed it *as a metaphor,* it became a *catachresis,* a wild, extravagant metaphor, a no-no. A pleasing fullness of utterance was *amplificatio,* but one you noticed was *bomphilologia,* a bombastic diatribe. Or, to take the most comprehensive case, if you used all the adornments with tasteful invisibility, according to the Aristotelian precepts, that was, well, that was *style.* If you used them in an obvious way, though, it could be any one of a dozen sins, from *aschematiston* (unskillful use of figures) on down to *cacozelia* (an affected use of foreign "inkhorn" terms).

The problem here was in telling the difference between the good version and the bad. Back to the original Aristotelian dilemma. I might notice what you don't. It all depends on custom, background, training. The really neutral terms were always getting mixed up with the evaluative ones, until they *all* came to carry an evaluative charge. All discussions of style soon reduced themselves to one cluster of questions: How do you tell when a stylistic "virtue" turns into its corresponding "vice"? How much is enough? At what point does enough become too much? Why? And why should it seem *enough* here but *far too much* there? Such questions could be discussed endlessly. That is just what has happened. The whole study of style came to focus on this single At/Through switch and what triggers it. All the stale advice about "good writing" depends upon this one event. We might diagram it thus:

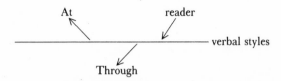

If, for whatever reasons, the reader reads *through* the verbal surface, he accepts the "content" to be as stated. He may not agree with it, of course, but he doesn't challenge its verbal presentation. He accepts that rendering as a possible world and then proceeds to argue with the world if he wishes, but not with the rendering. Quite otherwise with the *at* vision. Here the reader trips on the opaque surface and then pauses to "correct" the text. The composition teacher reading a student paper defines this case, wheeling the revising machinery into position to attack the prose. The reader, distracted from the message by the medium, starts to fiddle with the medium until it is no longer noticeable—at least to that reader. Then the content snaps into focus and the style is no longer noticed. It has become transparent. The writing has been "corrected."

We have lived with this model for so long that, again, it is hard to see how severely it conditions our thinking. It allows us, for a start, only two possible judgments, At or Through, Bad or Good, Style or Content. By doing this it gratuitously dichotomizes style and content, medium and message. Our response to verbal style is reduced to the kind of either/or choice that perception psychologists invoke with bi-stable illusions, those which can be seen either of two ways but not both at once. The old duck/rabbit figure, for example:

We do find it hard, perhaps impossibly hard, to read for "style" and "content" at the same time. The harsh simplicity of the At/Through choice reveals a fundamental truth about how we read. Yet it is not the whole truth. Our response to a verbal surface varies in self-consciousness by degree, too; it does not simply click on or off. Our response here, like the brain's functioning as a whole, seems both digital and analog. Nor is there any reason in the nature of things, rather than in the Platonic-Aristotelian tradition, why the At/Through choice should equal a good/bad choice. Ever since the Greeks, people have thought styles infinitely varied in their self-consciousness, and sometimes for good, sometimes for ill. We must find a way to resolve this seeming paradox. Can we envisage a scheme which measures this crucial variable of self-consciousness to its full extent both analogically and digitally, and in a neutral way?

Let's posit a spectrum of self-consciousness for verbal styles which measures the whole range from transparent to opaque.

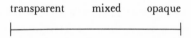

transparent     mixed     opaque

No point on this spectrum will be any more virtuous than any other. We aim only to chart the full range of variation. At the transparent extreme we might locate the military orders we examined in the last chapter. At the opaque extreme, or close to it, we could place the passage from James' *The Wings of the Dove* considered earlier for its compulsive parentheticality. Well to the opaque side we might locate the *Variety* passage reporting the profits of "One Flew Over the Cuckoo's Nest." Far to the transparent side, we might locate the Burns passage on theatricality analyzed in chapter 1. Every passage we've looked at can be located on this spectrum. Try it.

The spectrum does not plot any single verbal pattern, remember. Two styles may be equally self-conscious but for very different reasons. Hemingway and Faulkner, to take two familiar examples, would occupy about the same position on the spectrum but for very different reasons. Faulkner's stylistic self-consciousness comes from the density and variety of his verbal ornamentation; Hemingway's, from the severity with which he restricts himself to a plain diction and a simple or compound syntax. A style can choose to call attention to itself by ornament or its absence, Latinate diction or Anglo-Saxon, convoluted syntax or simple. A high style can occupy the same position as a low style. Let's examine a few styles from this point of view, place them on this spectrum, and then ask what advantages accrue from this catholic and neutral way of measuring stylistic self-consciousness.

We can begin by a passage from Swinburne's *Notes on Poems and Reviews* (London: Bonchard, 1863) where he is dwelling on beauties in his own verse which reviewers have stubbornly failed to notice.

Next on the list of accusation stands the poem of Dolores. The gist and bearing of this I should have thought evident enough, viewed by the light of others which precede and follow it. I have striven here to express that transient state of spirit through which a man may be supposed to pass, foiled in love and weary of loving, but not yet in sight of rest; seeking refuge in those 'violent delights' which 'have violent ends,' in fierce and frank sensualities which at least profess to be no more than they are. This poem, like *Faustine,* is so distinctly symbolic and fanciful that it cannot justly be amenable to judgement as a study in the school of realism. The spirit, bowed and discoloured by suffering and by passion (which are indeed the same thing and the same word), plays for awhile with its pleasures and its pains, mixes and distorts them with a sense half-humorous and half-mournful, exults in bitter and doubtful emotions:

Moods of fantastic sadness, nothing worth.

It sports with sorrow, and jests against itself; cries out for freedom and confesses the chain; decorates with the name of goddess, crowns anew as the mystical Cotytto, some woman, real or ideal, in whom the pride of life with its companion lusts is incarnate. In her lover's half-shut eyes, her fierce unchaste beauty is transfigured, her cruel sensual eyes have a meaning and a message; there are memories and secrets in the kisses of her lips. She is the darker Venus, fed with burnt-offering and blood-sacrifice; the veiled image of that pleasure which men impelled by satiety and perverted by power have sought through ways as strange as Nero's before and since his time; the daughter of lust and death, and holding of both her parents; Our Lady of Pain, antagonist alike of trivial sins and virtues: no Virgin, and unblessed of men; no mother of the Gods or God; no Cybele, served by sexless priests or monks, adored by Origen or Atys; no likeness of her in Dindymus or Loreto. The next act in this lyrical monodrama of passion represents a new stage and scene. The Worship of desire has ceased; the mad commotion of sense has stormed itself out; the spirit, clear of the old regret that drove it upon such violent ways for a respite, healed of the fever that wasted it in the search for relief among fierce fancies and tempestuous pleasures, dreams now of truth discovered and repose attained. Not the martyr's ardour of selfless love, an unprofitable flame that burnt out and did no service—not the rapid rage of pleasure that seemed for a little to make the flesh divine, to clothe the naked senses with the fiery raiment of faith; but a stingless love, an innocuous desire.

Pretty self-conscious, no? Look at the doublet habit, for a start:

> gist *and* bearing
> precede *and* follow
> foiled in love *and* weary of loving
> fierce *and* frank
> symbolic *and* fanciful
> bowed *and* discoloured
> by suffering *and* by passion
> the same theory *and* the same word
> its pleasures *and* its pains
> mixes *and* distorts
> half-humorous *and* half-mournful
> bitter *and* doubtful
> sports with sorrow *and* jests against itself
> cries out for freedom *and* confesses the chain

All these from only the first twenty lines. And notice all the alliteration that reinforces this pattern?

> *f*ierce and *f*rank
> *p*leasures and its *p*ains
> *s*ports and *s*orrow
> a *m*eaning and a *m*essage
> *b*urnt-offering and *b*lood-sacrifice
> *p*erverted by *p*ower
> a new *s*tage and *s*cene
> *f*ierce *f*ancies

And the *polyptoton* (repeating the same root-word in a different form): "foiled in *love* and weary of *loving*." And the rhyme: "real or ideal." And the *homoioteleuton:*

> small scale:    bow*ed* and discolor*ed*
> larger scale:   half-humorous and half-mourn*ful*
>                 bitter and doubt*ful*

All the doublets create a continuing *isocolon* that is intensified by the consistent *asyndetic parataxis.*

> She is *the darker Venus,* fed with burnt-offering
> and blood-sacrifice;
> *the veiled image . . .*
> *the daughter of lust and death . . .*
> *Our Lady of Pain*
> no *mother of the Gods or God*
> no *Cybele . . .*
> no *likeness*

*Anaphora* plays a strong part here too, of course. And we could discuss at length the *epitheton,* the repeated naming, either through proper name or adjectival coloration.

Good heavens, what would Aristotle think! A prose too much like poetry, for one thing. (And too much like Swinburne's poetry, for another.) People usually just wrinkle their noses at this "purple patch" and pass on. But instead of simply condemning it, we might ask how it throws the At/ Through switch. Clearly, here, by the repetition of a very limited range of figures, a range forming a rigid pattern. Exaggeration, then, and repetition. No problem with where to put this on the spectrum: well over toward the opaque extreme.

How about the next passage? It's from the famous philosopher F. H. Bradley's *Appearance and Reality* (London: Oxford University Press, 1930):

> It may repay us to discuss the truth of this last statement. Is there, in the end and on the whole, any progress in the universe? Is the Absolute better or worse at one time than at another? It is clear that we must answer in the negative, since progress and decay are alike incompatible with perfection. There is of course progress in the world, and there is also retrogression, but we cannot think that the Whole either moves on or backwards. The Absolute has no history of its own, though it contains histories without number. These, with their tale of progress or decline, are constructions starting from and based on some one given piece of finitude. They are but partial aspects in the region of temporal appearance. Their truth and reality may vary much in extent and in importance, but in the end it can never be more than relative. And the question whether the history of a man or a world is going forwards or back, does not belong to metaphysics. For nothing perfect, nothing genu-

inely real, can move. The Absolute has no seasons, but all at once bears its leaves, fruit, and blossoms. Like our globe it always, and it never, has summer and winter.

Such a point of view, if it disheartens us, has been misunderstood. It is only by our mistake that it collides with practical belief. If into the world of goodness, possessing its own relative truth, you will directly thrust in ideas which apply only to the Whole, the fault surely is yours. The Absolute's character, as such, cannot hold the relative, but the relative unshaken for all that, holds its place in the Absolute. Or again, shutting yourself up in the region of practice, will you insist upon applying its standards to the universe? We want for our practice, of course, both a happening in time and a personal finitude. We require a capacity for becoming better, and, I suppose too, for becoming worse.

Look at the patterns in the early sentences. Anaphora, and in a nice ABBA structure just as in Swinburne:

> It may repay us to discuss . . .
> Is there . . . any progress
> Is the Absolute better . . .
> Is it clear

And notice how the pattern is suggested, at greater intervals, throughout the first paragraph:

> There is . . .
> The Absolute . . .
> These, with their tale . . .
> They are . . .
> Their truth . . .
> The Absolute . . .

And, like Swinburne, a fondness for doublets:

> in the end and on the whole
> better or worse
> at one time than at another
> progress and decay
> progress . . . and . . . retrogression
> progress or decline
> truth and reality

> going forwards or back
> it always, and it never
> for becoming better . . . for becoming worse

And, as perhaps benefits a philosopher, a fondness for the intellectual balance of *chiasmus:*

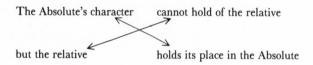

The Absolute's character     cannot hold of the relative

but the relative     holds its place in the Absolute

Or, in a more condensed form:

A                             B
Like our globe it always,     and it never,
B                             A
has summer                    and winter

Here you can reverse both A and B in both halves and it still makes sense. It was designed to. Or, in a more loosely etiolated form:

A                                     B
If into the world of goodness         possessing its own *relative* truth
B                                     A
you will directly thrust in           the fault surely is yours
ideas which apply only to the
*Whole*

Here the contrast on the B axis is clear. The connection on the A axis is only the implied causality: "If into the world of goodness . . . the fault is yours." The causality here is strengthened by the B axis but it is still not quite a full chiasmus. It is looser than the first chiasmus example, just as the second was much tighter.

Where on the spectrum for Bradley? A very different style from Swinburne's, clearly, in spite of the superficial likeness. Here the verbal patterns all aim to underline and refine the thought. Aristotle would have approved. If we were not by this time inveterate lemon squeezers, we would probably not have noticed the patterns at all. Yet they are there and they do work in a clearly demonstrable way. This puts Bradley's prose in the middle of our spectrum, or perhaps a shade toward the transparent end.

How about this example of psychoanalytic prose?

> There are perhaps no endeavors that illuminate more poignantly certain aspects of the dilemma of human identity then the seemingly kaleidoscopic rearrangement of human identities in the historical process. For this reason I shall begin with the discussion of David Riesman's *The Lonely Crowd,* a work that sets itself the task of studying changes in the American character during the last four or five decades. To give an adequate presentation of Riesman's hypotheses and to discuss them intelligently within the scope of this paper, offers many difficulties. Some of the difficulties are due to the fact that I am not a social scientist. I am therefore inadequately informed about many subjects that Riesman deals with in his work. (Heinz Lichtenstein, M.D., "The Dilemma of Human Identity," *Journal of the American Psychoanalytic Association,* [1963] vol. 11.)

Scholarly prose like Bradley's, on a scholarly subject, working out a conceptual argument. But the argument gets no help from the prose, a flat, boring, rhythmless, unemphatic noun style. A style meant to be not-noticed for sure. Here all the noun-style patterns are wholly inadvertent. This is formula-writing by someone who has never himself looked *at* a piece of prose rather than *through* it. It fits close to the transparent extreme on the spectrum—the kind of prose both written and read by people who would just as soon do away with words in favor of ideas.

Now another kind of prose altogether, an excerpt from Michael Herr's book on the Vietnam War, *Dispatches* (New York: Knopf, 1977). It poses the question of self-consciousness in a more complex way than the previous passages:

> In the months after I got back the hundreds of helicopters I'd flown in began to draw together until they'd formed a collective meta-chopper, and in my mind it was the sexiest thing ever going; saver-destroyer, provider-waster, right hand-left hand, nimble, fluent, canny and human; hot steel, grease, jungle-saturated canvas webbing, sweat cooling and warming up again, cassette rock and roll in one ear and door-gun fire in the other, fuel, heat, vitality and death, death itself, hardly an intruder. Men on the crews would say that once you'd carried a dead person he would always be there, riding with you. Like all combat people they were incredibly superstitious and invariably self-dramatic, but it was (I knew) unbearably true that close exposure to the dead

sensitized you to the force of their presence and made for long reverberations; long. Some people were so delicate that one look was enough to wipe them away, but even bone-dumb grunts seemed to feel that something weird and extra was happening to them.

Helicopters and people jumping out of helicopters, people so in love they'd run to get on even when there wasn't any pressure. Choppers rising straight out of small cleared jungle spaces, wobbling down onto city rooftops, cartons of rations and ammunition thrown off, dead and wounded loaded on. Sometimes they were so plentiful and loose that you could touch down at five or six places in a day, look around, hear the talk, catch the next one out. There were installations as big as cities with 30,000 citizens, once we dropped in to feed supply to one man. God knows what kind of Lord Jim phoenix numbers he was doing in there, all he said to me was, "You didn't see a thing, right Chief? You weren't even here." There were posh fat air-conditioned camps like comfortable middle-class scenes with the violence tacit, "far away"; camps named for commanders' wives, LZ Thelma, LZ Betty Lou; number-named hilltops in trouble where I didn't want to stay; trail, paddy, swamp, deep hairy bush, scrub, swale, village, even city, where the ground couldn't drink up what the action spilled, it made you careful where you walked.

Sometimes the chopper you were riding in would top a hill and all the ground in front of you as far as the next hill would be charred and pitted and still smoking, and something between your chest and stomach would turn over. Frail gray smoke where they'd burned off the rice fields around a free-strike zone, brilliant white smoke from phosphorus ("Willy Peter/Make you a buh liever"), deep black smoke from 'palm, they said that if you stood at the base of a column of napalm smoke it would suck the air right out of your lungs. Once we fanned over a little ville that had just been airstruck and the words of a song by Wingy Manone that I'd heard when I was a few years old snapped into my head, "Stop the War, These Cats Is Killing Themselves." Then we dropped, hovered, settled down into purple lz smoke, dozens of children broke from their hootches to run in toward the focus of our landing, the pilot laughing and saying, "Vietnam, man. Bomb 'em and feed 'em, bomb 'em and feed 'em."

Description here, not argument. The passage provides, in fact, one of those set-piece descriptions we often find in classical epic. Only here it is not the shield of Achilles which is described but the central weapon—the helicopter—of a very different kind of war. On the analogy of the special terms classical rhetoricians used for certian kinds of description—*topographia, dendrographia*, etc.—we've earlier coined one of our own—*astrographia.* Here, obviously, *choppergraphia;* the formal description of "a collective meta-chopper" in action.

The chopper is clearly personified, alive, but whether it is female, "the sexiest thing going" or a male animal settling deep into the "deep hairy bush" of landing zone Thelma, isn't altogether clear. Herr has a wonderfully onomatopoetic name to begin with—chopper—nonhuman, already loaded with metaphoric associations of cutting, bleeding, danger, and death. He doesn't intensify this pattern, however, but chooses to take it in the opposite direction, toward philosophy: "a collective meta-chopper." He's going to describe the machine *in action,* its collective life to all who see it. The "meta" comes from the fashionable world of university discourse in literature and philosophy. Greek μετά means "with" or "after," and as usually employed in philosophical talk refers to what *comes after* objects themselves, the level of reflection built on top of them. Meta-drama is drama about drama, self-conscious drama, drama which notices itself in the same way that an opaque style notices itself. Here the helicopter is made maximally self-conscious, given a human "life" stronger than even personification can bestow.

The passage begins with a basic antithetical pattern:

saver-destroyer, provider-waster, right hand-left hand

The first two pairings in the series work clearly enough: the chopper is the agency both of death and of life, machine-gun fire and food. This antithesis builds throughout the passage to the pilot's final ironic laughter: "Vietnam, man. Bomb 'em and feed 'em, bomb 'em and feed 'em." But what of the third pairing in the series—"right hand-left hand." It's a different *kind* of pairing, not descriptive but, like the *meta* chopper, abstract and philosophic, a reference to the Latin words for left and right, *sinistra* and *dextra,* and the superstition which derives from them, the left as *sinister* and unlucky, the right *dextrous,* able and honest. Gears change between the second pairing and the third, and in a very self-conscious way. We're meant to notice that triple pairing and to notice how different the third term is from the first two.

A similarly self-conscious change of gear occurs in the series of adjectives following:

nimble, fluent, canny and human

"Nimble" is easy enough. Just what we would expect for a helicopter. But "fluent"? Well-spoken, conversing easily, as in "fluent" French? Yes, clearly. But the word works not only on this metaphorical level but on the literal level as well, full of fluids: oil, gas, the blood of machines and the blood of man. This pun on "fluent" makes for self-conscious prose indeed. And what about "canny and human"? The root word for "canny" is the Anglo-Saxon word for "to know": *can,* the central act of human intelligence. In ordinary use nowadays it is used to mean "streetwise," "naturally clever," "alert"—all the intuitive aspects of animal intelligence. The word functions here metaphorically, strengthens the personification of the chopper. Its pair-word, however, works just the opposite way. "Human" simply *asserts* what all the metaphors have been implying. Back to the philosophical world of meta-chopper, even of F. H. Bradley's appearance and reality.

The breaking down of the subject into good and bad alternatives *(antanagoge)* continues with:

> sweat cooling and warming up again
> cassette rock and roll in one ear and door-gun fire in the other
> fuel, heat, vitality and death, death itself, hardly an intruder

What happens when "death" is repeated *(epizeuxis)?* Again, it signals a gear-change. We move from description to allegory, from matter to abstraction, from the fact to what we make of the fact, death itself, the grim reaper with a scythe, meta-death.

Then the same kind of pairing on a larger, sentence scale. First, a straight narrative:

> Men on the crews would say that once you'd carried a dead person he would always be there, riding with you.

Then the philosophic, academic, meta-reflection and restatement of the same truth:

> Like all combat people they were incredibly superstitious and invariably self-dramatic, but it was (I knew) unbearably true that close exposure to the dead sensitized you to the force of this pressure and made for long reverberations; long.

Sounds a little like Swinburne, doesn't it? The doublet, the homoioteleuton, the emotional adjectival and adverbial qualifications, the isocolon,

> incredibly superstitious and
> invariably self-dramatic . . .
> unbearably true

And the internal rhyme: "I *knew*—unbearably *true*." And the very showy and melodramatic repetition of "long": "made for long reverberations; long." The prose here reveals a sensitivity very like that of the battle scene it describes. The prose is trying to make us self-conscious and yet carried away with excitement (another paradoxical pairing); to rub on our nerves just as the Vietnam War rubbed on the nerves of those who fought it. The At/Through switch is being flipped on practically every line.

How, for example, do we read the sentence that follows the very literary and self-conscious repetition of "long reverberations; long"?

> Some people were so delicate that one look was enough to wipe them away,
> but even bone-dumb grunts seemed to feel that something weird and extra
> was happening to them.

Low style slang: "wipe them away," "something weird," "bone-dumb grunts." Yet a high style occasion, supernatural in fact. The gear-change we've come to expect occurs here in "extra." An abstract word in amongst the slang, yet suggesting feelings extra-rational, mystical, beyond control. "Grunt" in the war became an antiheroic heroic term, the perfect embodiment of dogged bravery built on incredible mistakes and hopeless wrong. It is a slang word but, like the whole passage, you must *notice it,* feel its full force, be as "delicate" as the "some people" who are blown away. That vulnerability, that sensitivity, makes the point of the sentence, of the whole passage.

The second and third paragraphs present a series of vignettes, quick vigorous units of description (*energia* is the term for this technique). The sequence begins with a paratactic series of participle and absolute phrases:

> Helicopters and people jumping out of helicopters
> people in so close
> choppers rising

> wobbling down
> cartons thrown off, dead and wounded loaded on

Then the changes of scene are rung with routine, often metaphoric, pivot words:

> Sometimes they were
> There were installations
> There were
> Sometimes the choppers
> Once we fanned
> Then we dropped. . . .

The way the scenes change is not haphazard but carefully wrought. We notice not only the scene changes but how they change and *how the writer describes* the changes.

The punning language of layered metaphor and literary self-consciousness noticed in the first paragraph never sinks far below the surface:

> There were installations as big as cities with 30,000 citizens, once we dropped in to feed supply to one man. God knows what kind of Lord Jim phoenix numbers he was doing in there, all he said to me was, "You didn't see a thing, right Chief? You weren't even here."

Notice the force of "citizens"? Gear-changing again, here by describing a wartime jungle camp as a peaceful city. And the neutral "supply" comes with a "feed" which is both literal—they are giving him food—and metaphorical, as when you "feed" ammo belts into a machine gun. And with what kind of self-consciousness do we respond to "God knows what kind of Lord Jim phoenix numbers he was doing in there"? Does the literary allusion dominate? Conrad's novel *Lord Jim* and what lonely stress does to that hero? Or the allusion to the CIA's PHOENIX campaign to assassinate Vietcong members? Or the counterculture pun on "numbers," as both the CIA plot and "do a number"—i.e., "smoke a joint"? Or just the plain weirdness—the "something extra"—of the event itself? This passage seems to layer kinds of self-consciousness one above the other, and to ask us always to be quick-witted, able to move from one to the other.

All this clearly does not make for the kind of prose of which Aristotle could approve. Too much like poetry, for a start. Continually calls attention to itself. That, precisely, is how it works, what it tries to say. The prose models the war: self-conscious, mannered, media-aware to within an inch of its life, yet suddenly switching to impossibly real and bloody and pointless. Vietnam *was* unlike other wars. Herr was trying to tell us how and why this was so. It was not a war fought on one level of self-consciousness. It was not a war whose emotional and moral and psychic orientation we could all agree on, as, say, World War II was. It was fought in extreme self-consciousness. This the prose both says and embodies. Who is to say that such prose is not "clear"? Does not let us *see* that war as it was? Yet the Aristotelian scheme can do nothing with such prose except condemn it. It can even be called "incorrect"—comma splitting, anacoluthon, anastrophe, the lot.

The uselessness here of the Aristotelian scheme brings up several important general problems. Perhaps the most obvious are the prose/poetry and the fiction/nonfiction distinctions. For Aristotle, these must be absolute distinctions. Just there the At/Through trigger operates. You are allowed to look *at* poetry but only *through* prose. The fictional prose/nonfictional-prose distinction did not present itself to Aristotle so strongly as it presents itself to us, but he could not have handled it if it had. How do you decide what is fictional and what is not? All you can do is *decide* that there are two categories and that you should look *through* the nonfictional prose but can look *at* fictional prose, much as if it were poetry. In such a scheme the typography which sets off poetry from prose, like the subtitle "A Novel" which sets a novel off from nonfictional prose, both point to absolute differences. When you have a prose which is too poetic for prose, like Herr's frequently, you make up a special name for it—*kunstprosa* or *art prose*—and then forget the problem. If you have a prose that is halfway between fictional and nonfictional prose, again like Herr's New Journalism, you make up a special name for that too—"faction" (fact + fiction) seems the preferred new noun—and again forget about the theoretical problem. What else can you do?

Our neutral spectrum simply dissolves all these pseudoproblems. A prose style is allowed to call any amount of attention to itself that it wishes. Herr's style, far over toward the opaque side of the spectrum, still takes its place in a full and comprehensive range of verbal effect. The difference between prose and poetry becomes simply a typographical signal, as indeed our earlier discussions have shown it to be. And the fictional/nonfictional distinction becomes part of a much more complex transaction between reader and writer which allows both of them to delineate degrees of self-consciousness in the kind of reality indicated, just as Herr is trying to do here.

Perhaps the most surprising thing about the Aristotelian prohibition of self-consciousness is that it has lasted so long. Here is a method for stylistic judgment that reduces what is obviously a complex gradient of response to a simplistic on-off switch, and by so doing involves us in manifold and continual difficulties and self-contradictions. Yet it has persisted virtually unchallenged ever since, so dominated our thinking that even questioning it demands a major intellectual readjustment. What does it have going for it? Why has it lasted so long? I can suggest two answers, a general one taken from current thinking in evolutionary biology and a narrow one taken from perception psychology. Let's start with the general one.

Why should we want to resist becoming self-conscious about style? Why have students of style for so long wanted to equate self-consciousness with sin? What do we gain? We protect, finally, a specific conception of the self and of the world's reality. If the natural state of words is transparent, then they do not by nature interfere with the structure of ideas or the structure of the world. Ideas are just "out there," self-standing and absolutely real. We use words to *reveal* them or *point to* them, but not to construct them. Words at best are deceivers ever and ideas our only true friends. This was, of course, exactly the conception of an idea Plato sought to defend. It was not a social product, conditioned by use, but constituted an independent order of reality. The West has always desperately wanted to believe this—especially America. Nowhere has the fallacy of the self-existent idea been more firmly held. "Don't bother about my words, teacher. Look at my wonderful ideas!" Ideas are things, bottom-line grown-up stuff. Words are sissified and artistic. I'm exaggerating here but not much. As soon as you look *at* a verbal surface, though, rather than *through* it, this independence of ideas comes into question. Ideas seem to depend on the words.

From here only a step leads to the idea that the world itself—as Plato would say, "the world itself as in itself it really is"—does not just sit out there waiting to be observed. We create it by perceiving it. Perception is active, creative. Words are part of this process. For the structure of ideas, they form the central part. And in reading, when we become self-conscious about words, they come to symbolize our participating creation of the external reality. A transparent theory of language, or assumption about language, invites us to ignore this co-creation. And if your theory of style makes such self-consciousness *a sin,* then you command the reader to ignore this participation and the consequent undependable fragility of the world perceived. This is what Plato wanted to do. A theory of value judgments in verbal style became a potent allegory for a philosophy of the self-standing Idea.

The same kind of argument holds for the *social* reality we live in. If language is a passive and transparent medium, then human society exists independently of it, just stands "out there," like rocks and stones and trees. Again, just this Plato wanted to urge. Plato wished to defend a conception of society which had only recently emerged from orality into written literacy. A society's sense of itself in an oral culture depends on the language which expresses it. Plato wanted to break this dependence once and for all. He succeeded.

A persistent strand of the opposite opinion lasted through antiquity though, the recurrent idea that the world is a stage, a vast drama. And, as the Burns passage in chapter 1 points out, this idea stands central to our current thinking about social reality: it is radically dramatic, radically mediated by words, essentially self-conscious. A transparent theory of language pretends that this is not so. So too with the individual self. The argument for "naturalness," "sincerity," is an argument for an unself-conscious self, located halfway between the ears, and existing—or capable of existing—outside human society. To admit self-consciousness into verbal styles is to imply that the self is a social being, created by human society and existing only in it, finding in society its natural and necessary audience. Again, much sociological thinking in the last hundred years has been arguing just this case. Plato wanted to move in the opposite direction, toward a self which existed outside the social matrix. And in a very deep way so do we all. This wish is documented by everything from Stoic philosophy to our own sense of normal autonomy, the sense that makes us feel our free will. It takes an injury or a health scare to remind us that the self exists only in process, physical and perceptual. We don't savor these reminders. They get in the way of enjoying life in the same way that stylistic self-consciousness gets in the way of reading for content.

Stylistic self-consciousness, then, parallels behavioral self-consciousness, and we resist both for the same reasons. They are intellectual reasons when they assume the Platonic guise but they also run deep into our evolutionary past. Stylistic behavior is enormously expressive. Gesture, costume, posture, tone of voice, all of these nonverbal communicators carry heavy loads of meaning. How much they carry we find out every time we try to write and have to find verbal equivalents for them. In daily life we usually find our way around through these intuitive clues. They allow people to communicate their feelings and attitudes in a very efficient way. Usually there isn't time to "prove" one's feelings, to explain them fully. You have to depend on a stylistic code. For that reason, we must think that code an unfakeable one, "sincere." There just isn't time to ask for a copy of someone's diploma; you have to ask yourself if the person "acts like" a college graduate. We are so concerned about a "sincere" manner, and about an affected one, because so much rides on this means of social communication. And for the same reason we resist learning too much about this kind of nonverbal communication. If we spend a lot of time talking about it, we'll learn how to fake it. And that will prove very uncomfortable for all concerned—even for the fakers.

A similar behavioral argument from perception psychology has underlain and supported Aristotle's equation of stylistic self-consciousness with sin. If a writer shows himself a manipulator of words, he can fake what we want to think an unfakeable code. He can fabricate an alternative reality, another self. This fear of hypocrisy reaches far back into our evolutionary past. Students often manifest this fear when asked to analyze a poem which has moved them deeply. They'd prefer not to. They might find something bogus in their elation. Best to leave the feeling alone rather than "murder to dissect." The At/Through switch is thought to be equal to a good/bad one because it models a similar fault-line in human behavior itself. Human behavior also offers deep support for its absolute discontinuity, its on/off nature. The bi-stable illusion mentioned earlier does seem to allegorize the nature of our verbal attention in a deep way. When we read for "content" it is very hard to notice style, at least to notice it consciously. And vice versa. Attending to one kind of thing blocks out the other.

Perhaps this has to do with the two hemispheres of the brain so much discussed now, left brain working with content and right with style. I don't know. But clearly, from a behavioral point of view, it is adaptively useful to be able to fix our attention on a "meaning" and block out the surrounding signals. Perhaps the most obvious illustration of this selective attention, for our purposes, comes from the act of writing itself. Writing and revising are, for most of us, two different kinds of acts. When you write you are writing for "content," trying to shape and fix an argument. When you revise you reverse this process, look At rather than Through. The whole act of writing, as a process, is an oscillation of these two kinds of vision, Through and At. Write and revise, write and revise, in a continuing alternation.

Reading too, we might remark parenthetically, must work through the same oscillation. But just as we feel we "ought" to be able to write well without revision, ought to fix and focus our ideas purely in the mind, without the intermediation of words, just so we think that reading ought to be purely unself-conscious, not an oscillation of At and Through, but all Through. When you ask yourself, "How do I know what I think until I see what I write?" you've made a rueful admission not only about writing but about reading as well. And it isn't surprising that it upset Plato and Aristotle. It upsets all of us. It is embarrassing if not downright humiliating that, in order to bring the world into focus, one has to play games with one's own perceptual machinery. And so we want to freeze this oscillation, admit to only half of it, and deny the other half. This simplification has fatal effects for any workable theory of value judgments about prose, as we shall see.

In the Aristotelian prohibition of self-consciousness, another kind of insidious flattery is at work. The transparent, unself-conscious prose ideal models plain utilitarian purpose. We are trying to get on with the world of "real" objects and "real" ideas and not linger over words. Think of all the formulas for "readability" that pepper the writing textbooks. The business community fancies these formulas so ardently because that community likes to flatter itself even more than the rest of us do about the practicality and realism of its motives, the "bottom line" profit-and-loss simplicity of its behavior. This sense of bluff practical purpose grotesquely deludes us all, of course, both the bottom-liners and the rest of us. Homo sapiens belongs to the order of primates and primates have motives radically "unpurposive," at least in a short-range sense. What obsesses us is status. Recall, for example, my meditation on cars in the Introduction. Cars can stand as the central symbol of the "real" world of practical purpose. Yet how many people buy cars just for transportation? I know. I know. A lot of people *say* they do, but how do they *behave?* Do they buy the $1500, seven-year-old, faded and dented veteran that has always constituted the best value for basic transportation? Not often. They buy the car that expresses their personality and their sense of social rank, a fact as true of a Rockefeller's Chevrolet as of a prizefighter's Cadillac. Yet in spite of such demonstrable, material, behavioral evidence, we like to pretend to ourselves that we are much more purposive than we are. Maximizing the unself-conscious transparency of words, both in how we use words and how we think about them, preserves just this dowdy but seductive delusion. It allows us to kid ourselves about our own motives. Stylistic self-consciousness moves in just the other way, reminds us that we like to idle and play, to show off, to dress up, to win—to act, that is, like normal human beings.

Here the stylistic virtue/vice pairing comes very close to the ethical one. Much of what the Judeo-Christian tradition has called "sin" is just the whole range of nonpurposive behavior we have been discussing. Christianity usually calls it Pride, but often it masquerades as one of the other deadly sins. Again, value judgments about style seem to parallel value judgments about behavior. Our fondness for the Platonic-Aristotelian model has informed our whole cultural heritage. Perhaps that is why its obvious contradictions and limitations have never seemed very obvious.

Thus, when we try to replace this simple and absolute virtue/vice pairing with a neutral and descriptive one, we are doing something like what behavioral science has done in the last 150 years: trying to describe the full range of human behavior, and understand it, rather than simply dividing it into two virtually exclusive categories of good and bad. That effort has always seemed threatening to the ethical imagination for the same reasons an awareness of style threatens human behavior: it brings into self-consciousness signals and motives which, often for good reasons, we want to keep below the level of daily attention.

A full spectrum such as ours, then, represents a judgmental act before we have used it to make a single judgment. It introduces a new variable to measure, and proposes to measure it in a neutral way. Self-consciousness, it argues, constitutes the central variable for analyzing prose and especially for making value judgments. The failure to measure self-consciousness has caused endless confusion. It stands behind most of the basic terminological problems we've come across in our efforts at descriptive analysis thus far. How can a "low" style seem "high"? How can a paratactic, asyndetic, unparenthetic style yet seem—like Hemingway's—continually reflective and judgmental in the ordinary business of neutral description? How can a sublime style transport us without seeming to work upon our emotions? One is talking, in all these cases, about how the At/Through switch works, how our attention oscillates, at different frequencies and magnitudes, from one mode to the other.

When we understand the centrality of measuring this self-conscious variable, it becomes obvious that we need more than one spectrum to measure the complex process of reading. For if a text can vary in how self-consciously it asks to be read, a reader can willfully vary his attention in the same way, whatever the textual switch. So we have something like what appears in the diagram below.

|  | Transparent | Opaque |
|---|---|---|
| Text | | |
|  | (prose; nonfiction) | (poetry; fiction) |
|  | Through | At |
| Perceiver | | |
|  | (common reader) | (critic) |

We can choose to look *at* a style whether it invites this attention or not—just as we've been doing in analyzing prose throughout this book. We thus become literary critics rather than common readers, professional students of prose with purposes of our own.

This second spectrum has a behavioral analogy as well. We can behave as full and unself-conscious members of society, participate fully in its ideas, joys, and sorrows, or we can stand outside it as an observer. The behavioral counterpart of the literary critic is the visiting anthropologist, someone who studies a culture much as we have been studying verbal texts. But you don't have to be an anthropologist to project this detachment: I make an impassioned, heartfelt speech for something I believe in, ecology say, and you reply, "Wonderful, Dick! Who writes your stuff?" You've implied that my universe was an *at* one rather than a *through* one. It is a neat put-down because there is no defense against it. Once you've become self-conscious, there is no going back—at least for as long as that conversation lasts.

"Who writes your stuff?" implies, obviously, a third spectrum, one for social reality itself. Text, perceiver, and now the reality perceived.

|  | Primate Biogrammar | Ordinary Life | Drama |
|---|---|---|---|
| Reality | | | |
|  | (dream, myth) | (central, "serious" self) | (the actor) (social pageantry) |

At the right extreme, society as drama and all of us as avowed bit-players. All the admitted drama of social ceremony and ritual. At the left, totally unself-conscious behavior, the deeply felt world of dream-myth that resists our thinking about or understanding its power. I've used a fancy phrase from sociobiology here, primate biogrammar, as an umbrella term for the whole inherited baggage of our evolutionary past. Our "biogrammar" is our inherited repertoire of behavior, our urge for pair-bonding, for mother-child bonding, for status competition, and so on. I'm not concerned to argue here whether this is entirely genetically transmitted or not. However it comes to us, it seems to live far back of thought, to supply the unquestioned, unself-conscious groundwork of our being. We can write about life as it seems to be at any point along the spectrum. The same prejudices have operated here as on the other spectra. Each of us will think one point on the spectrum, or one area, more "real" than the others. For Freud, the final "reality" for man was well over to the left; for Shakespeare, it was way over to the right, as dramatistic as the Globe Theater where he earned his living. For the president of General Motors, it presumably falls somewhere in the middle.

I want to add a fourth and final spectrum to complete our matrix, though the strict logic of text/observer/reality observed does not seem to require it. This spectrum measures individual human motive.

| | Ludic | Ethical | Aesthetic |
|---|---|---|---|
| Motive | | | |
| | (hierarchy; $; game) | (practical purpose) (factual communication) | (play; hobbies; honor; "good form") |

This spectrum spells out the basic range of motive that underlies the other spectra and makes them work. At the left, the intensely absorbing pleasures of competition, the unself-conscious concentration of the player while inside the game. At the right, behavior "for its own sake," activity pursued just for the pleasure of pursuing it. In the middle, General Motors again, the "ordinary world" and the rules for good and evil that make it tolerable. You'll say that each of these kinds of motive implies the other, that there are no pure states. Of course. And this is true of the other three spectra as well. Motives are inextricably mixed. But for analytical purposes, to visualize how they are mixed, we must try to unmix them. This visualization is what a descriptive method of value judgments is all about, and what our matrix is constructed to make possible. Let's look at it entire.

|  |  |  |  |
|---|---|---|---|
| *Text* | Transparent | | Opaque |
|  | (prose; non-fiction) | | (poetry; fiction) |
| *Perceiver* | Through | | At |
|  | (common reader) | | (critic) |
| *Reality* | Primate Biogrammar | Ordinary Life | Drama |
|  | (dream, myth) | (central, "serious" self) | (the actor) (social pageantry) |
| *Motive* | Ludic | Ethical | Aesthetic |
|  | (hierarchy; $; game) | (practical purpose) (factual communication) | (play; hobbies; honor; "good form") |

Here is the *range* of experience to be described. The *act* of description is the At/Through oscillation of attention we've discussed. We might diagram it thus:

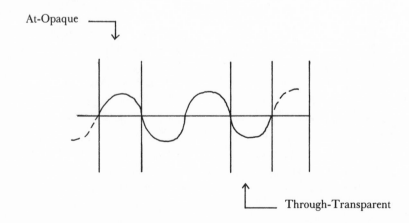

At-Opaque

Through-Transparent

We can now see how to resolve our root paradox: how can an act of attention, a self-consciousness that seems to vary by degrees, yet turn itself on and off in one simple and absolute motion, like a neuron which either fires or does not. The At/Through oscillation *does* work like a simple on/off switch, but the frequency with which it switches varies infinitely. Sometimes the switch gets flipped very slowly, sometimes very fast. At the left extreme, it works so slowly it seems stuck in the Through wave of the oscillation; at the right extreme, it seems stuck in the At wave. In the middle, our attention moves rapidly back and forth between the two.

This conceptual charting may seem a little cumbersome and elaborate. It's not, really. It is built on a basic oscillation, remember, and it measures but a single variable, self-consciousness. And we shouldn't begrudge the time it has taken to construct this matrix; we are, after all, hunting big game. We are trying to go beyond Aristotle.

# X

# Value Judgments

The Aristotelian scheme of stylistic vices and virtues introduced a fundamental distortion into Western thought about language and style. The scheme denied the whole self-conscious side of human life. Furthermore, it radically confused the relationship between reader, text, and reality; by insisting on the self-standing idea and the transparent verbal surface, it made the continuing oscillation between At and Through vision seem to be an either/or choice only, sliced the full wave-form in half, as it were. It made a dynamic interchange seem a static tableau. As a result, it was seldom clear in the subsequent rhetorical tradition whether a statement was being made about a text or a reader's response to it; about a "high" style or a "high style" subject; about a "decorum" that adjusted style to subject or one that fit subject to style. To dispel these confusions, a framework was needed which permitted a full range of evaluative and descriptive statements. We've needed, all this time, a "Periodic Table of the Elements" for verbal style. This the matrix assembled in the last chapter aims to be—a neutral framework within which meaningful statements about style can be made.

Here at the start we must be clear about what such a framework can and cannot do. It cannot make value judgments which then become "objective," stand outside individual interpretation. It cannot make you like what I like. Nor can it, except in a very limited way, suggest that you *should* like what I like. Value judgments will always remain private and unique. They exist at the interface between private experience and whatever is "out there"; this is what makes them so rare and cherishable. But if we cannot predict what they will be, or lend them objective validity, we can chart how they occur. We can explain historical consensus where it occurs and analyze disagreement into its constituent parts. We can chart on the matrix both consensus and disagreement and why they come about. We can *describe* with some objective rigor where and how value judgments occur. To do this much carries us far. Especially so since even what can be done has in fact so rarely been done.

Why choose self-consciousness as the measured variable? Why don't the kinds of descriptive patterns dealt with earlier form part of the matrix? The easy answer: because the mistake Aristotle bequeathed to us was about self-consciousness. This was the mistake to be corrected, the fundamental error confusing discussions of style ever since. True enough, but why was the initial mistake made? That's what really stands at issue here. It was made because a basic strand of Western reality, a strand Plato was the first to formulate, wanted to deny the whole area of self-conscious behavior and motive. And it is just that range of behavior which creates and sustains the verbal patterns that I have spent the first eight chapters of this book trying to describe. The Aristotelian framework has always stumbled over these patterns because it outlaws the styles where they naturally occur! Such patterns, if the Aristotelian framework were logically consistent, ought not exist at all, even as "vices." The matrix allows us to chart the areas of verbal experience where descriptive patterns occur. By doing so, it allows us to see what kind of behavior the descriptive patterns represent, and thus to make value, i.e., behavioral, judgments about them. The point bears repeating. Value judgments mean judgments about behavior. To make value judgments about prose, we must connect verbal patterns with behavioral patterns. That is what the matrix does.

By conceiving of the self-conscious variable as central we can see why value judgments about verbal style have always been so heavily moralistic. Why, in fact, all statements about verbal style have tended to be value judgments. Because verbal style so closely parallels human behavior in how it reflects self-consciousness, verbal style is immediately, if subconsciously, read as an allegory of behavior. Measuring and controlling self-consciousness in human behavior is, as we saw in the last chapter, extraordinarily important for man, evolutionarily as well as politically adaptive. And so we stay acutely aware of corresponding changes in verbal style.

We can see this even in how we respond to common mistakes in spelling, grammar, and usage. With our customary illusions about the purposefulness of our motives, we object to these solecisms because they confuse us, hide the meaning. But they seldom do. Enough redundancy is built into most messages so that no harm comes to the message. The harm comes to the writer's public self. We are rendered self-conscious about a verbal habit well-bred people don't call attention to. Sometimes a group of intellectuals will single out an "error," as the literary establishment has recently done with the misuse of "hopefully," and make such misuse a stigma of exclusion from the inner group. Often, as with "hopefully," the dimension of incorrectness is small and harmless, but that's irrelevant. The "mistake" becomes a litmus paper for membership in the proper intellectual class.

By measuring self-consciousness we can connect style with other kinds of behavior, and even, as we shall see, with value judgments in the nonverbal arts as well. Let's put the matrix before us again, and then comment briefly on how it permits us to reformulate some traditional difficult questions.

| | | | |
|---|---|---|---|
| *Text* | Transparent | | Opaque |
| | (prose; non-fiction) | | (poetry; fiction) |
| *Perceiver* | Through | | At |
| | (common reader) | | (critic) |
| *Reality* | Primate Biogrammar | Ordinary Life | Drama |
| | (dream, myth) | (central, "serious" self) | (the actor) (social pageantry) |
| *Motive* | Ludic | Ethical | Aesthetic |
| | (hierarchy; $; game) | (practical purpose) (factual communication) | (play; hobbies; honor; "good form") |

One can, for a start, sort out the four basic theories of verbal style which are usually advanced. Each group chooses one spectrum as defining, takes one of these basic variables as a constant, and then discusses the other three in terms of it. What we usually call "mimetic" theories take the reality spectrum as fundamental and interpret the other three in terms of it. The central term for these theories—the term that is synonymous with "success"—is "realism," and all kinds of verbal behaviors are measured in terms of final loyalty to a preexistent "reality." The transparent theory of prose style is the mimetic theory par excellence. But every time a writing textbook talks about "exact correspondence between the matter to be communicated and its written expression," and every time a critic talks about a novel as being "faithful to life as it is actually lived," we stand on the reality spectrum.

When we talk about the writer and his or her motives as the constant against which the other spectra vary, then we have to do with "expressive" theories of verbal creation. The artist's Herculean search for pure form, his equally heroic efforts to top a rival artist, build a higher cathedral, carve a more sublime statue, and so on, all depend on the motive spectrum as defining. The central "success"-term here is not "reality" but "sincerity." You can, as with all four "success"-terms (this is why they are both so vague and so indispensable), locate "sincerity" at any point on the spectrum. If you feel that the act of writing should be utterly disinterested, you'll want your writer to write "for its own sake." If you believe, as do many professional writers, that the best motive for long-term verbal productivity is money, then "sincerity" for you will be well over on the left hand side of the spectrum rather than the right. If you feel that the motive for writing is the neutral and disinterested communication of ideas, you'll find your "sincerity" right in the middle.

The theories that take the perceiver-spectrum as their basic measurement all talk about "clarity" as the central "success"-term, the main value. Again it can be found at any point along the spectrum. I may always choose to look At a text and you Through it and we each choose to call the comfortable success felt in so doing by the loaded name "clarity." The word's usual meaning probably comes in mid-spectrum, the oscillation of At and Through vision we have already noted. Theories based on the perceiver are often called pragmatic. Recently, reader-response theories have re-thought this whole spectrum in terms of its At extreme, admitted this "clarity" is a synonym for "success" rather than the description of a text, and attempted to redefine the whole act of reading on the basis of this admission.

Theories based on the text itself, the New Criticism for example, are called "formal" theories. The "success"-term here for nonliterary texts is "brevity." For literary texts, it is the natural perfection of form which Blake found in all literature, the assumption that everything in the poem must be there, that the poet, like nature, *nihil agit frustra,* does nothing in vain.

The matrix thus offers a little insight into some basic terms—clarity, brevity, sincerity, realism—which are both impossibly vague and so indispensable that they keep being reinvented under one guise or another. There is no reason not to keep on using them, provided we use the matrix to chart how they are being used.

We can also begin to think methodically about the differences between literary and nonliterary kinds of writing. You can, for a start, discuss this distinction based on any one of the spectra. Take the reality spectrum, for example. When a critic insists that only certain subjects are fit subjects for poetry, the statement argues from the reality spectrum. One can think that mythic reality (at the far left of the spectrum) is reality itself, and that literary texts deal only with a contrived and dramatic social reality. Or, on the motive spectrum, one can argue that the form-for-its-own-sake motive is *the* motive for artistic creation and money its perfect opposite. Or one can argue from the perceiver spectrum. Here, "literature" is not a verbal text but a way of looking at one. You can read anything "literarily" by looking At rather than Through it. You don't posit an external reality against which to measure the reality presented in the literary work. You accept that literary reality as reality itself. You suspend your disbelief, as Coleridge said. Or you can choose to consider the text itself. You can give it typographical clues that indicate an At vision as appropriate, as we do with a text printed as verse. Or you can call it a "novel," and print and bind it to look like one. Or you can measure the density of verbal ornament in some way. In all these judgments on the four spectra, the "literary" position stands at the right "opaque" extreme and the nonliterary position at the left. We can begin to plot and thus make sense of the various ways that "literariness" or "ordinariness" have been defined, without invoking an absolute either/or distinction impossible to sustain in practice.

The ease of charting brings with it an incidental pedagogical benefit. The teaching of prose composition and the teaching of literature are often done under the same roof, or within the same skull, but they usually depart from opposite theories of value. Composition instruction, under the Aristotelian Clarity-Brevity-Sincerity theory of value, depends on the transparent side of the matrix. The teaching of literature depends on the opposite opaque side. Students are often confused by this ("If you correct my comma splice, why can't I correct Shakespeare's?"), and instructors even more so ("Because you're not Shakespeare!"). The matrix allows us to plot both

kinds of theory on a common ground, to rationalize the difference in pedagogy through a common theory which includes both attitudes toward language and all the mixtures in between. A common theory of language
resolves the Aristotelian dichotomy which has so bemused us.

The matrix also suggests a resolution of the old style/content dichotomy
confusion. This turns out to be the literature/not-literature distinction on a
lower plane of regard. The composition teacher often argues that expository
prose is best when the style becomes maximally transparent and allows the
content to shine through. As one handbook has it, "When it works, the
reader doesn't even know it's there. He is simply aware of clear meaning."
The bifurcation between form and content is total. This allows us to talk
about the "ideas" in an essay, for example, while ignoring the words that
present those ideas. This is just what we must *not* do, we are told, when
reading literature. There the form *is* the content. You can't "correct" Shakespeare, or even chide him for his low tastes, as Samuel Johnson was wont
to do. Again, the matrix provides a framework for plotting both of these
form/content definitions and reconciling them. At the transparent side of
the matrix, form and content *are* totally discrete. And this separation can be
found in the text, the perceiver, the reality perceived, and the artist's motive.
At the opaque extreme, form and content are one. Since the perceiver is
looking At the verbal surface and not Through it, that surface *is* the content,
much as the dramatic surface of a Beckett play, for example, *is* the theme,
the "meaning," of that play. On the text spectrum, an opaque style *is* the
subject, the thing imitated and gazed at, the referent reality. Language has
become its own subject, maximized its self-conscious self-reference. The
matrix does not prohibit or applaud either extreme or any point in between.
They are all equally God's children, all equally legitimate models for a corresponding kind of self-consciousness in nonverbal behavior. Again, we have
converted a moralized dichotomy into a neutral spectrum.

Looked at in this way, the matrix explains something which is surprisingly seldom remarked—the genesis of stylistic error, of the "vices" of rhetoric. The Platonic-Aristotelian framework doesn't have to explain them.
Rhetorical vice equals self-consciousness and self-consciousness is just there,
an unhappy but undeniable reality. If all degrees of self-consciousness are
permissible, however, then we can't depend on original sin. Stylistic vices
seem caused by a positive rather than a negative attribute, by the love of
another kind of worth, an opaque one rather than a transparent one. Opac-

ity, the matrix suggests, is something part of our nature seeks. It does not simply happen through carelessness or inadvertence, by "abandoning our mind to it." We want it. This hunger has been rarely acknowledged by rhetoricians from Plato's time to ours. "Yes, people do seem fond of putting things in obscure ways, fooling others and themselves, inventing jargons far beyond specialized descriptive needs. Yes, some people do become famous simply because they write so obscurely everyone thinks them profound. I wonder why? Oh well, that's human perversity for you." The matrix suggests that this hunger for verbal play is normal, that like self-conscious behavior generally, it has a legitimate place in human life.

We do make intellectual mistakes. We fail to think things through. Adding 2 and 2, we get 5. Much of our misunderstanding, though, comes from a hunger for opaque styles or opaque attitudes. We want to color our communications, flood our human relationships with feeling. Jargons which stiff-arm one kind of audience do so because they want to embrace another kind of audience. Often utterances don't make sense in one frame of reference just because they *do* make sense in another. You puzzle me until I "see where you are coming from." Human beings don't just want to do things, they want to "do things with style," and the same goes for how they speak and write. We can generate such "failures of communication" intentionally by insisting on looking Through a text that was meant to be looked At, noticed as a style.

This insistence on a perceiving attitude uncalled for by the text can generate the kind of willful misunderstanding we see when I "just don't speak your language." It can also generate the comic distance that allows us to look At rather than Through the behavior of our fellow men, thus converting it to a comic banquet and dining off it. The matrix supplies then a diagram of possible human misunderstandings. Just create inappropriate linkings between the four spectra.

If you were an enemy of Churchill, for example, you might choose to look at one of his inspirational wartime addresses, mock his stylistic habits, the anaphora and tricolon climax, as hypocritical affectation. You would push him from left to right across the whole matrix. Or, as a second example, consider my revision of the Elizabeth Burns passage in chapter 1. I deliberately chose to notice stylistic attributes that were not meant to be noticed. I failed to adopt the "blindness," the resolute Through vision, such a style implicitly requires. "Not fair!" she might rejoin. I could then counter her argument by insisting that such a resolute noun style does not work even in the Through mode appropriate to it. Or, as another example, I might read Michael Herr's Vietnam account as if it were a neutral account like the military orders at the end of chapter 8; read his prose, that is, as General Westmoreland would have read it. I could then accuse him of lacking clarity (text spectrum), of looking at a "real" war as if it were self-conscious drama (reality spectrum), and so on. Often enough, such misreading comes from inappropriate assumptions rather than a will to misunderstand. Learning to find the appropriate positioning on the matrix for a particular style is, in a literary sense, what it means to learn to read.

To explain the genesis of stylistic vice leads us to a yet more fundamental distinction, the difference between ornament and essence, figure and ground. Once you see that this distinction is a matter of choice, an arrangement that inheres in a particular connection across the four spectra, rather than something inherent in the nature of an unchanging reality, then some unexpected reversals suggest themselves. The Platonic-Aristotelian scheme of things aims to maximize the life and power of ideas. Ideas can take on a rhetorical coloration, be made to look more or less attractive than they really are, but they still remain referential. When we contend about ideas or play with them, it is the ideas and the ideological yield which motivate the transaction. Ideas are essential, words—and the motives they represent—ornamental. But what if this relationship is reversed? What if the ideas are merely an excuse to play or contend? The Aristotelian theory of language seems designed to deny this possibility but it immediately suggests itself when the matrix supplies our framework for thinking. The matrix does not discriminate between possible ranges of motive. For the traditional scheme, ideas are essential and words ornamental; purposive thought essential, play and competition ornamental. Our traditional intellectual and moral orientation is built on this distinction. Plain purpose is o.k.; proud display is not. The whole of our traditional scheme of satire, for example, comes from juxtaposing the "good sense" of plain purpose with the idiocy of stylistically motivated games and play. When Thorstein Veblen, the great satirist of American capitalism, contrasted "ordinary" need with "conspicuous consumption," he was making a distinction based on the traditional illusions about the primacy of purpose. But what if human motive works just the other way? If transportation supplies the excuse rather than the reason for a fancy car?

To the extent that this "Great Reversal" of essence and ornament, of figure and ground, has to be admitted, the nature of prose style itself undergoes a similar radical reversal. We think—automatically, in the Platonic-Aristotelian tradition—of prose style as the handmaiden, willing or not, of an idea, a practical purpose which is already there. We are hungry, our body makes us so, and then someone figures out a fancy spiel which gets us to eat Product X rather than Product Y. But what if the hunger and the eating are caused by the spiel? What if purpose is created by style? Look at the motive spectrum again.

| *Motive* | Ludic | Ethical | Aesthetic |
|---|---|---|---|
|  | (hierarchy; $; game) | (practical purpose) (factual communication) | (play; hobbies; honor; "good form") |

Does the energy flow in both directions? Can plain purpose be established, motivated, from the outside in, by the power of the extremes? Are the extremes the essentials, the central plain purpose a mixture of the two major determining forms? It is a shock, isn't it, even to consider this possibility? It is like moving from Ptolemaic to Copernican astronomy. We are so used to thinking of it the other way, to saying that our central self is just *there,* the essential predeterminant of all else. So with purpose: We ordinarily think that we do things because we need to, and that these needs are the preexistent determinants of our behavior.

People have argued it the other way but we usually don't pay attention to them. When King Lear's daughters deprive him of all his courtiers, the visible panoply of his kingly identity, they tell him that he should not be upset. An old man does not "need" them. He cries out in agony, "O reason not the need!" The Christian tradition has said from the beginning, even when cautioning against pride, that man does not live by bread alone. And the whole Stoic tradition tells us to adjust our expectations down to our reality and not vice versa. Want what you've got. Define your "need" as what you already have. None of this expostulation has had any effect just as no one has tried to reason through the self-contradictions of a transparent theory of prose style. The primacy of purpose has remained too flattering to question.

And so prose becomes the workaday vehicle, a happy slave heard but not seen. The other ranges of human motive are given away to literature, another kind of language with another legitimating premise. The matrix, however, suggests a far different picture of prose. It makes prose, both dia-grammatically and metaphysically, the central means of utterance. And prose style is nothing less than the main way that practical purpose is moti-vated. It models how work gets done in the world. In its essence, then, it is deeply political. It stands to language as a politician stands to a democracy. The "men of principle" despise the politician as a mere convenience. He knows better. Nothing would get done without him. He orchestrates the powerful motives of play on the one side and competition on the other into the needful purposes of daily life. And so does prose.

Plato hated politics and politicians, just as he hated the democracy they both create and preserve. He had, therefore, to denigrate the means of ordi-nary conscious life. This denigration has lasted a long time and done immense harm. It is about time we put it aside. The matrix, by measuring the crucial variable of self-consciousness, allows us to do just this. It shows us clearly what the relationship between style and behavior is, and suggests how value judgments about prose may be legitimately made. It suggests the truth behind our epigraph, Οἷος ὁ βίος τοῖος ὁ λόγος: "As with life, so with words."

How does the matrix work in practice? What we are trying to do is chart a complex intersection between reading, text, and reality. The "object" mea-sured, remember, doesn't stand still. We stand to it not like a carpenter measuring wood, but far more like a bullion dealer checking the price of gold. He takes daily "fixings" on a continuously varying process. The matrix allows us to diagram that process and so think about it more clearly. It will not, to repeat, prevent disagreements, lead to a harmonious unan-imity about value judgments. We all start from far too many different prem-ises, perceive in too many different ways. But it will allow us to make sense of our disagreements, see where they come from and what they amount to. It will render us self-conscious about value judgments.

Now, some prose to work on:

The object of this Essay is to explain, as clearly as I am able, the grounds of an opinion which I have held from the earliest period when I had formed any opinions at all on social or political matters, and which, instead of being weakened or modified, has been constantly growing stronger by the progress of reflection and the experience of life: That the principle which regulates the existing social relations between the two sexes—the legal subordination of one sex to the other—is wrong in itself, and now one of the chief hindrances to human improvement; and that it ought to be replaced by a principle of perfect equality, admitting no power or privilege on the one side, nor disability on the other.

The very words necessary to express the task I have undertaken, show how arduous it is. But it would be a mistake to suppose that the difficulty of the case must lie in the insufficiency or obscurity of the grounds of reason on which my conviction rests. The difficulty is that which exists in all cases in which there is a mass of feeling to be contended against. So long as an opinoin is strongly rooted in the feelings, it gains rather than loses in stability by having a preponderating weight of argument against it. For if it were accepted as a result of argument, the refutation of the argument might shake the solidity of the conviction; but when it rests solely on feeling, the worse it fares in argumentative contest, the more persuaded its adherents are that their feeling must have some deeper ground, which the arguments do not reach; and while the feeling remains, it is always throwing up fresh intrenchments of argument to repair any breach made in the old. And there are so many causes tending to make the feelings connected with this subject the most intense and the most deeply rooted of all those which gather around and protect old institutions and customs, that we need not wonder to find them as yet less undermined and loosened than any of the rest by the progress of the great modern spiritual and social transition; nor suppose that the barbarisms to which men cling longest must be less barbarisms than those which they earlier shake off.

A revolutionary argument—the feminist case in its deepest essentials— but hardly a revolutionary style. Nothing in it asks to be noticed; it stands at the transparent end of the text and perceiver spectra. The motive, like the subject, is rational persuasion, so place it at the center of the motive spectrum. And the kind of the reality imitated? Not self-conscious either. At the center of the reality spectrum. "Normal" argumentative prose. Is it "good" prose? An answer starts by consulting an implied norm. What kind of prose do we expect to go with a feminist pronouncement? More fire and less ponderous argument. And so we notice the ponderousness as we would not were the subject Kant's theory of knowledge. The text-perceiver relationship moves, in fact, well over toward the opaque side. We notice, for the first time, that the opening sentence is a paragraph long and that it is built on a technique of continued parenthetical interruption. The basic argument looks like this:

*The object of this Essay is to explain*
  (as clearly as I am able)

*the grounds of an opinion*
> (which I have held from the earliest period)
>> ((when I had formed any opinions at all on social
>>> (or political) questions)
> (and which ((instead of being weakened (or modified)))
>> (has been constantly growing stronger (by the progress of
>> reflection and the experience of life))

*That*
> (the principle which regulates the existing social relations between the
> two sexes)

*the legal subordination of one sex to the other is wrong*
> (in itself)
> (and now one of the chief hindrances to human improvement)

*and that it ought to be replaced by a principle of perfect equality*
> (admitting no power or privilege on the one side, nor disability on the
> other.)

A kind of periodic suspension here, I suppose. Does it strengthen the argument or drag it down? Do we notice it as interfering with what is being said? A modern reader is likely to; a contemporary nineteenth-century reader much less so. It would not have seemed to its own time as wordily self-indulgent as it does to us. And, as always happens, an anonymous writer might seem a tedious windbag but a famous philosopher—here, John Stuart Mill—majestically judicious. (The passage is from *The Subjection of Women* [London: J. M. Dent, 1929].)

The crucial issue remains whether we notice the style as a style and, if so, what makes us do so. I think we do, and for two reasons. The modern reader expects, for such a topic, more passion and less periodicity. A more immediate voice. And, too, the periodicity organizes the argument but it does not energize it. We notice it just because it does *not* add any force to the issue. Its self-consciousness is not justified by any fixing on the matrix. Suppose we rewrote it to meet these objections? Here is a modern "translation" rendered by one of my students.

> This essay explains a long-held, deep-seated opinion that sexual inequality, wrong in itself, also wrongs society. Only perfect equality, which admits neither male power nor female privilege, can save us.
> If I find it difficult to choose the right words—and I do—don't think my opinion lacks support. Remember, I struggle against a mass of feeling—feeling so strongly rooted that to argue against it is to invite conservative reaction. An opinion based on feeling protects itself by excluding logic. Its adherents

assume, inevitably, that an opponent misunderstands the real issue—how else explain his opposition? And our subject—the relationship between the sexes—incites feeling so intense that social progress, effective in other areas, has left this virtually untouched. But tradition never insures sanctity. Let's face it: modern domesticity means ancient barbarism.

Is this better? A verb style rather than a noun style, half as long, with no harm, certainly, to the argument; a direct and colloquial modern voice that fits the "modern" feminist argument; a transparent style that calls for an unself-conscious perceiver. We are primed now to notice all of these things just because we are analyzing them; normally we'd look right through them to the feminist argument. I think we *can* call it better, with these stipulations: we want transparency here, and the nineteenth-century nominal style gets in the way; a verb style fits the revolutionary subject better anyway; we get there twice as fast with no loss of power to the argument. There are losses. The new speaker hasn't the philosophic weight bestowed on the old by all those ponderous parentheses. And a revolutionary argument can be strengthened by a well-dramatized lack of passion. Only the cold facts and these suffice here. I don't think Mill's prose works like this, though. It just gets in the way. Henry James may make art out of parentheticality but Mill does not. You may disagree. The disagreement doesn't matter but agreeing on the grounds for disagreement is crucial. Which spectrum? Where positioned? How altered by revision? And a cost-benefit analysis of the trade-offs the revision inevitably brings.

John Stuart Mill is protected both by his name and his historicity. We hesitate to tamper with either one, even if the At/Through switch is thrown and we are tempted to. There are times, though, when no hesitation at all seems called for.

### INSTRUCTIONS

#### HOW TO USE ENAMELED TEA KETTLE

*Enamel is one of glass materials so do not give any shock to your TEA KETTLE.

*Do not heat the KETTLE without water in it. When the KETTLE is heated and hot, make sure it cool down slowly, otherwise chipping problem may be caused.

*Do not give heat directly on handle.

*Avoid using metal brush or cleanser for cleaning as it will damage surface. After cleaning, the moisture should be wiped off.

*If with full capacity of water, it will boil over so it is recommended to use it just with 60 to 70% full of water.

We've all read hundreds of examples of this genre—the instructions that come with a Japanese product. We chuckle at the unidiomatic and incorrect English and immediately start to revise in our own minds. It is an easy plot on the spectrum: ordinary life, practical purpose, and a perceiver/text relationship that has gotten self-conscious but should not be.

And yet the "Japanese instruction" often teaches a more interesting lesson than this. The self-consciousness here, at least for me, makes the instructions work much better. To be told to treat enamel carefully is one thing: to be told "do not give any shock to your TEA KETTLE" is quite another. The tea kettle, as it happens, is a very dainty little one and I will now, whenever I pick it up, remember not to shock it by any of the dangers tea kettles fall heir to. Error here works *as art*. It makes us look At, contemplate for pleasure, possess by metaphor, what we would ordinarily look Through. The "Japanese instruction" often works this way, tells us not only how to use the product but the spirit in which to use it. To correct the "Japanese instruction" is always more justified than to correct the likes of John Stuart Mill. And yet the loss is sometimes greater than when we translate Mill. Self-consciousness often collaborates with chance for a happy result.

A famous case of revising for clarity: what about value judgments here?

> I returned and saw under the sun, that the race is not to the swift, nor the battle to the strong, neither yet bread to the wise, nor yet riches to men of understanding, nor yet favor to men of skill; but time and chance happeneth to them all.

> One more thing I have observed here under the sun: speed does not win the race nor strength the battle. Bread does not belong to the wise, nor wealth to the intelligent, nor success to the skillful; time and chance govern all.

The translators of the New English Bible held before them only one purpose—clarity of meaning. The reader was the common reader, looking through an ideally transparent text to find, ultimately, his spiritual salvation. The King James version now seems strange in both syntax and usage to the modern reader. These obstacles to understanding the divine text have been removed in the new translation.

Several other things have been removed as well. The King James version is an opaque text to us by virtue of the very "faults"—Renaissance syntax, diction, and so on—which the New English Bible seeks to remedy. The opaque triggers did not operate on the audience in 1623—or at least not so strongly. They have accrued over the centuries. But this does not make them less important. Self-consciousness, numinosity, is the first attribute a Scripture must possess. To present the wisdom of God in transparent prose ensures that it will never seem like the wisdom *of God*. The same violent change occurs on the reality spectrum. The reality presented in the King James version is highly ritualized, allegorical. We have always read it as larger than ordinary life, both at the right, ritual end of the reality spectrum and at the left extreme of dream and myth. The New English Bible cancels both kinds of power and pushes the human drama into the narrow center of ordinary life. What had been a drama with eternal salvation at stake turns into just another day's work.

So, too, on the motive spectrum. The extremes are cancelled in favor of the center. The intense sense of word play in the King James vanishes—and so does its ludic daring, its continual striving for the memorable, and hence authoritative, statement. This authority above all the New English Bible throws away. The King James style manages to exemplify as well as imply the whole range of human motive; the New English Bible reduces this power and grandeur to an exercise in Freshmen Composition.

The King James—and here I am going beyond the passage in question—represents English prose at its greatest. The New English Bible translation, compared with the King James on the matrix, suggests why and begins to suggest what "greatness" in prose really means. First of all, the King James oscillates rapidly and continually on all four spectra from transparent to opaque and back. It shows our full wave form.

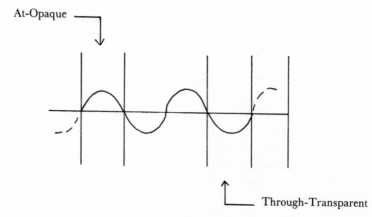

At-Opaque

Through-Transparent

The New English Bible wants to shut this oscillation down, restrict scriptural reading to the transparent side of text and perceiver spectra and to the middle of the bottom two spectra. By doing so it fatally narrows the emotional range of Scripture. For when you choose a fixing like this on the matrix of verbal style you have chosen a similar fixing in your theory of behavior. Western literature and art at its best have always shown man as both profoundly isolated and profoundly social, a continual oscillation of central and social self. Scripture needs to heal this split, not reinforce it. "Greatness" in prose, this comparison suggests, comes from harmonizing in some way the full range of human self-consciouness, offering a series of fixings across the matrix that brings its disparate extremes of motive together in the mind at once. It is, as we have just been discovering, much easier to make value judgments about prose if you compare examples selected for their comparability to begin with. But if we can make absolute statements beyond the "good or bad, given the intended purpose," it is by looking for this harmonization of disparate motives which prose at its best always displays.

The matrix suggests, in fact, that when we make absolute judgments of this sort, we are still making a basic comparative judgment, a measurement of figure against ground. At the transparent extreme, we choose an external reality as referential and measure the prose style against that. At the opaque extreme, we accept the prose style as referential and measure reality against it. Sometimes we can see this figure/ground oscillation flitter back and forth right before our eyes. Grammatical or syntactical errors, when they encourage this figure/ground instability, often strike us as funny. Here's a sentence from a discussion of primate behavior:

> Brachiation allowed prehumans to throw things which ultimately made them successful (farmers/hunters/tree-dwellers).

The scholar who wrote this would object that the mistake didn't matter because no real misunderstanding occurred. True enough, but the passage also pushes the text way over toward the opaque side when the author doesn't want this. It makes him look like, well, a monkey. It makes us self-conscious in a way disastrous for the dignity of a scientific report. But what kind of sentence has the author—however inadvertently—managed to create? On the one hand, the sense the writer intended. On the other: No comma after "things" makes "which ultimately made them successful" refer to "things" and not to prehumans' ability to throw them; this in turn leads us to interpret the parenthetical "farmers/hunters/tree-dwellers" as an appositive which enumerates the "things" brachiation allowed them to throw. And so we have our distant ancestors rising to wealth and honor by using brachiation to toss their fellow farmers, hunters, and tree-dwellers hither and yon. Because this vision makes very good sense—at least in terms of human behavior—we want to perceive it as "correct" too. Two meanings share the same words. This kind of unintended syntactic punning allows us to hold two different positions on the matrix at once, accept a figure as also a ground, and vice versa. All value judgments involve this figure/ground relationship and at the extremes constitute reverse images of it.

Let's try this idea out on a kind of prose we've already seen, the compulsively mannered prose of John Lyly:

> Philautus by how much the less he looked for this discourse, by so much the more he liked it, for he saw all qualities both of body and mind in Euphues; unto whom he replied as followeth:
> "Friend Euphues—so your talk warranteth me to term you—I dare neither use a long process, neither a loving speech, lest unwittingly I should cause you to convince me of those things which you have already condemned. And verily I am bold to presume upon your courtesy, since you yourself have used so little curiosity, persuading myself that my short answer will work as great an effect in you as your few words did in me. And seeing that we resemble, as you say, each other in qualities, it cannot be that the one should differ from the other in courtesy. Seeing the sincere affection of the mind cannot be expressed by the mouth and that no art can unfold the entire love of the heart, I am earnestly to beseech you not to measure the firmness of my faith by the fewness of my words, but rather think that the overflowing waves of good will leave no passage for many words. Trial shall prove truth. Here is my hand, my heart, my lands, and my life at thy commandment. Thou mayest well perceive that I did believe thee that so soon I did love thee, and I hope thou wilt the rather love me in that I did believe thee."
> Either Euphues and Philautus stood in need of friendship or were ordained to be friends. Upon so short warning to make so soon a conclusion might seem, in mine opinion, if it continued, miraculous; if shaken off, ridiculous. But after many embracings and protestations one to another, they walked to dinner, where they wanted neither meat, neither music, neither any other pastime; and having banqueted, to digest their sweet confections, they danced all that afternoon. They used not only one board, but one bed, one book—if so be it they thought not one too many. Their friendship augmented every day, insomuch that the one could not refrain the company of the other one

minute. All things went in common between them, which all men accounted commendable. (*Euphues, The Anatomy of Wit* [London, 1578])

"Through" vision here obviously makes no sense. Bring those expectations to bear and you can only call this kind of prose insane and go your way— as most modern readers do. But put on the "At" side of the spectrum, it begins to make sense. What such a text is "about" is verbal play. Its style *is* the content, that metronomic balancing into alternatives *is* Lyly's wild and compulsive search for verbal and psychic balance, for a self stable enough to permit the kind of friendship he is talking about here. The "motive" for such a search comes from both extremes of the motive spectrum, from pure play and from a desire to attract attention with a bizarre game of stylistic extremity. The kind of life imitated is that of ritualized drama, of compulsive self-consciousness. But Lyly is using it, not to put off his reader, but to become at one with him, to share his compulsive need for balance and order. Looked at in this way, Lyly's style is not "mannered" at all. It is *realistic,* but "realistic" to, that is faithful to, a strange and private world, a world Lyly wants to share with us, to socialize and thus to make real. Whatever in prose leads us to allow this alternative world, to suspend the "correcting" urge of Through vision, is what we mean by "authority" in prose style. It comes in all sizes and shapes; its common ingredient is only that it flips the switch. It can do so by rewarding the transparent expectation or as here by denying it.

The great virtue of Lyly's style lies in teaching us to keep the At mode continually working in the perceiver. In fact, we must do this even when "correcting" in the most schoolmasterly way. Revision is a continuing At/ Through oscillation, trying always to tailor prose to the reality you want to reveal or create. Prose like Lyly's insures that we will not become accustomed to a narrow range of possible realities. The impossible styles like Lyly's allow our vision to grow. They are often called "decadent" but in fact work in the opposite way, toward novelty and vigor, not decay. Only because they represent a self-conscious dramatization of reality anathema to the Platonic view of style are they called decadent. Lyly's prose is a good prose indeed, once it is correctly plotted on the matrix.

Good but not great. Great prose is always an affair of the center. It heightens the sense of life, but of ordinary life. It animates, energizes social purpose. It confers power. Here is an example of great prose, from an Eliz-

abethan contemporary of John Lyly, a schoolmaster named Richard Mulcaster. He is talking about the need for a new kind of elementary school
curriculum and commenting on the strong feelings that such changes always
elicit. A serious purpose then, but not what we usually think a heroic one:

> For who am I to persuade the liking of so full an Elementary, not allowed
> of the most, neither tried of the best? A simple teacher. And yet that teaching
> name is not plain nothing, in a matter of school. A mean companion. That is
> a great something, where the persuaders countenance, is to carry away the
> thing. Nay a newfangle. That is very odious, where the old current will not
> lightly be changed, and the opinion of right hath both the countenance of the
> best, and contentment of the most, whereupon to make stay. To me it may be
> replied: you meddle in this matter alone, you do but trouble yourself; you can
> not turn the course, which is ordinary & old, and therefore very strong for
> you to strive against this thing which you commend is not every man's ware.
> It will not be compassed. Do you let it alone. If you will needs write, turn
> your pen to other matters, which the state will better like of, which this time
> will soon allow, which you may persuade with credit, if they be new, and
> suitable: or confirm with praise if they be old and need the file. If these and
> such objections were not always ordinary even to every one, in all attempts
> of turning, either from the ill to good, or from the good to better, I would
> answer them with care, but now I need not, because to win a resolute good,
> he that wisheth to have it must think to wrestle for it, both with words and
> writing, against the corruption of time, against the aloneness of the attempt,
> against the prejudice of parties, against the difficulties of performance, &
> whatsoever else. Neither must he be discouraged with any ordinary thwart-
> ing, which is a thing well known to well travelled students, and of least
> account where it is best known, how fearful a thing forever it seems to weak
> fancies, by crossing of corruption to strive against the stream. For both the
> stream will turn, when a stronger tide returns, and if there be no tide, yet an
> untired traveller will still on against it, until he be above it. And more hon-
> orable it were for some one or some few to hazard their own credit and esti-
> mation for the time in favor of such a thing, as they know to be of credit,
> though not in account, then by too timorous a conceit, too sore afraid of a
> popular opinion, not always the soundest, though most of swing, to leave
> excellent arguments either destitute of defense, if they be pleaded against, or
> defeated of delivery, if they fortune to be called for. For may it not fall out,
> that such a thing as this is may be called for hereafter, though presently not
> cared for through some other occasion, which hath the rudder in hand? (*The
> First Part of the Elementary (1582)* [Menston, England: Scolar Press,
> 1970]); I have modernized the spelling.)

Read it aloud. It comes alive. The looseness of syntax and awkward changes of direction characteristic of so much Elizabethan prose smooth right out and the power shines through. Part of the power comes from the series of commands, the emphatic interior monologue.

> To me it may be replied, you meddle in this matter alone, you do but trouble yourself: you cannot turn the course. . . . Do you let it alone. If you will needs write, turn your pen to other matters.

Part comes from the anaphora and isocolon, as here:

> Turn your pen to other matters,
>     which the state will better like of,
>     which this time will soon allow,
>     which you may persuade with credit,
>         if they be new, and suitable
>             or confirm with praise
>         if they be old, and need the file.

Or in this great sequence which adds alliteration:

> . . . to win a resolute good,
>     he that wisheth to have it
>     must think to wrestle for it,
>         both with words and writing,
>     against the corruption of time,
>     against the aloneness of the attempt,
>     against the prejudice of parties,
>     against the difficulties of performance,
>         and whatsoever else.

Mulcaster had a natural sense of prose climax:

> For both the stream will turn, when a stronger tide returns, and if there be no tide, yet an untired traveller will still on against it, until he be above it.

And he can build a crescendo over a longer span, and without using the precise antithetical balance of the formal period:

And more honorable it were for some one or some few to hazard their own credit and estimation for the time in favor of such a thing, as they know to be of credit, though not in account, then by too timorous a conceit, too sore afraid of a popular opinion, not always the soundest, though most of swing, to leave excellent arguments either destitute of defense, if they be pleaded against, or defeated of delivery, if they fortune to be called for. For may it not fall out, that such a thing as this is may be called for hereafter, though presently not cared for through some other occasion, which hath the rudder in hand?

Prose like this enlists motives from either extreme of the spectrum to serve the center. It galvanizes practical purpose, energizes ordinary life. We remain prisoners here too of the Platonic way of thinking about style and motive. We think practical purpose self-motivated, ordinary life purposefully motivated by nature. Not so. The motive power lurks at the extremes. When someone is very good at bringing that power into the center, orchestrating ordinary life with the energies of game and play, he becomes a politician, despised—as Plato has taught us to despise him—but essential. Great prose like Mulcaster's is political in just this sense. It orchestrates power in the service of plain purpose. It mixes our motives for us and puts them to work. Purpose, like clarity, is not a self-standing inevitability that has only to be revealed. It must be created from its counterbalancing opposites and this, in the great moments, the prose writer does.

In oral cultures, cultures without writing, poetry preserves and transmits the culture through memorable meter and rhyme, harmonizes and preserves its traditional mixtures of motive, patterns of acceptable behaviors. In written, literate cultures, prose inherits this central task of transmission and renewal. It must not only do the work of the world but tell us in what spirit that work is done. That is why we feel so strongly about prose style, fuss so over solecisms which go unnoticed in poetry. Prose style in a written culture provides a direct readout of behavior, allegorizes the current mixtures of motive. No wonder we want always to talk about it in moral terms. It points directly to the essence of morality, the mixture of our motives.

The oscillation of prose is closer to the oscillation of the self than that of verse or of mathematics. That is why we are moral—and moralistic—about prose, why we so naturally use the vocabulary we have developed to talk about the self to talk about prose. Great prose is thus fundamentally moral, and moral in the same way that we are ourselves, moral in trying to hold two kinds of self, social and central, public and private, together. Obviously prose could not have developed until this kind of complex self was somehow sensed and approved. It is this sane, everyday balance of the two selves that great prose enshrines. It would seem to follow that a culture's value judgments for prose style will reflect the degree of its need for self-consciousness. If it needs little—Enlightenment France or Victorian England, for example—it will value a transparent style. If it needs a lot—Elizabethan England or contemporary America—it will develop a range of opaque styles.

In the Platonic model, self-consciousness is bad, its absence good. But Aristotle, whose at times melancholy duty it was to reconcile Plato with common sense, knew that this good-bad dichotomy wouldn't work in practice. He thus contrived an awkward compromise: art, the self-conscious invention, shall be there but not show. *Ars celavit artem.* This sleazy compromise has lasted as a stylistic bromide ever since. It has done so because it points to a real and a positive truth. Too much self-consciousness *is* paralyzing, as Hamlet discovers. None at all puts you in the world of dream and myth, cancels your individuality. An active and vigorous self—and an active and vigorous society—clearly stand somewhere between the two extremes. But it is just because the stance is not static that they can stand just there. The stance may be more like a dance, a rhythmic to-ing and fro-ing between the extremes. It comprehends what we have just called the oscillation of revision, the rapid alternation of self-consciousness and self-forgetting. This happens at all frequencies and wavelengths but creates always a continual oscillation, one as cyclical and as necessary as breathing in and breathing out.

The talent for cultivating and regulating this oscillation is what a great Renaissance social philosopher, Baldassare Castiglione, called *sprezzatura.* Thought of as a static talent, *sprezzatura* seems hopelessly self-contradictory, an artistic kind of artlessness, a carefully studied but unself-conscious presentation of self, a contrived naturalness. Aristotle's sleazy compromise embodied in behavior. If, however, we view it not as a static talent but as an active oscillation between the two behavioral extremes, it makes perfect sense. Castiglione's great insight was to see this oscillation as the center of human sociality. The At/Through switch testifies to the radical discontinuity between the two extreme states. You cannot be both self-conscious and unself-conscious at the same time. It is this oscillation that brings them together, that finally makes us human.

The Western self has been both so vital and so unstable precisely because it has been built on an oscillation, an alternation of radical opposites. So tense has been this oscillation, so hard both to sustain and bear, that Plato has engendered a horde of spiritual descendants wanting to shut this oscillation down, decide once and for all in favor of one extreme or the other. Plato decided for the Through extreme and Oscar Wilde decided for the At extreme, but they were both striving for the same ontological release and reassurance. The great texts in Western literature have taken the opposite path, sought for peace in governing the oscillation rather than shutting it down. Thucydides was the first of these and he set down the archetypical pattern of Western narrative structure, the alternation of historical event and formal speech about it, of an unself-conscious and a self-consciously rhetorical style. Infinite variations have been played on this pattern since then, but the pattern has remained the same, this because the split self which it seeks to heal has remained the same.

Prose style has developed along the same axis of self-consciousness. The great prose stylists have always galvanized the center by embodying the self-creating oscillation in styles that also do the work of the world. That is why the question of *norm* is so important in studying prose style, and also why it's so hard both to learn and to describe. To make value judgments you must always consult a norm of some kind. You need one simply to read a text, meaning being conveyed by variations from that norm. But this norm is implied, intuitive. It exists only in the minds of all the readers of English. You have to cultivate it by wide and continued reading. The point of reading is to allow you to do more reading better. The wider and more elastic your prose norm, the more easily you will like and understand unfamiliar styles. This is why experience of a full range of English prose, not simply modern prose, is so needful and why I have drawn on this range in the examples we have considered. The catholic taste that comes from this broad experience is very adaptive. It allows us to imagine possible mixtures of motive, balances of the two selves, try them without trying them out in life and taking the consequences. Prose style models motive. This is why we think it so important. To participate fully in the prose norms of a society means that you participate fully in its social norms, that you have internalized its full range of motive. The existence of that prose norm as a model for social norm is what a literate society is all about. When we lose that prose norm, as we stand in danger of losing it today, we lose the intuitive center of Western society itself, the vital oscillation between action and awareness.

The matrix is not, then, a set of rules for making value judgements. It does not tell us why beauty is beautiful, allow us to make rules for interpretation, invent a teacher-proof curriculum. It is not a set of rules but a piano to practice on, a diagram of how the intuitive norms of prose style operate—and how they model the norms of human behavior. A fixing across all four spectra provides a way of freezing a verbal event and thus allowing it to be described. This fixing is not a mechanical routine. It is a talent. True, some people are born with more of it than others. But it is also a teachable skill; you can get better at it with practice. In behavior, we usually call it tact. In prose analysis, as in the rest of art, the best word for it is taste. You learn which fixings across the spectrum harmonize the self, regulate self-consciousness in productive and peaceful ways. This is both an act of prose analysis and a participation in social harmony. Prose style acts thus, in a humble as well as an elevated way, as an agency of citizenship and of civility. When we analyze it, we are exploring what makes us at one with one another, and with ourselves.

# A Brief Glossary
# of Rhetorical Terms*

Classical rhetoric was divided into five parts:
1. Invention
2. Arrangement
3. Style
4. Memory
5. Delivery

And into three areas of use:
1. Deliberative (to debate in political bodies)
2. Judicial (to plead in law courts)
3. Epideictic or Panegyric (to praise, blame, or show off)

*alloiósis.* Breaking down a subject into alternatives:
> Your tax accountant, on the pros and cons of taking a chancy deduction: "You can either eat well or sleep well."

*amplificátio.* A generic term for all the ways an argument can be expanded and enriched.

*anadiplósis.* Repetition of the last word of one line or clause to begin the next.

*anacolúthon.* Ending a sentence with a different construction from that with which it began.

*anáphora.* Repetition of the same word at the beginning of successive clauses or verses:
> It is the most grievous consequence of what we have done and of what we have left undone in the last five

*For a fuller listing, see Richard A. Lanham, *A Handlist of Rhetorical Terms* (Berkeley: University of California Press, 1969).

years—five years of futile good intentions, five years of eager search for the line of least resistance, five years of uninterrupted retreat of British power, five years of neglect of our air defences.

**anthiméria.**

Using one part of speech for another:
Who *authored* this tripe, anyway?

**antístrophe.**

See *epiphora.*

**aporía.**

True or feigned doubt or deliberation about an issue:
"Dora is rather difficult to—I would not, for the world, say, to rely upon, because she is the soul of purity and truth—but rather difficult to—I hardly know how to express it, really, Agnes."

**apóstrophe.**

Breaking off a speech or conversation to address a person or thing absent:
"Mother, dear, you should have lived to see this!"

**catachrésis.**

A wildly unlikely metaphor:
"Mom will have kittens when she hears this."

**chiásmus.**

The order in the second half of an expression reverses that of the first:
"When the going gets tough, the tough get going."

Or, as in the old Mark Cross slogan:
"Everything for the horse but the rider and everything for the rider but the horse."

The term is derived from the Greek letter X (chi), whose shape, if the two halves of the construction are diagrammed, it resembles.

When the going gets      tough

the tough ←              get going.

**climax.**

Mounting by degrees through words or sentences of increasing weight and in parallel construction:
So a Victorian schoolmaster rebuked a dilatory student who wouldn't learn Latin vowel quantities: "If you do not take more pains, how can you ever expect to write good longs and shorts? If you do not write good longs and shorts, how can you ever be a man of taste? If you are not a man of taste, how can you ever be of use in the world?"

**conduplicátio.**

Repetition of a word or words in succeeding clauses.

**corréctio.**

Correction or revision of a word or phrase used previously.

**diácope.**

Repetition of a word or phrase with one or more words in between:
"Give me strength, O Lord, give me strength!"

*effíctio.*    The head-to-toe inventory of a person's charms once so common in English poetry:
> "My Lady's hair is threads of beaten gold, Her front the purest Chrystal eye hath seen, Her eyes the brightest stars the heavens hold . . ." and so on.

*enárgia.*    A general term for vivid, vigorous description.

*enumerátio.*    Division of subject into adjuncts, cause into effects, antecedent into consequents:
> "How do I love thee? Let me count the ways. I love thee to the depth and breadth and height. . . ."

*épanaphora.*    Intensive *anaphora.*

*epímone.*    Frequent repetition of phrase or question, dwelling on a point.

*epíphora.*    Opposite of *anaphora,* repetition of a word or phrase at the end of several clauses or sentences:
> "When I was a child, I spake as a child, I understood as a child, I thought as a child."

*epithéton.*    Repeated or regular qualification of a noun by an appropriate adjective; an adjective that regularly accompanies a noun, as in "heartfelt thanks."

*epizeúxis.*    Emphatic repetition of a word with no words in between:
> "O Horror! Horror! Horror!"

*ethopoeía.*    Putting oneself into the character of another so as to express that person's thoughts and feelings more vividly.

*éthos.*    The character or set of emotions which a speaker reenacts in order to affect an audience.

*homoioteleúton.*    Use of a series of words with similar endings:
> "The expres*sion* of the func*tion* of the facilita*tion* of the condemna*tion* of the amputa*tion*," as a licensed bureaucrat might put it.

*hypóphora.*    Raising questions and answering them.

*hypozeúxis.*    Every clause in a sentence has its own subject and verb:
> "Madame, the guests are come, supper served up, you called, my young lady asked for, the nurse cursed in the pantry, and everything in extremity."

*isócolon.*    A succession of phrases of equal length and corresponding structure:
> "Never in the history of mankind have so many owed so much to so few."

*lítotes.*    Denial of the contrary, understatement in order to intensify:
> "I am not unacquainted with the pleasures of money, for I love the stuff!"

*meiósis.*  Belittling comparison:
> "Banker's hot rod" for a Ferrari coupe

*metónymy.*  Substitution of cause for effect (or vice versa) or proper name for quality (or vice versa):
> So Winston Churchill wrote to his wife during WW II, "I can't tell you how we are coming but we're coming by puff-puff."

*occupátio.*  Emphasizing a point by pointedly seeming to pass it over:
> "I will not discuss his criminal record, his several jail terms, the daring escape and bloody recapture—bygones are bygones."

*oxymóron.*  A condensed paradox:
> "Icy hot," "darkness visible," "act naturally"

*paramológia.*  Conceding a point to seem fair; giving away a weaker point to make a stronger:
> "Of course I stole; what mother with starving children would do otherwise?"

*parechésis.*  Repeating the same sound in words close together:
> "Gaunt as the ghastliest of glimpses that gleam through the gloom of the gloaming when ghosts go aghast."

*paromoiósis.*  Use of similar sounds to reinforce isocolon:
> "Seeing the sincere affection of the mind cannot be expressed by the mouth and that no art can unfold the entire love of the heart, I am earnestly to beseech you not to measure the firmness of my faith by the fewness of my words."

*páthos.*  A general term for any kind of rhetorical figure which appeals directly to the emotions of an audience. *Ethos,* then, is the emotional set of the speaker; *pathos,* the emotional set the speaker wants to evoke in the audience.

*plóce.*  Repetition of a word with a different meaning after the interval of another word or words:
> "On the walls were pictured groups of early Americans signing things and still earlier Americans shooting arrows at things. But all over the immaculate mushroom-coloured carpet, and in what could be seen of a sort of Empire-style room opening off on the left, stood groups of present-day Americans drinking things."

*polýptoton.*  Repetition of words from the same root but in different forms or with different endings:
> "Society is no comfort to one not sociable."

*synécdoche.*  Substitution of part for whole, genus for species, or vice versa:
> "All hands on deck."

*tapinósis.*  Debasing language or epithet:
"Rhymester" for "poet"
Often synonymous with *meiosis.*

*tricolon.*  The pattern of three phrases in parallel, so common in Western writing after Cicero:
"Clear leadership, violent action, rigid decisions, one way or the other, form the only path not only of victory, but of safety and even of mercy."

*trópe.*  A rhetorical figure (metaphor, for example) which changes the meaning of a phrase. A *trope* is usually contrasted with a *scheme* (*isocolon,* for example), which only changes the shape of a phrase.

*zéugma.*  One verb is made to govern several objects, each in a different way:
"Here thou, great *Anna!* whom three realms obey.
Dost sometimes counsel take—and sometimes Tea."